Dog Whistle Politics

DOG WHISTLE POLITICS

HOW CODED RACIAL APPEALS HAVE REINVENTED RACISM AND WRECKED THE MIDDLE CLASS

IAN HANEY LÓPEZ

OXFORD
UNIVERSITY PRESS

OXFORD
UNIVERSITY PRESS

Oxford University Press is a department of the University of Oxford.
It furthers the University's objective of excellence in research, scholarship,
and education by publishing worldwide.

Oxford   New York
Auckland   Cape Town   Dar es Salaam   Hong Kong   Karachi
Kuala Lumpur   Madrid   Melbourne   Mexico City   Nairobi
New Delhi   Shanghai   Taipei   Toronto

With offices in
Argentina   Austria   Brazil   Chile   Czech Republic   France   Greece
Guatemala   Hungary   Italy   Japan   Poland   Portugal   Singapore
South Korea   Switzerland   Thailand   Turkey   Ukraine   Vietnam

Oxford is a registered trade mark of Oxford University Press
in the UK and certain other countries.

Published in the United States of America by
Oxford University Press
198 Madison Avenue, New York, NY 10016

Library of Congress Cataloging-in-Publication Data
Haney López, Ian.
  Dog whistle politics : how coded racial appeals have reinvented racism and wrecked
the middle class / Ian Haney López.
    p.   cm.
  ISBN 978-0-19-996427-7 (hardback : alk. paper); 978-0-19-022925-2 (paperback : alk. paper)
  1. Racism—Political aspects—United States—History—20th century. 2. United States—Race relations—
Political aspects—History—20th century. 3. Racism—Political aspects—United States—History—
21st century. 4. United States—Race relations—Political aspects—History 21st century.
5. Communication in politics—United States—History—20th century. 6. Communication in politics—
United States—History—21st century. 7. United States—Politics and government—1945–1989. 8. United
States—Politics and government—1989– 9. Post-racialism—United States—History.   I. Title.
  E185.615.H278 2014
  323.1196'073—dc23
                                                                    2013015913

9 8 7 6 5 4 3 2 1

Printed in the United States of America
on acid-free paper

To family members across four generations,

each compassionate and generous in his or her own manner:

in memory of my father, Terry, and brother, Garth;

and for my stepdaughter, Chelsea, and granddaughter, Lennea.

Contents

Preface

■ LEARNING ABOUT RACISM AT HARVARD LAW

Two themes dominate American politics today: at the forefront is declining economic opportunity; coursing underneath is race. This book connects the two. It explains popular enthusiasm for policies injuring the middle class in terms of "dog whistle politics": coded racial appeals that carefully manipulate hostility toward nonwhites. Examples of dog whistling include repeated blasts about criminals and welfare cheats, illegal aliens, and sharia law in the heartland. Superficially, these provocations have nothing to do with race, yet they nevertheless powerfully communicate messages about threatening nonwhites. In the last 50 years, dog whistle politics has driven broad swaths of white voters to adopt a self-defeating hostility toward government, and in the process has remade the very nature of race and racism. American politics today—and the crisis of the middle class—simply cannot be understood without recognizing racism's evolution and the power of pernicious demagoguery.

I initially sketched the ideas elaborated here in the Sixteenth Annual Derrick Bell Lecture on Race in American Society, delivered at New York University in the fall of 2011. The professor honored by the lecture series, Derrick Bell, passed away less than a month before the lecture he had invited me to deliver. You may have heard of him. Leading up to the 2012 election, a rightwing media outfit promised a "bombshell" about President Barack Obama. It turned out to be a grainy video of Obama as a student at Harvard Law School introducing Bell at a rally, and then giving him a hug. The warm clasp, media provocateur Andrew Breitbart's group claimed, symbolized Obama's full embrace of an intellectual leader they described as "the worst Johnny Appleseed of a nasty racialist legal theory [that argues] that the law is a weapon of the majority whites to oppress 'people of color.' "[1]

As a contemporary of Obama's at Harvard Law, let me add my voice to the chorus of those saying that Obama was no militant minority.[2] Obama did not study with Bell, nor take any course that focused on race and American law.[3] On a campus highly polarized around racial issues, as it was in those years, this may have been an early harbinger of Obama's tendency to hold himself aloof from racial contentions. Then there was Obama's election to the prestigious presidency of the *Harvard Law Review*. It's widely known that Obama won as the consensus candidate after conservative and liberal factions fought themselves to exhaustion.[4] Less well known is that these camps were racially identified, with almost all of the African American review members and their allies on one side. When conservatives threw their support to Obama, they ended a racial as well as political standoff.[5] As others have observed, Obama's conciliatory above-the-fray political style from those years has carried over to his presidency. I would say the same regarding the approach to race Obama seemed to cultivate as a student—that one can heal racial divisions by standing apart from racial conflict, simply letting race play itself out. This is far from what Derrick Bell taught.

My focus at this point is not on Obama, though, but on Bell and my relationship with him. I had the enviable opportunity to study with Bell in the late 1980s and early 1990s, at the start of my own lifelong intellectual engagement with race and racism in the United States. This is not to say that I was close to Bell during my student days, or that I stayed in contact with him over the last two decades. On the contrary, I had hoped to use the lecture in his honor to finally fully repair a strained relationship. Over just the past few years I had been able to reconnect with Bell, and we had even joked about my having been a "difficult" student in one of the last courses he taught while still at Harvard. But we had never discussed the source of the estrangement—an estrangement so deep that mid-semester I simply stopped attending class. That long-ago conflict bears directly on my arguments in the pages that follow.

Bell taught his course through weekly engagements with chapters from a book he was then writing, *Faces at the Bottom of the Well: The Permanence of Racism*.[6] The crux was the subtitle. I thought then, and until the last several years, that Bell's central claim—that there had been little genuine progress in American race relations—was silly, even absurd. Bell explained his thesis thus: "Black people will never gain full equality in this country. Even those herculean efforts we hail as successful will produce no more than temporary 'peaks of progress,' short-lived victories that slide into irrelevance as racial patterns adapt in ways that maintain white dominance."[7] The end of slavery, and of Jim Crow segregation, were merely temporary peaks of progress sliding into irrelevance? The claim seemed ridiculous.

To explain away his thesis, I focused not on its substance but instead on Bell's psychology. He was then in a particularly challenging place: his beloved wife Jewel was dying of cancer. And as if that wasn't enough, two decades after becoming the first tenured black professor at Harvard Law, he was in the midst of protesting that school's insistence year after year that no woman of color qualified to serve on its august faculty. True to his background as a civil rights lawyer and activist, Bell had taken an unpaid leave of absence to pressure the institution, and we students staged rallies in support—including the event at which Obama introduced Bell. The school administration responded by demanding that Bell return to full-time teaching, or resign his tenured professorship. He resigned. I thought then that he was at a bitter point in life, infecting his insights and his pedagogy.

In retrospect, it was my mindset that mattered more. Young and liberal, I burned with impatience, emboldened by an "arc of history bends toward justice" certainty about the world. I didn't have much tolerance for deep pessimism. Plus, my own biography suggested that Bell was wrong. Like Obama (we overlapped at high school too), I grew up in Hawaii as a biracial kid, albeit white and Latino. Rarely encountering the racially pejorative views more common on the mainland, I learned to move easily among different groups. Also, I was privileged—not to the degree of most of my peers at HLS, to be sure, but after all wasn't I there walking its hallowed halls and studying in its storied classrooms? Wasn't my life, and indeed even Bell's Harvard professorship, proof positive that at least some progress had been made, clear evidence that the civil rights movement, though it hadn't achieved nearly enough, still had moved this country dramatically forward? I viscerally rejected Bell's dismal analysis, for it assaulted my confidence in the moral universe and drew into question the meaning and security of my own position.

Things came to a head the week we debated Bell's "space trader" allegory.[8] Suppose, he said, aliens arrive from space and offer America riches to solve the debt problem, new technology to heal the environment, and a steady source of clean energy. In return, though, they ask for the nation's entire black population, and re-enslavement seems likely. Would America accept? I raised my hand and said "no," unable to countenance a future for myself in a society still capable of selling blacks into slavery. The country would not again reduce people to property, not in the present, I protested. I remember distinctly Bell's rejoinder mocking my "pie-in-the-sky" optimism. He argued that, in many ways, metaphorically the United States has often sold nonwhites down the river to achieve short-term and short-sighted benefits for whites. Other students piped up to support his dire analysis. I fumed and thought they were all playing at being radicals, with their unfairly biting attacks on a society that had already given me, us, so much. After that class, discouraged and upset, I left the course and did not return.

On a personal level, I now wince at my misplaced certitude and also lament squandering the chance to continue to learn from the best thinker on race and law in a tumultuous era. I also keenly regret never having taken a moment to talk about all of this with Bell, to seek some sort of closure on this faded conflict. But most especially, I'm sorry that my former professor did not live long enough to join me in rueful laughter following the lecture in his honor. After all, in that lecture I explained how I reluctantly came to conclude that he was correct all along about the permanence of racism.

My mistake had been to think that "permanent" meant fixed and unchanging. It did not. Rather, the key lay plainly visible in another phrase within Bell's thesis: "short-lived victories that slide into irrelevance *as racial patterns adapt* in ways that maintain white dominance." Racial patterns adapt. Or, to switch from the passive voice, strategic individuals adapt race.

Dog Whistle Politics explains how politicians backed by concentrated wealth manipulate racial appeals to win elections and also to win support for regressive policies that help corporations and the super-rich, and in the process wreck the middle class. The book lays out the details. For now, though, the bottom line is that Professor Bell was correct: racism is not disappearing, it's adapting. True, by virtually every measure things aren't as bad as in the 1850s, when the southern half of the country was still a slavocracy and the northern half practiced ferocious racism. Even compared to the 1950s, things are much, much better. Today the routine bigotry of publicly endorsed white supremacy is largely past, and the country remarkably elected and re-elected a black president, a triumph against racism of incredible magnitude. But racial progress in the United States is not a steady march toward equality. Valleys of reversal follow peaks of progress, and after the promising advances of the civil rights era we are deep in one such valley now. Moreover—and here's the crucial point—nonwhites have not been the only victims of the recent slide. Instead, racism has been harnessed to a right-wing politics that bankrupts the middle class writ large. Someday I fervently hope to say—as the result of open-minded and careful analysis rather than self-protecting, self-deluding anger—that Bell has been proven wrong, that racism is no longer surreptitiously adapting but genuinely over. Today, though, that day seems further off even than it did two decades ago, when a young student precipitously abandoned Bell rather than confront a painful truth about our society and our future.

One final lesson from my law school days bears directly on this book: the realization that racists are often decent folks. Taking a year off from HLS, I spent the fall of 1988 researching human rights violations in apartheid South Africa. Ironically, my greatest education came when I stopped reading and writing and spent a month hitchhiking around South Africa and Namibia. With striking openness and sincerity, white drivers earnestly volunteered their racial views. They seemed eager to do so, perhaps because they worried that as a foreigner I might misunderstand the nature of apartheid. Also, they seemed to see me foremost as an American and therefore as a fellow white; despite my light brown skin tone, I was far from the color of the Africans who marked the opposite pole in their racial world. Almost invariably initiating the conversation on race, they spoke breezily, confident that the reasonableness of their reprehensible ideas would shine through.

Some conversations bordered on the farcical, as for instance when a kind couple asked about conditions in the United States, and shared their fear that the threat from blacks would soon be dwarfed by the troubles pouring across the southern border as Latin American hordes invaded. I couldn't help but highlight the folly of their assumption about their rider, and so I explained that I was unconcerned given my own Latin American heritage, with a mother from El Salvador.

Other conversations, however, completely upturned how I thought about racism. One in particular stands out. In Namibia, then under South African control and also an apartheid state, the towns were widely spaced in a desert of sere geologic beauty. A farmer who gave me a lift lived some hundred-plus kilometers outside of the next town, but recognizing that there would be little traffic and so virtually no chance that I could secure an onward ride, he drove on past his homestead in the fading sunlight. This generous act added hours of needless driving to an already long day for the farmer. As we got close to town, though, he apologized and explained he would have to drop me off several hundred meters from the outskirts. He had killed a "kaffir"—the local equivalent of "nigger"—for poaching, and the constable had asked him to stay out of town for a few weeks until pressure for his arrest subsided. I was stunned speechless. Then the routines of normal etiquette kicked in and carried me through a ritual of thanks, goodbye, good luck with your travels.

Like most, I had been conditioned to think of racism as hatred, and racists as pathologically disturbed individuals. To be sure, sadistic racists exist, and racism is frequently bound up with the emotional heat of fear and hatred. But as I began to intuit while hitchhiking through the landscape of apartheid, *most racists are good people*. That bears emphasizing, since it runs so profoundly contrary to the dominant conception. Even the farmer who killed another human being for the petty act of poaching, I came to understand, was not a homicidal lunatic but a complex person capable of both brutal violence and real generosity.

What follows in this book is an effort to understand racism as it works in American society, and especially as it has evolved and impoverished the whole country over the last five decades. In the process, I will call out both Republican and Democratic politicians for being racial demagogues, and will rebuke individuals and organizations that craft racist appeals. But I will not conduct a witch-hunt for malevolent racists, nor demean whole groups as benighted bigots. Typically, those in thrall to racist beliefs are just people, reared and living in complicated societies that esteem human interconnection and also condone dehumanizing violence. This book is not about bad people. It is about all of us.

Introduction

Racial Politics and the Middle Class

Let's start with an open secret: Republicans rely on racial entreaties to help win elections. In 2010, the chairman of the Republican National Committee, Michael Steele, acknowledged that "for the last 40-plus years we had a 'Southern Strategy' that alienated many minority voters by focusing on the white male vote in the South."[1] Steele was echoing the remarks of another head of the Republican National Committee, Ken Mehlman. In 2005, he used a speech before the NAACP to admit that his party had exploited racial divisions, and had been wrong to do so. "By the seventies and into the eighties and nineties," Mehlman said from a prepared text, "Republicans gave up on winning the African American vote, looking the other way or trying to benefit politically from racial polarization. I am here today as the Republican chairman to tell you we were wrong."[2]

These apologies at once confess to racial pandering and also implicitly promise to sin no more. This is a promise that the GOP will struggle to fulfill, for this party is now essentially defined by race: it is almost exclusively supported by and composed of whites. In the 2012 presidential election, 88 percent of the voters who pulled the lever for the GOP candidate were white.[3] That means that whites made up roughly nine out of every ten persons who threw in with Mitt Romney. Even more startling, among state-level elected Republican officials nationwide, 98 percent are white.[4] Notwithstanding some prominent minority faces pushed to the fore to suggest otherwise, this is a party of white persons.

Yet this open secret receives surprisingly little attention. From conservatives, there's the occasional mea culpa, but much more typically there's a firm insistence that the GOP does not notice race, followed by the outraged retort that any suggestion otherwise is not only unfounded but a contemptible playing of the race card. From the Democratic Party, there's a resounding silence. Even from liberal commentators there's only murmured objections. A few point out GOP demographics, but beyond noting the striking numbers and the challenge this poses for assembling majorities in an increasingly diverse society, they have little to say about how and why Republicans became a white party. A smaller handful go somewhat further, accusing Republicans of sometimes engaging in racial pandering. But even the most trenchant critics seem to treat race-baiting as a marginal dynamic—a vestigial remnant of ugly racial practices lingering from the pre-civil rights era, a despicable ploy that crops up at moments of electoral desperation, one more telltale sign of a party in decline, but never a central feature of American democracy today.

The pattern of perceiving GOP racial pandering as largely irrelevant can be seen in the impulse to mock that party for appealing to a small and shrinking sliver of the population—"middle-aged white guys," in one version. Upon President Barack Obama's re-election, the *New York Times* ran a generally celebratory piece that closed with a Republican operative lamenting, "there just are not enough middle-aged white guys that we can scrape together to win. There's just not enough of them."[5] But the GOP did not win among only a narrow slice of whites: it triumphed among every major demographic cohort of whites. In 2012, Romney won 59 percent of the white vote, and compared to the previous election the GOP's margin of victory among white voters almost doubled, from 12 percent to 20 percent. Moreover, while women as a whole voted Democratic, giving rise to talk of a "gender gap" that hurt the GOP, white women nevertheless favored Romney 56 percent to 42 percent—not that far off from the rate of white male support for Romney, at 62 percent. What about white youth? Obama won among those under 45, fueling an uplifting narrative about a post-racial youth free from the fears of their more racially tremulous elders. Yet even among the youngest age bracket of white voters, only 44 percent voted for Obama.[6] Finally, what about by region? As *The Nation* reported, "If only white people had voted . . . Mitt Romney would have carried every state except for Massachusetts, Iowa, Connecticut and New Hampshire."[7] Among whites, race more than gender, age, and region drives how individuals vote, and across all these divisions whites overwhelmingly support the Republican Party.

So we need to be clear: the connection between race and the Republican Party is not accidental, vestigial, or comical, and it's certainly not trivial. Instead, as we will see, over the last half-century conservatives have used racial pandering to win support from white voters for policies that principally favor the extremely wealthy and wreck the middle class. Running on racial appeals, the right has promised to protect supposedly embattled whites, when in reality it has largely harnessed government to the interests of the very affluent. The result is an economic crisis that has engulfed the nation, combining dramatic increases in wealth at the very top along with severe strains for almost everyone else. Today's grossly unequal economy reflects decades of government policies favoring the very rich but justified as a response to threatening minorities. Republican racial pandering is an enormous problem for the country—and in particular for the middle class.

Some will be quick to retort that minorities overwhelming vote Democratic, implying that this symmetry undercuts the argument that there is any great problem with the GOP being identified almost exclusively with whites. But the important questions are, first, why different racial groups vote as they do, and second, whether they are helped or harmed by doing so. Many minorities vote Democratic because they have been repelled by the GOP and also because it's in their economic interests. As we will explore, many whites vote Republican out of racial anxiety and, as members of the broad middle, lose out when they do so.

Dog Whistle Politics aims to lay bare how race has become, and at least in the medium term will remain, central to American electoral politics and the fate of the middle class. Even when willing to concede that race matters when talking about the lives of poor minorities, members of the middle class nevertheless typically harbor an unfounded certainty that race holds little relevance to them or their future. They could not be more wrong, for race constitutes the dark magic by which middle-class voters have been convinced to turn government over to the wildly affluent, notwithstanding the harm this does to themselves. This book's primary goal is to grab the attention of middle-class readers, white and nonwhite alike, to awaken them to the importance of race to their fate. We will not pull government back to the side of the broad middle until we confront the power of racial politics.

■ BLOWING A DOG WHISTLE

How has the GOP managed to elicit racial loyalty despite a national revulsion toward racism? The answer lies in the GOP's use of coded language. Its racial entreaties operate like a dog whistle—a metaphor that pushes us to recognize that modern racial pandering always operates on two levels: inaudible and easily denied in one range, yet stimulating strong reactions in another.

The new racial politics presents itself as steadfastly opposed to racism and ever ready to condemn those who publicly use racial profanity. *We fiercely oppose racism and stand prepared to repudiate anyone who dares utter the n-word.* Meanwhile, though, the new racial discourse keeps up a steady drumbeat of subliminal racial grievances and appeals to color-coded solidarity. *But let's be honest: some groups commit more crimes and use more welfare, other groups are mainly unskilled and illiterate illegals, and some religions inspire violence and don't value human life.* The new racism rips through society, inaudible and also easily defended insofar as it fails to whoop in the tones of the old racism, yet booming in its racial meaning and provoking predictable responses among those who immediately hear the racial undertones of references to the undeserving poor, illegal aliens, and sharia law. Campaigning for president, Ronald Reagan liked to tell stories of Cadillac-driving "welfare queens" and "strapping young bucks" buying T-bone steaks with food stamps. In flogging these tales about the perils of welfare run amok, Reagan always denied any racism and emphasized he never mentioned race. He didn't need to because he was blowing a dog whistle.

In general, using a dog whistle simply means speaking in code to a target audience. Politicians routinely do this, seeking to surreptitiously communicate support to small groups of impassioned voters whose commitments are not broadly embraced by the body politic. The audiences for such dog whistles have included, at different times, civil rights protesters, members of the religious right, environmentalists, and gun rights activists. Dog whistling has no particular political valence, occurring on the right and left, nor is it especially uncommon or troubling in and of itself. Given a diverse public segmented by widely differing priorities, it is entirely predictable that politicians would look for shrouded ways to address divergent audiences.

Throughout this book, I use "dog whistle politics" to mean, more narrowly, coded talk centered on race; while the term could encompass clandestine solicitations on any number of bases, here it refers to racial appeals. Beyond emphasizing race, racial dog whistle politics diverges from the more general practice because the hidden message it seeks to transmit violates a strong moral consensus. The impetus to speak in code reflects more than the concern that many voters do not embrace the target audience's passions. Rather, the substance of the appeal runs counter to national values supporting equality and opposing racism. Those blowing a racial dog whistle know full well that they would be broadly condemned if understood as appealing for racial solidarity among whites.

This makes racial dog whistling a more complicated phenomenon than other sorts of surreptitious politics. It involves, as we shall see, three basic moves: a punch that jabs race into the conversation through thinly veiled references to threatening nonwhites, for instance to welfare cheats or illegal aliens; a parry that slaps away charges of racial pandering, often by emphasizing the lack of any direct reference to a racial group or any use of an epithet; and finally a kick that savages the critic for opportunistically alleging racial victimization. The complex jujitsu of racial dog whistling lies at the center of a new way of talking about race that constantly emphasizes racial divisions, heatedly denies that it does any such thing, and then presents itself as a target of self-serving charges of racism.

A final important difference between routine coded political speech and racial dog whistling lies in what the target audience hears. To be sure, some voters clearly perceive a message of racial resentment and react positively to it; *politician W is with us and against those minorities*, they may say to themselves. But many others would be repulsed by such a message, just as they would reject any politician who openly used racial epithets. For these voters, the cloaked language hides—even from themselves—the racial character of the overture. Terms like gangbanger and sharia law superficially reference behavior and religion. Even as these terms agitate racial fears, for many voters this thin patina suffices to obscure from them the racial nature of their attitudes. Consider Tea Party supporters: "They are all furious at the implication that race is a factor in their political views," writes *Rolling Stone* journalist Matt Taibbi, "despite the fact that they blame the financial crisis on poor black homeowners, spend months on end engrossed by reports about how the New Black Panthers want to kill 'cracker babies,' support politicians who think the Civil Rights Act of 1964 was an overreach of government power, tried to enact South African-style immigration laws in Arizona and obsess over . . . Barack Obama's birth certificate."[8] No doubt very few of the Tea Partiers stampeded by race are racist in the hate-every-black-person sense; indeed, the overwhelming majority are decent folks quick to condemn naked racism. But this is a far cry from saying that racial fears do not motivate them. Dog whistle entreaties often hide racism even from those in whom it triggers strong reactions.

■ RACE AND LIBERAL GOVERNMENT

It would be bad enough if race provided a routine way to win elections; but beyond this, dog whistling underlies efforts to dismantle government commitments essential to supporting a vibrant and growing middle class. As we learned in response to the last great economic calamity to confront the country, to ensure broad prosperity government has four crucial roles to play: first, to help people weather the vicissitudes that easily plunge families into poverty, for instance job loss or ill health; second, to provide escalators of upward mobility, such as quality schooling, higher education, and mortgage assistance; third, to build the nation's infrastructure, thus laying the groundwork for the next great economic boom; and fourth, to rein in marketplace abuses through regulation, and to prevent excessive concentrations of wealth through progressive taxation.

This is the New Deal liberal vision that propelled the largest expansion of the middle class ever seen, and that once enjoyed broad support across the whole country. Throughout this book, I use "middle class" in a manner inspired by the New Deal and its conception of those it sought to help: as a term that encompasses persons in the broad economic middle as well as those in poverty struggling to gain economic security.

These basic liberal commitments are now under sustained attack, and the weapon of choice is race. The New Deal itself was originally limited largely to whites, until under pressure from the growing number of black voters outside the South as well as the burgeoning civil rights movement, beginning in the 1960s the Democratic Party began to fold nonwhites into the broad middle that government sought to help.[9] But sensing an opportunity, Republicans moved in the opposite direction: they began to stoke hostility toward integration in schools and neighborhoods and to enflame resentment toward government initiatives to help nonwhites move into the middle class.

This racial strategy succeeded in winning white votes; more direly, it also worked to turn whites against liberal government. New Deal opponents had long repeated a tired mantra: the undeserving poor abuse government help, robbing hardworking taxpayers. This tale had little traction when whites saw themselves as the beneficiaries of government help, but once convinced that government aimed to shower minorities with their hard-earned tax dollars, this suddenly propelled many whites to reject liberalism. Attacks on integration quickly segued into broadsides against an activist state that funded welfare, schooling, job training programs, and so forth. Hostility toward the New Deal surged among whites—once it came to be seen as a repudiation of lazy, threatening nonwhites and the big government that coddled them.

As an example of how conservatives continue to frame political choices in racial terms, consider two telling responses to Obama's re-election. On election eve 2012, as swing states one by one went for Obama, Fox News commentator Bill O'Reilly rationalized the looming outcome this way: "There are 50 percent of the voting public who want stuff. They want things and who is going to give them things? President Obama. He knows it and he ran on it. Twenty years ago President Obama would have been roundly defeated by an establishment candidate like Mitt Romney. The white establishment is now the minority."[10] Parroting this analysis at the highest level of the Republican Party, Romney himself a few days later privately justified his loss by saying, "the Obama campaign was following the old playbook of giving a lot of stuff to groups that they hoped they could get to vote for them and be motivated to go out to the polls, specifically the African American community, the Hispanic community and young people."[11] As it has for the last five decades, casting whites as victims of an activist government that rains gifts on grasping minorities remains the most potent rhetoric available to conservatives.

■ THE STAKES

The present economic catastrophe confronting the middle class shows what's at stake. Look at median family income. According to the US Census Bureau, the average family income in 2011 was $50,054.[12] This represents an 8 percent decline since the Great Recession began in 2008. It also represents almost no movement since 1970, when dog whistle politics first gathered steam on the national stage and when the average family's income hovered around $45,000 a year. Rather than reflecting at least some stability, this actually betrays considerable lost ground. On average, when adjusted for inflation the pay of a typical male worker was lower in 2010 than in 1978.[13] Only because so many women have entered the workplace have middle-class families in the United States maintained their incomes.[14]

The hardship imposed on the middle class becomes even more unpardonable when compared to the increasing wealth at the very top of the income scale.[15] In the 1970s, the chief executives of major corporations earned roughly 40 times what an average worker made. In 2013, CEOs at the top 500 corporations averaged compensation packages totaling 354 times the typical worker's pay—in other words, they made each day what most workers earned in a whole year.[16] And even beyond chief executives, there's the obscene money going to those who manage money. In 2012, four hedge fund bosses each received payouts of over $1 billion—just one carried off $2.2 billion, thus averaging over $6 million every single day.[17] Or put it this way: if he clumsily dropped a $100 bill, that would represent just over a second of his time, and in the seven seconds it took him to bend down to pick it up, he would have made another $500. The six heirs to the Wal-Mart empire currently hold the same amount of wealth, roughly $90 billion, as the poorest 30 percent of Americans combined—something possible not only because the rich are so rich, but because the poor are so poor.[18] No wonder escalating economic insecurity dominates the public's fears. Not since the gilded years preceding the Great Depression has the United States been so economically unequal, and so financially precarious for those in the middle.

But is dog whistle racism really to blame for the economic calamity confronting the middle class, or is it something else? For instance, do structural changes to the economy or the increasing penetration of money in the political system better explain middle class vulnerability? One answer is that it's impossible to say, since these developments cannot be disaggregated from dog whistle politics. Race-baiting shoved the entire political culture rightward, reflecting but also contributing to other large scale changes in politics and the economy.

But here's a more definitive response: whether it matters most, dog whistle racism matters tremendously because party politics matters tremendously. Notwithstanding other large scale dynamics, whether a Democrat or a Republican occupies the White House directly shapes the economic destiny of the middle class as well as the poor. Noting that "a great deal of economic inequality in the contemporary United States is specifically attributable to the polices and priorities of Republican presidents," Princeton political scientist Larry Bartels reports that, "on average, the real incomes of middle-class families have grown twice as fast under Democrats as they have under Republicans, while the real incomes of working poor families have grown *six times* as fast under Democrats as they have under Republicans."[19] Dog whistle politics is central to the GOP's success, and thus central to the fate of the middle class.

We are in the midst, not at the tail end, of a sustained attack against liberal government. Much has been lost, yet much remains under assault. This is true at the national level, as evident in the agenda of the Republican-dominated House of Representatives, though perhaps it is most obvious at the state level. Look at what has happened where Republicans have captured both the executive and legislative branches, including in states like Wisconsin and North Carolina that until recently stood out as relatively progressive. Despite large public demonstrations protesting GOP extremism, Republicans have set to destroying liberal achievements with a vengeance, slashing funding to education, attacking unions, and gutting unemployment insurance, while ramping up efforts to further disenfranchise minority and working-class voters. How did these extremists come to power in the first place, and what makes voters support their cruel agendas? All too often the answer is race-baiting and other cultural provocations, for instance around abortion, guns, or gay marriage. This book's ultimate goal is to lay bare dog whistle politics, the better to help protect and revive a government that cares for people, provides routes for upward mobility, invests in infrastructure, and regulates concentrated wealth.

■ A BRIEF OUTLINE

In the pages that follow I offer five narrative chapters detailing dog whistle politics from the 1960s to the present, interweaving these with four chapters providing deeper conversations about racism. The narrative chapters proceed chronologically but eschew a steady pace through the last five decades of presidential politics, instead emphasizing turning points in coded race-baiting's development that illuminate the most salient features of contemporary dog whistle politics. Interspersed with the narrative chapters, I braid in complementary chapters that parse evolutions in racism directly connected to political dog whistling.

Chapter One begins with the 1960s, a decade that culminated in the emergence of the Southern strategy and Richard Nixon's election. Examining the decision by politicians to turn to racial demagoguery, Chapter Two follows by introducing the notion of "strategic racism"—the cold, calculating decision to use racial divisions to pursue one's own ends—and argues that this forms the heart of dog whistle politics.

Chapter Three focuses on Ronald Reagan, showing that dog whistle politics centrally involves using race to attack liberal government. Reagan's presidency also corresponded with the conservative popularization of colorblindness, which urges everyone to avoid race as the surest way to get past racial problems. This racial etiquette is widely embraced, including among liberals, yet as Chapter Four shows, colorblindness bolsters dog whistle politics in numerous ways.

Chapter Five explores two important evolutions in dog whistling: first, its adoption by many Democrats, including Bill Clinton; and second, a critical shift during the presidency of George W. Bush in the minority groups presented as threats to whites. Today, Latinos cast as illegal aliens and Muslims portrayed as terrorists are as likely as African Americans to be assigned the role of racial specter. Exploring the developing racial rhetoric used by demagogues, Chapter Six details how dog whistlers constantly manage to trade on racial stereotypes, and also how they defend themselves in a culture that strongly condemns racism.

The last two narrative chapters grapple with the racial politics enveloping the nation's first black president: Chapter Seven places the Tea Party as well as Mitt Romney within the larger trajectory of anti-government racial demagoguery; Chapter Nine explores how Obama seeks to sidestep, and yet ultimately reinforces, dog whistle politics. Sandwiched between these, Chapter Eight uses the notion of "commonsense racism" to answer perhaps the most pressing question raised by dog whistle politics: how race convinces many whites to vote against their own apparent interests.

Dog Whistle Politics concludes with a solutions chapter that warns against complacently assuming that demographic changes alone will resolve dog whistle racism. Organized around agendas for different social actors, this chapter offers a way forward for politicians, civil rights groups, liberal foundations, and unions, as well as for individuals in their daily lives. The proffered suggestions stop well short of asking everyone concerned with escalating economic inequality to work on racial issues first and foremost. But all who care about our society's well-being must understand the role racism plays in garnering votes, and more particularly its role in attacking liberalism and wrecking the middle class. We must hear the dog whistle for what it is if we are to repudiate its constant use to foment a populist hysteria against good government. We are all the victims of dog whistle politics. This book's project is to explain how so—and also, what we can do to fight back.

■ A WORD ON "WHITES"

Before turning to the main text, a last word seems warranted regarding the awkwardness of so much talk about "whites," for instance in the ubiquitous references to white voters and a white political party. Partly, there may be a sensitivity to references to whites accentuated by the context, a book that aims to contest racism. Anti-racist efforts have sometimes gone astray in critiquing whites. Yet even when they haven't done so, repeatedly they have been accused of promoting anti-white prejudice. As a result, today some hear almost any reference to whites coming from minorities or the political left as betraying a supposed "hate whitey" undercurrent. Also, discussing whites may come across as jarring because it violates an increasingly stringent norm that race should not be discussed openly. This preference for colorblindness, for a public blindness surrounding all things connected to race, holds broad attraction across the political spectrum. Yet conservatives have converted colorblindness into an ideology that facilitates and also protects dog whistling. We cannot assess how appeals to white identity shape modern politics without carefully talking about whites, and also without transgressing—and parsing—colorblindness.

Yet even tempered references to whites may generate discomfort: the term seems to treat as a monolith a group that comprises tens of millions of unique individuals who relate to their racial identity in innumerable, complicated ways. Thus, to be absolutely clear, in repeatedly talking about whites (and nonwhites) in the aggregate, I do not mean to imply a false uniformity that treats all group members as if they hold an identical relationship to race. Like all major social torsions, race influences individuals in myriad ways, some less, some more, some almost not at all. Nevertheless, "white" identity—complex, historically produced, constantly evolving—remains a potent social force, one we can only grapple with by naming and discussing it. In *Dog Whistle Politics*, we are principally concerned with voters who respond to appeals directed to their sense of themselves as white persons. Even as we take care to respect the complicacy of this phenomenon, we can hardly move forward without treating white identity as socially meaningful. "White" in this book serves as a necessary shorthand for a colossally powerful social entanglement.

A final thought: the constant references to whites stimulated by race-baiting may lead some readers to say, *all this talk about white voters is not about me.* Staunch liberals may feel that since they will never vote Republican, the whites at the center of this book's analysis are others, not them. They may especially hold this conviction if they already consider themselves wise to the dog whistle game, because this puts them on the outside looking in (and perhaps down) on the victims of the con. With even more certainty that they are not implicated, nonwhites may read these pages as an anthropological tour of unfamiliar others perceived as permanently on the other side of an impassable racial boundary. But as the Preface cautions, this book is about all of us. The pages that follow show that many confirmed liberals, white and nonwhite alike, subscribe to racial ideas that help empower dog whistle politics. Moreover, we will also see that racial pandering is evolving to pull in some minorities. Just as "white" does not denote a monolithic entity, neither does it denote a safely distant essence. The very complexity and dynamism of whiteness ensures that we are all caught to some extent within its morass.

1

The GOP's Rise as "the White Man's Party"

Dog whistle politics originates with two politicians in the 1960s, and each reveals a core feature of modern race-baiting: George Wallace illustrates the drive to use racial appeals to garner votes; Barry Goldwater evidences race's potential to turn whites against New Deal liberalism. Racial pandering during this era culminates in the "Southern strategy" adopted by Richard Nixon. This term remains in circulation today as a way to describe dog whistle politics, but it carries serious conceptual limitations.

F ew names conjure the recalcitrant South, fighting integration with fire-breathing fury, like that of George Wallace. The central image of this "redneck poltergeist," as one biographer referred to him, is of Wallace during his inauguration as governor of Alabama in January 1963, before waves of applause and the rapt attention of the national media, committing himself to the perpetual defense of segregation.[1] Speaking on a cold day in Montgomery, Wallace thundered his infamous call to arms: "Today I have stood, where once Jefferson Davis stood, and took an oath to my people. It is very appropriate then that from this Cradle of the Confederacy, this very Heart of the Great Anglo-Saxon Southland . . . we sound the drum for freedom. . . . In the name of the greatest people that have ever trod this earth, I draw the line in the dust and toss the gauntlet before the feet of tyranny . . . and I say . . . segregation now . . . segregation tomorrow . . . segregation forever!"[2]

The story of dog whistle politics begins with George Wallace. But it does not start with Wallace as he stood that inauguration day. Rather, the story focuses on who Wallace was before, and on whom he quickly became.

Before that January day, Wallace had not been a rabid segregationist; indeed, by Southern standards, Wallace had been a racial moderate. He had sat on the board of trustees of a prominent black educational enterprise, the Tuskegee

Institute. He had refused to join the walkout of Southern delegates from the 1948 Democratic convention when they protested the adoption of a civil rights platform. As a trial court judge, he earned a reputation for treating blacks civilly—a breach of racial etiquette so notable that decades later J.L. Chestnut, one of the very few black lawyers in Alabama at the time, would marvel that in 1958 "George Wallace was the first judge to call me 'Mr.' in a courtroom."³ The custom had been instead to condescendingly refer to all blacks by their first name, whatever their age or station. When Wallace initially ran for governor in 1958, the NAACP endorsed him; his opponent had the blessing of the Ku Klux Klan.

In the fevered atmosphere of the South, roiled by the 1954 *Brown v. Board of Education* decision forbidding school segregation, the moderate Wallace lost in his first campaign for governor. Years later, the victor would reconstruct the campaign, distilling a simple lesson: the "primary reason I beat [Wallace] was because he was considered soft on the race question at the time. That's the primary reason."⁴ This lesson was not lost on Wallace, and in turn, would reshape American politics for the next half-century. On the night he lost the 1958 election, Wallace sat in a car with his cronies, smoking a cigar, rehashing the loss, and putting off his concession speech. Finally steeling himself, Wallace eased opened the car door to go inside and break the news to his glum supporters. He wasn't just going to accept defeat, though, he was going to learn from it. As he snuffed out his cigar and stepped into the evening, he turned back: "Well, boys," he vowed, "no other son-of-a-bitch will ever out-nigger me again."⁵

Four years later, Wallace ran as a racial reactionary, openly courting the support of the Klan and fiercely committing himself to the defense of segregation. It was as an arch-segregationist that Wallace won the right to stand for inauguration in January 1963, allowing him to proclaim segregation today, tomorrow, and forever. Summarizing his first two campaigns for governor of Alabama, Wallace would later recall, "you know, I started off talking about schools and highways and prisons and taxes—and I couldn't make them listen. Then I began talking about niggers—and they stomped the floor."⁶

Wallace was far from the only Southern politician to veer to the right on race in the 1950s.⁷ The mounting pressure for black equality destabilized a quiescent political culture that had assumed white supremacy was unassailable, putting pressure on all public persons to stake out their position for or against integration. Wallace figures here for a different reason, one that becomes clear in *how* he upheld his promise to protect segregation.

During his campaign, Wallace had vowed to stand in schoolhouse doorways to personally bar the entrance of black students into white institutions.

In June 1963, he got his chance. The federal courts had ordered the integration of the University of Alabama, Tuscaloosa, and US Deputy Attorney General Nicholas Katzenbach flew down from Washington, DC, to enforce the order. More than 200 national reporters and all three of the major broadcast networks were on hand for the promised confrontation. From behind a podium, Wallace stood in the June heat and raised his hand to peremptorily bar the approach of Katzenbach. Then he read a seven-minute peroration that avoided the red-meat language of racial supremacy and instead emphasized "the illegal usurpation of power by the Central Government." In footage carried on all three networks, the nation watched as Wallace hectored Katzenbach, culminating with Wallace declaiming, "I do hereby denounce and forbid this illegal and unwarranted action by the Central Government."[8] It was pure theater, even down to white lines chalked on the ground to show where the respective thespians should stand (Katzenbach approached more closely than expected, but ultimately that only heightened the drama). Wallace knew from the start that he would back down, and after delivering his stem-winder, that is what he did. Within two hours, as expected, the University of Alabama's first two black students were on campus.

Lecturing US Deputy Attorney General Nicholas Katzenbach on states' rights, Governor George Wallace stands in the schoolhouse door blocking integration at the University of Alabama, Tuscaloosa. Library of Congress (Warren K. Leffler, photographer)

Over the next week, the nation reacted. More than 100,000 telegrams and letters flooded the office of the Alabama governor. More than half of them were from outside of the South. Did they condemn him? Five out of every 100 did. The other 95 percent praised his brave stand in the schoolhouse doorway.[9]

The nation's reaction was an epiphany for Wallace, or perhaps better, three thunderbolts that together convinced Wallace to reinvent himself yet again. First, Wallace realized with a shock that hostility toward blacks was not confined to the South. "He had looked out upon those white Americans north of Alabama and suddenly been awakened by a blinding vision: 'They all hate black people, all of them. They're all afraid, all of them. Great god! That's it! They're all Southern. The whole United States is Southern.'"[10] Wallace suddenly knew that overtures to racial resentment would resonate across the country.

His second startling realization was that he, George Wallace, had figured out how to exploit that pervasive animosity. The key lay in seemingly non-racial language. At his inauguration, Wallace had defended segregation and extolled the proud Anglo-Saxon Southland, thereby earning national ridicule as an unrepentant redneck. Six months later, talking not about stopping integration but about states' rights and arrogant federal authority—and visually aided by footage showing him facing down a powerful Department of Justice official rather than vulnerable black students attired in their Sunday best—Wallace was a countrywide hero. "States' rights" was a paper-thin abstraction from the days before the Civil War when it had meant the right of Southern states to continue slavery. Then, as a rejoinder to the demand for integration, it meant the right of Southern states to continue laws mandating racial segregation—a system of debasement so thorough that it "extended to churches and schools, to housing and jobs, to eating and drinking . . . to virtually all forms of public transportation, to sports and recreations, to hospitals, orphanages, prisons, and asylums, and ultimately to funeral homes, morgues, and cemeteries."[11] That's what "states' rights" defended, though in the language of state-federal relations rather than white supremacy. Yet this was enough of a fig leaf to allow persons queasy about black equality to oppose integration without having to admit, to others and perhaps even to themselves, their racial attitudes.

"Wallace pioneered a kind of soft porn racism in which fear and hate could be mobilized without mentioning race itself except to deny that one is a racist," a Wallace biographer argues.[12] The notion of "soft porn racism" ties directly to the thesis of *Dog Whistle Politics*. Wallace realized the need to simultaneously move away from supremacist language that was increasingly unacceptable, while articulating a new vocabulary that channeled old, bigoted ideas. He needed a new form of racism that stimulated the intended audience without overtly transgressing prescribed social limits. The congratulatory telegrams from across the nation revealed to Wallace that he had found the magic formula. Hardcore racism showed white supremacy in disquieting detail. In contrast, the new soft porn racism hid any direct references to race, even as it continued to trade on racial stimulation. As a contemporary of Wallace marveled, "he can use all the other issues—law and order, running your own schools, protecting property rights—and never mention race. But people will know he's telling them 'a nigger's trying to get your job, trying to move into your neighborhood.' What Wallace is doing is talking to them in a kind of shorthand, a kind of code."[13]

Finally, a third bolt of lightening struck Wallace: he could be the one! The governor's mansion in Montgomery need not represent his final destination. He could ride the train of revamped race-baiting all the way to the White House. Wallace ran for president as a third-party candidate in 1964, and then again in 1968, 1972, and 1976. It's his 1968 campaign that most concerns us, for there Wallace ran against a consummate politician who was quick to appreciate, and adopt, Wallace's refashioned racial demagoguery: Richard Nixon. We'll turn to the Wallace-Nixon race soon, but first, another set of weathered bones must be excavated—the remains of Barry Goldwater.

■ THE RISE OF RACIALLY IDENTIFIED PARTIES

The Republican Party today, in its voters and in its elected officials, is almost all white. But it wasn't always like that. Indeed, in the decades immediately before 1964, neither party was racially identified in the eyes of the American public. Even as the Democratic Party on the national level increasingly embraced civil rights, partly as a way to capture the growing political power of blacks who had migrated to Northern cities, Southern Democrats—like George Wallace— remained staunch defenders of Jim Crow. Meanwhile, among Republicans, the racial antipathies of the rightwing found little favor among many party leaders.[14] To take an important example, *Brown* and its desegregation imperative were backed by Republicans: Chief Justice Earl Warren, who wrote the opinion, was a Republican, and the first troops ordered into the South in 1957 to protect black students attempting to integrate a white school were sent there by the Republican administration of Dwight Eisenhower and his vice president, Richard Nixon. Reflecting the roughly equal commitment of both parties to racial progress, even as late as 1962, the public perceived Republicans and Democrats to be similarly committed to racial justice. In that year, when asked which party "is more likely to see that Negroes get fair treatment in jobs and housing,"

22.7 percent of the public said Democrats and 21.3 percent said Republicans, while over half could perceive no difference between the two.[15]

The 1964 presidential election marked the beginning of the realignment we live with today. Where in 1962 both parties were perceived as equally, if tepidly, supportive of civil rights, two years later 60 percent of the public identified Democrats as more likely to pursue fair treatment, versus only 7 percent who so identified the Republican Party.[16] What happened?

Groundwork for the shift was laid in the run-up to the 1964 election by right-wing elements in the Republican Party, which gained momentum from the loss of the then-moderate Nixon to John F. Kennedy in 1960. This faction of the party had never stopped warring against the New Deal. Its standard bearer was Barry Goldwater, a senator from Arizona and heir to a department store fortune. His pampered upbringing and wealth notwithstanding, Goldwater affected a cowboy's rough-and-tumble persona in his dress and speech, casting himself as a walking embodiment of the Marlboro Man's disdain for the nanny state. Goldwater and the reactionary stalwarts who rallied to him saw the Democratic Party as a mortal threat to the nation: domestically, because of the corrupting influence of a powerful central government deeply involved in regulating the marketplace and using taxes to reallocate wealth downward, and abroad in its willingness to compromise with communist countries instead of going to war against them. Goldwater himself, though, was no racial throwback.[17] For instance, in 1957 and again in 1960 he voted in favor of federal civil rights legislation. By 1961, however, Goldwater and his partisans had become convinced that the key to electoral success lay in gaining ground in the South, and that in turn required appealing to racist sentiments in white voters, even at the cost of black support. As Goldwater drawled, "We're not going to get the Negro vote as a bloc in 1964 and 1968, so we ought to go hunting where the ducks are."[18]

This racial plan riled more moderate members of the Republican establishment, such as New York senator Jacob Javits, who in the fall of 1963 may have been the first to refer to a "Southern Strategy" in the context of repudiating it.[19] By then, however, the right wing of the party had won out. As the conservative journalist Robert Novak reported after attending a meeting of the Republican National Committee in Denver during the summer of 1963: "A good many, perhaps a majority of the party's leadership, envision substantial political gold to be mined in the racial crisis by becoming in fact, though not in name, the White Man's Party. 'Remember,' one astute party worker said quietly . . . 'this isn't South Africa. The white man outnumbers the Negro 9 to 1 in this country.' "[20] The rise of a racially-identified GOP is *not* a tale of latent bigotry in that party. It is instead a story centered on the strategic decision to use racism to become "the White Man's Party."

That same summer of 1963, as key Republican leaders strategized on how to shift their party to the far right racially, the Democrats began to lean in the other direction. Northern constituents were increasingly appalled by the violence, shown almost nightly on broadcast television, of Southern efforts to beat down civil rights protesters. Reacting to the growing clamor that something be done, President Kennedy introduced a sweeping civil rights bill that stirred the hopes of millions that segregation would soon be illegal in employment and at business places open to the public. Despite these hopes, however, prospects for the bill's passage seemed dim, as the Southern Democrats were loath to support civil rights and retained sufficient power to bottle up the bill. Then on November 22, 1963, Kennedy was assassinated. His vice president, Lyndon Johnson, assumed the presidency vowing to make good on Kennedy's priorities, chief among them civil rights. Only five days after Kennedy's death, Johnson in his first address to Congress implored the assembly that "no memorial oration or eulogy could more eloquently honor President Kennedy's memory than the earliest possible passage of the civil rights bill for which he fought so long."[21] Even under these conditions, it took Johnson's determined stewardship to overcome three months of dogged legislative stalling before Kennedy's civil rights bill finally passed the next summer. Known popularly as the 1964 Civil Rights Act, it still stands as the greatest civil rights achievement of the era.

Indicating the persistence of the old, internally divided racial politics of both parties, the act passed with broad bipartisan support and against broad bipartisan opposition—the cleavage was regional, rather than in terms of party affiliation. Roughly 90 percent of non-Southern senators supported the bill, while 95 percent of Southern senators opposed it. Yet, heralding the incipient emergence of the new politics of party alignment along racial lines, Barry Goldwater also voted against the civil rights bill. He was one of only five senators from outside the South to do so. Goldwater claimed he saw a looming Orwellian state moving to coerce private citizens to spy on each other for telltale signs of racism. "To give genuine effect to the prohibitions of this bill," Goldwater contended from the Senate floor, "bids fair to result in the development of an 'informer' psychology in great areas of our national life—neighbor spying on neighbor, workers spying on workers, businessmen spying on businessmen."[22] This all seemed a little hysterical. More calculatingly, it could not have escaped Goldwater's attention that voting against a civil rights law associated with blacks, Kennedy, and Johnson would help him "go hunting where the ducks are."

Running for president in 1964, the Arizonan strode across the South, hawking small-government bromides and racially coded appeals. In terms of the latter, he sold his vote against the 1964 Civil Rights Act as a bold stand in favor of "states' rights" and "freedom of association." States' rights, Goldwater insisted, preserved state autonomy against intrusive meddling from a distant power—though obviously the burning issue of the day was the federal government's efforts to limit state involvement in racial degradation and group oppression. Freedom of association, Goldwater explained, meant the right of individuals to be free from government coercion in choosing whom to let onto their property—but in the South this meant first and foremost the right of business owners to exclude blacks from hotels, restaurants, movie theaters, and retail establishments. Like Wallace, Goldwater had learned how to talk about blacks without ever mentioning race.

No less than Wallace, Goldwater also demonstrated a flair for political stagecraft. A reporter following Goldwater's campaign through the South captured some of the spectacle: "to show the country the 'lily-white' character of Republicanism in Dixie," party flaks filled the floor of the football stadium in Montgomery, Alabama, with "a great field of white lilies—living lilies, in perfect bloom, gorgeously arrayed." To this tableau, the campaign added "seven hundred Alabama girls in long white gowns, all of a whiteness as impossible as the greenness of the field." Onto this scene emerged Goldwater, first moving this way and then that way through "fifty or so yards of choice Southern womanhood," before taking the stand to give his speech defending states' rights and freedom of association. If these coded terms were too subtle for some, no one could fail to grasp the symbolism of the white lilies and the white-gowned women. Much of the emotional resistance to racial equality centered around the fear that black men would become intimate with white women. This scene represented "what the rest of his Southern troops—the thousands in the packed stands, the tens of thousands in Memphis and New Orleans and Atlanta and Shreveport and Greenville—passionately believed they were defending."[23] Goldwater made sure white Southerners understood he was fighting to protect them and their women against blacks.

How would Goldwater fare in the South? Beyond his racial pandering, that depended on how his anti-New Deal message was received. The Great Depression had devastated the region, which lagged behind the North in industry. Federal assistance to the poor as well as major infrastructure projects, such as the Tennessee Valley Authority (TVA) that brought electricity for the first time to millions, made Southerners among the New Deal's staunchest supporters. Yet despite the New Deal's popularity in the South, Goldwater campaigned against it. While he was willing to pander racially, Goldwater also prided himself on telling audiences what he thought they needed to hear, at least as far as the bracing virtues of rugged individualism were concerned. Thus he made clear, for instance, that he favored selling off the TVA, and also attacked other popular programs.[24] As recounted by Rick Perlstein, a Goldwater political biographer, at one rally in West Virginia, Goldwater "called the War on Poverty 'plainly and simply a war on your pocketbooks,' a fraud because only 'the vast resources of private business' could produce the wealth to truly slay penury." Perlstein singled out the tin-eared cruelty of this message: "In the land of the tar-paper shack, the gap-toothed smile, and the open sewer—where the 'vast resources of private business' were represented in the person of the coal barons who gave men black lung, then sent them off to die without pensions—the message just sounded perverse. As he left, lines of workmen jeered him."[25]

Another factor also worked against Goldwater: he was a Republican, and the South reviled the Party of Lincoln. If across the nation neither party was seen as more or less friendly toward civil rights, the South had its own views on the question. There, it was the local Democratic machine that represented white interests, while the GOP was seen as the proximate cause of the Civil War and as the party of the carpetbaggers who had peremptorily ruled the South during Reconstruction. The hostility of generations of white Southerners toward Republicans only intensified with the Republican Eisenhower's decision to send in federal troops to enforce the Republican Warren's ruling forbidding school segregation in *Brown*. Most white Southerners had never voted Republican in their lives, and had vowed—like their parents and grandparents before them—that they never would.

Ultimately, however, these handicaps barely impeded Goldwater's performance in the South. He convinced many Southern voters to vote Republican for the first time ever, and in the Deep South, comprised of those five states with the highest black populations, Goldwater won outright. The anti-New Deal Republican carried Louisiana, Georgia, Alabama, Mississippi, and South Carolina, states in which whites had *never* voted for a Republican president in more than miniscule numbers. This was a shocking transformation, one that can only be explained by Goldwater's ability to transmit a set of codes that white voters readily understood as a promise to protect racial segregation. It seemed that voters simply ignored Goldwater's philosophy of governance as well as his party affiliation and instead rewarded his hostility toward civil rights. In this sense, Goldwater's conservatism operated in the South less like a genuine political ideology and more like Wallace's soft porn racism: as a set of codes that voters readily understood as defending white supremacy. Goldwater didn't win the South as a small-government libertarian, but rather as a racist.

If in the South race trumped anti-government politics, in the North Goldwater's anti-civil rights attacks found much less traction. Opposing civil rights smacked too much of Southern intransigence, and while there was resistance to racial reform in the North, it had not yet become an overriding issue for many whites. That left Goldwater running on promises to end the New Deal, and this proved wildly unpopular. To campaign against liberalism in 1964 was to campaign against an activist government that had lifted the country out of the throes of a horrendous depression still squarely in the rear view mirror, and that had then launched millions into the middle class. More than that, though, to campaign against liberalism in 1964 was to attack government programs still largely aimed at whites—and that sort of welfare was broadly understood as legitimate and warranted.

Goldwater's anti-welfare tirades produced a landslide victory, but for Lyndon Johnson. Voters crushed Goldwater's last-gasp attack on the New Deal state. Outside of the South, he lost by overwhelming numbers in every state except his Arizona home. Voters were offended by his over-the-top attacks on popular New Deal programs as well as by his penchant for saber rattling when it came to foreign policy. Goldwater especially suffered after the release of "Daisy," a Johnson campaign ad that juxtaposed a little girl picking the petals off a flower with footage of a spiraling mushroom cloud, sending the message that Gold-water's militarism threatened nuclear Armageddon. In the end, the Democrats succeeded in making Goldwater look like a loon. "To the Goldwater slogan 'In Your Heart, You Know He's Right,' the Democrats shot back, 'In Your Guts, You Know He's Nuts.' "[26] The country as a whole, it seemed, had solidly allied itself with progressive governance, and big-money/small-government conservatism was finally, utterly dead.

Or at least, this was the lesson most people took from the 1964 election. But like the clang of a distant alarm barely perceptible against the buzzing din of consensus, a warning was rising from the South: racial entreaties had convinced even the staunchest Democrats to abandon New Deal liberalism. If race-baiting had won over Southern whites to anti-government politics, could the same work across the country?

■ RICHARD NIXON

Notwithstanding the emerging racial strategy initiated by Goldwater, when Richard Nixon secured the Republican nomination in 1968, the new racial politics of his party had not yet gelled, either within the party generally, or in Nixon himself. Indeed, the moderate Nixon's emergence as the party's presidential candidate reflected the extent to which the Goldwater faction had lost credibility in the wake of their champion's disastrous drubbing. Nevertheless, the dynamics of the presidential race would quickly push Nixon toward race-baiting. Nixon's principal opponent in 1968 was Johnson's vice president, Hubert Humphrey. But running as an independent candidate, George Wallace was flanking Nixon on the right. By October 1, just a month before the election, Wallace was polling more support in the South than either Humphrey or Nixon. Nor was his support limited to that region. Wallace was siphoning crucial votes across the country, and staging massive rallies in ostensibly liberal strongholds, for instance drawing 20,000 partisans to Madison Square Garden in New York, and 70,000 faithful to the Boston Common—more than any rally ever held by the Kennedys, Wallace liked to crow.[27] Republican operatives guessed that perhaps 80 percent of the Wallace voters in the South would otherwise support Nixon, and a near-majority in the North as well.[28]

Late in the campaign, Nixon opted to publicly tack right on race. He had already reached a backroom deal with South Carolina Senator Strom Thurmond—an arch-segregationist who had led the revolt against the Democratic Party in 1948 when it endorsed a modest civil rights plank, and who switched to become a Republican in 1964 to throw his weight behind Goldwater. Nixon bought Thurmond's support during the primary season by secretly promising that he would restrict federal enforcement of school desegregation in the South.[29] Now he would make this same promise to the nation. On October 7, Nixon came out against "forced busing," an increasingly potent euphemism for the system of transporting students across the boundaries of segregated neighborhoods in order to integrate schools. Mary Frances Berry pierces the pretense that the issue was putting one's child on a bus: "African-American attempts to desegregate schools were confronted by white flight and complaints that the problem was not desegregation, but busing, oftentimes by people who sent their children to school every day on buses, including mediocre white private academies established to avoid integration."[30] "Busing" offered a Northern analog to states' rights. The language may have referred to transportation, but the emotional wallop came from defiance toward integration.

Nixon also began to hammer away at the issue of law and order. In doing so, he drew upon a rhetorical frame rooted in Southern resistance to civil rights. From the inception of the civil rights movement in the 1950s, Southern politicians had disparaged racial activists as "lawbreakers," as indeed technically they were. In the Jim Crow regions, African Americans had long pressed basic equality demands precisely by breaking laws mandating segregation: sit-ins and freedom rides purposefully violated Jim Crow statutes in order to challenge white supremacist social norms. Dismissing these protesters as criminals shifted the issue from a defense of white supremacy to a more neutral-seeming concern with "order," while simultaneously stripping the activists of moral stature. Demonstrators were no longer Americans willing to risk beatings and even death for a grand ideal, but rather criminal lowlifes disposed toward antisocial behavior. Ultimately, the language of law and order justified a more "quiet" form of violence in defense of the racial status quo, replacing lynchings with mass arrests for trespassing and delinquency.[31]

By the mid-1960s, "law and order" had become a surrogate expression for concern about the civil rights movement. Illustrating this rhetoric's increasingly national reach, in 1965 FBI Director J. Edgar Hoover denounced the advocacy of nonviolent civil disobedience by civil rights leaders as a catalyst for lawbreaking and even violent rioting: "'Civil disobedience,' a seditious slogan of gross irresponsibility, has captured the imagination of citizens. . . . I am greatly concerned that certain racial leaders are doing the civil rights movement a great disservice by suggesting that citizens need only obey the laws with which they agree. Such an attitude breeds disrespect for the law and even civil disorder and rioting."[32] This sense of growing disorder was accentuated by urban riots often involving protracted battles between the police and minority communities. In addition, large and increasingly angry protests against the Vietnam War also added to the fear of metastasizing social strife. Exploiting the growing panic that equated social protest with social chaos, one of Nixon's campaign commercials showed flashing images of demonstrations, riots, police, and violence, over which a deep voice intoned: "Let us recognize that the first right of every American is to be free from domestic violence. So I pledge to you, we shall have order in the United States." A caption stated boldly: "This time. . . . vote like your whole world depended on it . . . NIXON."[33]

Nixon had mastered Wallace's dark art. Forced bussing, law and order, and security from unrest as the essential civil right of the majority—all of these were coded phrases that allowed Nixon to appeal to racial fears without overtly mentioning race at all. Yet race remained the indisputable, intentional subtext of the appeal. As Nixon exulted after watching one of his own commercials: "Yep, this hits it right on the nose . . . it's all about law and order and the damn Negro-Puerto Rican groups out there."[34]

Nixon didn't campaign exclusively on racial themes; notably, he also stressed his opposition to anti-war protesters, while simultaneously portraying himself as the candidate most likely to bring the war to an end. Nevertheless, racial appeals formed an essential element of Nixon's '68 campaign. Nixon's special counsel, John Ehrlichman, bluntly summarized that year's campaign strategy: "We'll go after the racists." According to Ehrlichman, the "subliminal appeal to the anti-black voter was always present in Nixon's statements and speeches."[35]

NIXON'S SOUTHERN STRATEGY

Nixon barely won in 1968, edging Humphrey by less than one percent of the national vote. Wallace, meanwhile, had captured nearly 14 percent of the vote. Had Nixon's coded race-baiting helped? Initially there was uncertainty, and in his first two years in office Nixon governed as if he still believed the federal government had some role to play in helping out nonwhites. For instance, Nixon came into office proposing the idea of a flat wealth transfer to the poor, which would have gone a long way toward breaking down racial inequalities.[36] But over the course of those two years, a new understanding consolidated regarding the tidal shift that had occurred.

On the Democratic side, in 1970 two pollsters, Richard Scammon and Ben Wattenberg, published *The Real Majority*, cautioning their party that "Social Issues" now divided the base. "The machinist's wife in Dayton may decide to leave the Democratic reservation in 1972 and vote for Nixon or Wallace or their ideological descendants," Scammon and Wattenberg warned. "If she thinks the Democrats feel that she isn't scared of crime but that she's really a bigot, if she thinks that Democrats feel the police are Fascist pigs and the Black Panthers and the Weathermen are just poor, misunderstood, picked-upon kids, if she thinks that Democrats are for the hip drug culture and that she, the machinist's wife, is not only a bigot, but a square, then good-bye lady—and good-bye Democrats." How, then, could the party get ahead of these issues? Scammon and Wattenberg were frank: "The Democrats in the South were hurt by being perceived (correctly) as a pro-black national party." The solution was clear: the Democratic Party had to temper its "pro-black stance."[37]

On the Republican side, a leading Nixon strategist had come to the same conclusion about race as a potential wedge issue—though, predictably, with a different prescription. In 1969, Kevin Phillips published *The Emerging Republican Majority*, arguing that because of racial resentments a historical realignment was underway that would cement a new Republican majority that would endure for decades. A young prodigy obsessed with politics, Phillips had worked out the details of his argument in the mid-1960s, and then had gone to work helping to elect Nixon. When the 1968 returns seemed to confirm his thesis, he published his research—nearly 500 pages, with 47 maps and 143 charts. Beneath the details, Phillips had a simple, even deterministic thesis: "Historically, our party system has reflected layer upon layer of group oppositions." Politics, according to Phillips, turned principally on group animosity—"the prevailing cleavages in American voting behavior have been ethnic and cultural. Politically, at least, the United States has not been a very effective melting pot."

As to what was driving the latest realignment, Phillips was blunt: "The Negro problem, having become a national rather than a local one, is the principal cause of the breakup of the New Deal coalition." For Phillips, it was almost inevitable that most whites would abandon the Democratic Party once it became identified with blacks. "Ethnic and cultural division has so often shaped American politics that, given the immense midcentury impact of Negro enfranchisement and integration, reaction to this change almost inevitably had to result in political realignment."[38] Phillips saw his emerging Republican majority this way: "the nature of the majority—or potential majority—seems clear. It is largely white and middle class. It is concentrated in the South, the West, and suburbia."[39]

The number crunchers had spoken. The Southern strategy, incipient for a decade, had matured into a clear route to electoral dominance. The old Democratic alliance of Northeastern liberals, the white working class, Northern blacks, and Southern Democrats, could be riven by racial appeals. Beginning in 1970, Richard Nixon embraced the politics of racial division wholeheartedly. He abandoned the idea of a flat wealth transfer to the poor. Now, Nixon repeatedly emphasized law and order issues. He railed against forced busing in the North. He reversed the federal government's position on Southern school integration, slowing the process down and making clear that the courts would have no help from his administration. But perhaps nothing symbolized the new Nixon more than his comments in December 1970. Reflecting his initially moderate position on domestic issues, early in his administration Nixon had appointed George Romney—a liberal Republican and, incidentally, Mitt Romney's father—as his secretary of housing and urban development. In turn, Romney had made integration of the suburbs his special mission, even coming up with a plan to cut off federal funds to communities that refused to allow integrated housing.[40] By late 1970, however, when these jurisdictions howled at the temerity, Nixon took their side, throwing his cabinet officer under the bus. In a public address, Nixon baldly stated: "I can assure you that it is not the policy of this government to use the power of the federal government . . . for forced integration of the suburbs. I believe that forced integration of the suburbs is not in the national interest."[41] That dog whistle blasted like the shriek of an onrushing train.

In 1963, Robert Novak had written that many Republican leaders were intent on converting the Party of Lincoln into the White Man's Party. The following year, Goldwater went down in crushing defeat, winning only 36 percent of the white vote. Even so, less than a decade later, the racial transmogrification of the Republicans was well underway. In 1972, Nixon's first full dog whistle campaign netted him 70 percent of the white vote, leaving his opponent, George McGovern, with support from less than one in three whites. Defeated by the

Southern strategy, McGovern neatly summed it up: "What is the Southern Strategy? It is this. It says to the South: Let the poor stay poor, let your economy trail the nation, forget about decent homes and medical care for all your people, choose officials who will oppose every effort to benefit the many at the expense of the few—and in return, we will try to overlook the rights of the black man, appoint a few southerners to high office, and lift your spirits by attacking the 'eastern establishment' whose bank accounts we are filling with your labor and your industry."[42] McGovern erred in supposing that the Southern strategy pertained only to the South. Nixon had already learned from Wallace, and then later from the number crunchers, that coded racial appeals would work nationwide. Other than that, especially in its class and race dimensions, McGovern had dog whistle politics dead to rights.

■ THE SOUTHERN STRATEGY RECONSIDERED

The Southern strategy is surrounded by a whole slew of misconceptions that combine to diminish its seeming importance. It's thus crucial to be clear that dog whistle politics has always: transcended the South; involved Democrats as well as Republicans; extended beyond race to include other social issues as well as class; comprised much more than a simple backlash; and appealed not only to the white working class but also to white elites. With these misunderstandings stripped away, it becomes far easier to see how dog whistle racism has wrought fundamental changes in American party politics.

A national strategy. The most common misconception of the Southern strategy—though an understandable one, given its name—is that this is a regional dynamic that tells us little about areas outside the peculiar South.[43] Race is especially potent in the former Confederacy, of course, but even in 1970 dog whistling was a national, not regional, strategy. Recall Wallace's epiphany that "the whole United States is Southern." Kevin Phillips also saw clearly that success lay in stimulating racial antipathies among whites across the country. For Phillips, if there was a regional dynamic at work, it was instead an anti-Northeast one: he predicted that the whole country except the Northeast (and also the sparsely populated and largely white Northwest) would soon turn reliably Republican.[44] Phillips argued that those trending Republican included "Southerners, Borderers [those living in border states straddling the North and South], Germans, Scotch-Irish, Pennsylvania Dutch, Irish, Italians, Eastern Europeans and other urban Catholics, middle-class suburbanites, Sun Belt residents, Rocky Mountain and Pacific Interior populists." In contrast, he anticipated that the Democratic Party would soon be restricted to representing "silk-stocking Megalopolitans, the San Francisco-Berkeley-Madison-Ann Arbor electorate, Scandinavian progressives and Jews," in addition to the "Northeastern Establishment" and blacks.[45] Regarding white voters, Phillips proved largely prescient. While in the South whites vote much more aggressively for Republicans than in other regions, in every region except in the Northeast majorities of whites continue to vote Republican with very rare exceptions.[46]

There's a further reason to avoid dismissing the Southern strategy as merely regional: doing so tends to invite the dismissal of the South itself, as a backward, morally stunted area that we can safely ignore, or even insult.[47] Yes, the South inherits an ugly strain of racism, and nowhere is dog whistle politics more fecund. After 2012, Republicans controlled all 11 state legislatures of the former Confederacy, and their campaign tactics centered more than ever on depicting themselves as the white party and Democrats as beholden to minorities.[48] But this is a far cry from saying that what happens in the South stays there. On the contrary, the Republican's political dominance in the South, combined with its racial roots, ensures an outsize influence for racial politics nationally, especially in Congress. Moreover, beyond politics, since the 1970s, Southern white culture—in the form of country music and the adoption of a faux working class sensibility that embraces pick-up trucks, fishing holes, cheap beer, NASCAR, and "you know you're a redneck when . . . " humor—has spread throughout the nation.[49] The South's influence on the country's direction is increasing rather than diminishing, and the racial politics that plays well there inescapably affects us all. We should not think that the Southern strategy applies only to the South; and neither should we suppose that the South does not influence national culture and politics.

A bipartisan strategy. The Southern strategy is also mistakenly diminished when it is attributed only to Republicans. On the contrary, dog whistle politics originated with and continues to find a home in the Democratic Party. It was the Southern Democrats, not the GOP, that had been the white man's party for generations—using state law and party rules, and also economic coercion and violent mayhem, to disenfranchise blacks. Campaigning in 1946, Mississippi senator Theodore Bilbo intimated how Democrats kept politics white: "You and I know what's the best way to keep the nigger from voting. You do it in the night before the election. I don't have to tell you any more than that. Red-blooded men know what I mean."[50] As this bald language became publicly unacceptable, it was other Democrats such as George Wallace who pioneered more clandestine rhetoric. When Republicans first began to speak in the masked terms of states' rights and law and order, they were simply parroting the evolving language of the Southern Democrats. Though popularly associated with the Republicans, from the outset *both* parties adopted a Southern strategy based on dog whistle racism.[51] This is key, because as we'll see, the Democrats themselves would soon pick up the whistle at the national level, especially in the figures of two Southern politicians, Jimmy Carter and Bill Clinton. They could blow that whistle more easily because race-baiting lay deeply embedded in their party's DNA.

Beyond white and black. Another classic misunderstanding posits that the Southern strategy involves only white-black dynamics, or more generally, only race. On the contrary, Phillips was clear that whites would flee the Democratic Party in revulsion at "blacks *and* browns," citing in particular the ascendant Mexican American community in the Southwest.[52] To be sure, especially in the 1970s and 1980s, the portrayal of African Americans as criminals and welfare cheats provided the central themes in dog whistle assaults. Even during these decades, though, racial bogeymen varied by region, with Latinos in the Southwest, Asians in certain metropolitan areas, and Native Americans in the upper Midwest and in other pockets of the country also serving as racial scapegoats. The prominence of these other groups in racial demagoguery would increase over this period, and after the 2001 World Trade Center attacks, Muslims as potential terrorists and Latinos as illegal aliens would become core archetypes in dog whistle narratives. Dog whistling comes out of the South and its preoccupation with blacks, but it always involved equal opportunity racism, and never more so than today.

Culture wars. Beyond race, Phillips joined with the Democratic strategists Scammon and Wattenberg in seeing a host of "social issues" as driving a permanent wedge through the Democratic Party. Phillips looked forward to a "great electoral bastion of a Republicanism that is against aid to blacks, against aid to big cities and against the liberal life style it sees typified by purple glasses, beards, long hair, bralessness, pornography, coddling of criminals and moral permissiveness run riot."[53] Here we see a distinct meaning of "liberal" emerge: now not as a stance regarding good government and the dangers of concentrated wealth, but liberalism as "moral permissiveness," especially around issues of crime, gender, sexual orientation, and religion.[54]

As one among a range of "social issues" used by conservatives, racial dog whistle politics can be understood as a part of a larger effort to flimflam voters by substituting one meaning of liberalism for another. Demagogic politicians hector voters to oust the permissive liberals who coddle nonwhites, women, gays, criminals, and atheists, though often the actual target is the liberal policies that help the middle class and temper capitalism.[55] Righteously attacking social liberalism becomes a surreptitious way to defeat economic liberalism. This is not to portray race as simply one among many issues, each with equal weight; instead, race has been the principal weapon in the right's arsenal against New Deal liberalism. More than any other single concern, over the last half-century racial issues have transformed American politics.[56] Even so, however, racial appeals exist within a larger pattern wherein conservatives stoke cultural divisions as cover for a politics that primarily serves the very wealthy. The full assault on good government can only be understood by recognizing the many inter-related fronts in the culture wars.

Class. A related misapprehension is that the Southern strategy involves only race, but not class.[57] This fundamentally misses how dog whistle politics fuses together class and race in the term "middle class," a topic to which we will return in later chapters. Here, note that dog whistle politics has a strong class component in whom it blames and whom it exonerates.

Consider Kevin Phillips' class analysis of the tectonic shift in American politics: "For a long time the liberal-conservative split was on economic issues. That favored the Democrats until the focus shifted from programs which taxed the few for the many, to things like 'welfare' that taxed the many for the few."[58] This dialectical phrasing only works because of an important switch in who counted as the "few," and in turn this elision reveals the alchemical core of dog whistle politics: the "few" who threatened the middle class changed from the malefactors of great wealth to blacks and Latinos, Asians, and Muslims. We can see this by taking apart Phillips' phrasing.

Start with the first half of Phillips' statement, the claim that economic issues favored the Democrats when government programs "taxed the few for the many." This represents 1964, when Goldwater assailed the New Deal and lost in a landslide. To this point, liberalism still comprised programs primarily geared toward helping whites. Thus, the "many" were the white middle-class beneficiaries of government programs, and the "few" were the rich who were asked to pay more in taxes. But then Phillips flipped the order, and argued that Democrats began to lose when they began promoting " 'welfare' that taxed the many for the few." Here he was talking about the Johnson administration's effort to extend government aid across the color line, and the white hostility that ensued. Note what happened, though. While the "many" stayed the same, still referring to the white middle class, the "few" changed: it no longer referred to the rich who were to be taxed, but now to nonwhites who were consuming taxes.

Conservative dog whistling made minorities, not concentrated wealth, the pressing enemy of the white middle class. It didn't seem to matter that the actual monetary transfers to nonwhites were trivial. If all of the anti-poverty and social

welfare dollars paid to blacks during the Kennedy and Johnson administ.
had instead been given to low- and middle-income whites, it would have a
less than three-eighths of 1 percent to their actual disposable income.[59] W
mattered was the sense that blacks were getting more than they deserved, at
the expense of white taxpayers. The middle class no longer saw itself in opposition to concentrated wealth, but now instead it saw itself beset by grasping
minorities. And note a further, related shift evident in Phillips' phrasing: what
had been liberal "programs" when they helped whites became "welfare" when
extended across the colorline. Racial attacks on liberalism shifted the enemy of
the middle class from big money to lazy minorities, and transmuted economic
programs that helped to build the nation into welfare for undeserving groups.

Another element of Southern strategy class politics bears mention. In addition to reviling poor minorities at the bottom of the class hierarchy, dog whistle
politicians also targeted those at the top—not the very rich, though, but instead
cultural and intellectual elites. Phillips, for instance, saw the Southern strategy
as especially involving class- and culture-based resentments against Northeastern blue bloods—whom he derided as "Yankee silk stockings," "mandarins of
Establishment liberalism," and "limousine liberals."[60] Nixon too saw himself
as leading a middle-class revolt against the country's Eastern establishment.
This hostility against intellectual and cultural elites had antecedents in Senator
Joseph McCarthy's attacks in the 1950s, and arguably more generally forms a
persistent streak in American politics.[61] In terms of culture war politics, though,
the result is a particularly ironic charade. Politicians, themselves often quite
wealthy, do the bidding of the wealthiest segments of society—all while posturing as defenders of the common man against the greed of the grasping poor and
the high-handed dictates of Eastern snobs.[62]

Beyond backlash. Many commentators mistakenly view dog whistlers as
merely taking advantage of a naturally occurring reaction to social upheaval.
An important example can be found in Thomas and Mary Edsall's *Chain Reaction: The Impact of Race, Rights, and Taxes on American Politics* (1991), a book
accepted by many among the Democratic Party's intelligentsia as *the* guidebook
for understanding the Southern strategy. As a metaphor, backlash treats racial
reaction as if it were an act of nature: push too fast with civil rights and the extension of liberal programs, the backlash imagery implies, and a hostile eruption
ineluctably follows. Thus the naturalistic title: *Chain Reaction.* Once unleashed,
like atomic forces, racial backlash violently explodes with an enormous blast-
radius and decades of lethal fallout. Beyond the liberals who shoved too hard,
no one is really at fault, a backlash story says, for these surging forces are largely
beyond control and fully to be expected.

This story distorts reality, first by blaming liberalism while downplaying racism. "At the extreme," *Chain Reaction* contended, "liberalism inflamed resentment when it required some citizens—particularly lower-class whites—to put homes, jobs, neighborhoods, and children at perceived risk in the service of bitterly contested remedies for racial discrimination and segregation."[63] The ostensible culprit is liberalism's bitterly contested remedies which asked too much of whites. Yet this ignores the long history, in the North as well as the South, of white opposition to virtually any easing in racial oppression. Even modest efforts at ameliorating discrimination generated intense opposition, a phenomenon that played out repeatedly in the 1940s and 1950s. It did not require extreme liberal positions during the Johnson administration to generate white hostility; almost all efforts to improve the status of nonwhites generated resentment.[64]

Beyond absolving racism, the backlash story also exonerates demagoguery. True, *Chain Reaction* recognized that "this backlash was . . . fostered and driven for partisan advantage by the Republican opposition."[65] But by this the authors seem to mean principally that Republicans seized the moment and made the most of the situation. They thus diminish the role of dog whistle politicians, presenting them as mere opportunists rather than bold strategists. Racism undoubtedly generated intense resentment, but political entrepreneurs worked long and hard to stoke this fury and then to channel it into hostility toward liberal government in general. In addition, the reactionary think tanks that would prove so crucial to Southern strategy triumphs—a phenomenon we will explore later—are largely missing from the backlash story. Dog whistle racism certainly has elements of reaction to it, but it is much more than an inchoate flare-up of latent hostility. Instead, as we shall come to see, the Southern strategy represents first and foremost the *strategic* manipulation of racism; indeed, its purposeful reinvention.

The backlash metaphor is also dangerous because it suggests self-defeating short- and long-term solutions. The story it offers seems to counsel that the best immediate response to dog whistle politics is mimicry. Reasoning pessimistically that white resentment inevitably results when liberalism helps minorities, the defeatist conclusion follows that Democrats should pull back from helping nonwhites. The choice is often framed as staying true to liberal principles and losing elections, or winning by strategically pulling back from unpopular groups and liberalism too. As we shall see, this is precisely the "lesson" Democrats learned from *Chain Reaction*, for the year after the book came out, Bill Clinton opted to "win" by translating the Edsalls' logic into campaign slogans and governing policies that adopted dog whistle politics.

In contrast to its pessimism about short-term dynamics, backlash theory is naively optimistic about long-term prospects, which leads it to suggest that the best long-range response to dog whistling is to do nothing. In picturing racism as largely static and reactive, the backlash metaphor also implies that it is generationally bounded.[66] We're told that those who grew up under white supremacy, inculcated to a deep loathing of nonwhites, will naturally revolt against liberal efforts to foster racial equality. But take heart, the thesis suggests, for this generation will eventually pass, to be replaced by those reared with racially egalitarian values. Ostensibly, all will be well with the simple passage of time: the bigots will eventually die off. Imagine the dismay, then, when Obama's support among whites plummeted from 2008 to 2012. The backlash thesis cannot explain the persistence of racial politics past, say, 15 or 20 years after the civil rights movement shifted American race relations. But *50* years after George Wallace began blowing the whistle, racial demagoguery is as powerful as ever.

Liberal elites. A final misapprehension must be addressed, and this one may be the most damaging of all. According to most commentators on the Southern strategy, racial bias is a problem among backward whites—but not amid the commentators themselves or their esteemed peers. Often this manifests in analyses that attribute racial resentment exclusively to whites in the South, or to working-class whites. But sympathy for the stereotypes prevalent in dog whistle politics can be found among whites across the country and across classes, including among liberal elites. Liberal thought leaders have long identified with the racist grumblings undergirding the Southern strategy, and this has skewed how they respond to dog whistle racism.

Reconsider the backlash thesis itself. Why were so many liberal thinkers quick to accept the claim that white defection from the Democratic Party stemmed from liberalism's excesses? What made them so readily disposed to treat dog whistle politics as a predictable response to their own errors, leading them to favor retreat and even mimicry? One answer might be basic, disheartening pragmatism: they thought they couldn't win by challenging dog whistle racism, so they picked up the whistle themselves. But a deeper and more unsettling answer is that many liberal elites shared the sense that racial equality *was* disruptive, rather than morally just and long overdue.[67] Among elites, too, the dog whistle harping on welfare, forced busing, and law and order struck powerful chords, making it that much harder for Democratic leaders to see coded race-baiting for what it was—a strategy, not a natural reaction.

Challenging the Southern strategy must involve more than calling upon Wallace voters to examine their beliefs and self-defeating voting patterns. It also requires that committed liberals face their seeming sympathy for grievances framed and expressed in racist narratives. This sympathy is sometimes given voice. Perhaps more often, though, and with much greater significance, it finds expression in a silent acquiescence to dog whistle narratives. Like most in society, liberals often unwittingly accept and even routinely draw on racism in their thinking. When confronting dog whistle racism, this is a tremendous problem—for even those liberals who continue to vote Democratic often sympathize with the racial complaints animating the core attacks on their party's values. In turn, this sympathy largely incapacitates their response, inhibiting confrontation and instead engendering often silence and sometimes mimicry.

2

Beyond Hate: Strategic Racism

Exploring the link between race and crime emphasized by dog whistle politicians, this chapter concentrates on how race works for those who blow a dog whistle. To describe racial demagoguery, it argues that a new understanding of racism is necessary: strategic racism.

George Wallace and Barry Goldwater probably harbored prejudiced views; Richard Nixon certainly did. Nevertheless, none was especially racist in the hate-filled sense, and none was especially motivated to harm minorities. On the contrary, before they grasped the advantages of racial pandering, each had a reputation for being relatively moderate on racial issues. Still, all three intentionally sought to manipulate race as a means of getting elected. Wallace, Goldwater, and Nixon recognized and sought to take advantage of existing bigotry in the voting public, bigotry they did not create but which they stoked, legitimized, and encouraged. They did so not to inflict further pain and humiliation on nonwhites, though that consequence was sure to follow from their actions. Rather, they were willing to play racial hardball to get elected. These racial demagogues acted out of strategic racism.

This chapter's principal goal is to lay out a conception of strategic racism, contextualizing it in terms of other understandings of racism. Before turning to that project, though, it's important to explain why this book weaves deeper conversations on race into the larger dog whistle narrative.

We can start by noting two striking facts about the death penalty: first, blacks are about 12 percent of the population but roughly 43 percent of those on death row; second, support for the death penalty varies among whites if they are first told that capital punishment "is unfair because most of the people who are executed are African Americans"—it shoots up. One might expect that informing whites that capital punishment is racially unfair would produce a drop in support. But on the contrary, when so informed in a recent study, the number of whites favoring the death penalty surged by 18 percent, while among those who claimed to "strongly favor" the death penalty, support leaped a precipitous 44 percent.[1]

What explained this shocking increase in support? This was not because whites affirmatively favored discriminating against minorities, and piled on once they understood that the death penalty did just that. Rather, it seemed that whites were so sure that the death penalty was fair, that when told the opposite, they reacted angrily by reiterating and even increasing their support for the challenged practice. Resentful at the implication of bias, instead of reconsidering, many whites doubled-down on championing capital punishment.

This finding has major implications for those seeking to understand and combat dog whistle politics. First, it suggests that many and possibly most whites accept the connection between minorities and crime, and by extension widespread racial inequality in society, as part of the natural order of things. That is, they understand that our society is stratified by race, but do not see this as a social problem so much as an unpleasant fact of life. Racial beliefs in this conception work like commonsense: as an "obvious" truth that, while rooted in social structures and cultural beliefs, is nevertheless accepted simply as reality. Many of those who "hear" racial appeals likely draw on this sort of commonsense racism. They may harbor no active animosity toward nonwhites. Indeed, they may be completely committed to abstract principles of racial equality, and would find old-style bigotry abhorrent. Nevertheless, racial dog whistles resonate because, at the level of the taken-for-granted, they see the world in ways deeply colored by a foundational belief in the legitimacy of racial inequality.

In turn, this implies that those most prone to respond positively to clandestine race-baiting will also be those most prone to react hostilely to the claim that racial pandering in American politics is ubiquitous. Rather than expressing outrage over the news that politicians have been surreptitiously linking race and crime for decades, many may accept the linkage as fact, reasoning that minorities *are* more predisposed to commit crimes. To these whites, the use of coded messages demonizing minorities as predatory hoodlums—or welfare cheats, illegal aliens, or terrorists—may seem less like deceitful manipulation, and more like the legitimate recognition of objective societal problems. For this audience, the perceived outrage will lie instead in the act of labeling such appeals as racial dog whistles—and, as with the death penalty, some may react to the affront by intensifying their support for politicians they see as unfairly maligned. We would like to believe that if the polity understood that race-baiting continues to be widely practiced, people would repudiate it. Yet many whites may be so sure racial discrimination is *not* a problem that, when told it is, they will reject this information and compound their support for the discrimination.

Thinking through this implication in the context of the death penalty, the researchers in the study above came to a familiar conclusion: the best way to reduce racial unfairness is to use stealth strategies that do not mention race at all. "Our results," they argued, "suggest that a more effective argument for encouraging opposition to the death penalty is one that frames the unfairness of the policy more generally, without focusing on race, thereby avoiding whites' resistance to more direct racial appeals."[2] In effect, they proposed a colorblind approach. They suggested fighting racial bias in the death penalty by *not* talking about race. Far from being alone in this sort of thinking, they have prominent support: Barack Obama takes this position, for instance, as do most liberal thought leaders.

This position is not entirely without merit. If all that one provides is a mini-sermon on racial unfairness with no deeper discussion, talking about race tends to confirm rather than disprove negative stereotypes about nonwhites. Because many whites believe that major social institutions are racially fair *and* include vast racial disparities, simply informing them about dramatic race-correlated differences will not change their beliefs. Instead, and perversely, among those who accept dramatic racial inequalities as a normal and legitimate feature of society, hearing about discrepancies alone tends to solidify their beliefs regarding minority failings and society's basic fairness. *Of course there are striking imbalances in incarceration rates, health outcomes, test scores, unemployment numbers, and familial wealth*—the response will come—*and you've just shown that these natural differences are even greater than I realized.* More than ineffective, it's downright counterproductive to merely stress racial gaps or allege racial discrimination. And so colorblindness seemingly offers a promising way forward.

But avoiding race cannot be a long-term solution. Refusing to address race, either in the death penalty or in politics, insulates racial discrimination further, thus contributing to the sense that it is indeed a "natural" feature of American life. We have to discuss race—and when we do, we have to provide much more than numbers, or the equivalent, bald statements that politicians racially pander all the time. We have to dig deep to explain fundamental dynamics.

To provide that depth, I weave race chapters like this one between the chapters telling the dog whistle story. My goal is to explain how race works in a manner designed to illuminate the ubiquity and efficacy of present race-baiting. I've just introduced the notion of commonsense racism, suggesting that most voters drawn to racial demagogues are not hate-filled bigots but decent folks who see racial injustice as a normal feature of society. I will revisit this discussion briefly later in this chapter, and again in more depth in Chapter Eight when I explain why so many members of the middle class respond to racial appeals by voting against their apparent interests. Here at the book's beginning, as we seek to understand how dog whistling began and how its original contours shape today's politics, I primarily focus on those blowing the whistle. If racism operates as a form of accepted truth among those who hear the whistle, how does racism influence those who blast out its calls? To explore this question, I turn to convict leasing, a widespread but largely forgotten horror that arose just after the end of slavery. Convict leasing helps lay bare the social rather than natural connection between race and criminality. Even more importantly, it pushes us to recognize that currently popular conceptions of racism cannot explain the rise and persistence of dog whistle politics.

■ CONVICT LEASING

When Nixon began championing "law and order," he was drawing on a Southern tradition going back much further than the civil rights era. In Alabama in 1870, blacks comprised 74 percent of the prison population, but only two decades before, they had been just 2 percent.[3] What changed in those few years?

Slavery ended in 1865, and without slavery to control them, blacks suddenly gave over to their criminal nature—or at least, that's the tale the South liked to tell, though even on its own terms it was hardly a consistent story. During the slavery era, whites routinely depicted blacks as contented, happy, frivolous, and foolish—in short, in childish need of a paternalistic guardian in the form of an owner and master. Concurrent narratives of dangerous, lascivious blacks also existed, but the primary racial stereotypes painted blacks as joyfully enslaved. Post-emancipation, these notions faded as more threatening stereotypes quickly gained currency. Almost immediately, blacks came to be seen as wicked, vengeful, lust-filled, and violent—a menacing population prone to terrible crimes that had to be forcefully restrained. Slavery or prisons, the post-bellum South was wont to claim, were needed to control the treacherous nature of blacks.

But there's another, more sinister explanation for the rapid rise in black incarceration rates: the material interests of wealthy whites. The Civil War and the forcible ending of slavery shattered the Southern economy, abruptly terminating a massive system of labor exploitation. In the scramble to figure out what would replace it, Southern states quickly seized on a loophole. The constitutional amendment that banned slavery provided that "neither slavery nor involuntary servitude, *except as a punishment for crime whereof the party shall have been duly convicted*, shall exist within the United States."[4] Right there in the middle of the Thirteenth Amendment was a gaping hole—one big enough to allow the reestablishment of slavery by another name. Through innumerable stratagems, the South rapidly built a criminal justice system around imprisoning blacks.[5] Fines for minor infractions suddenly morphed into jail time. Selective prosecution of blacks surged. New crimes made their way onto the books. But of course the point was not to fill jail cells; rather, it was to fuel a new form of involuntary servitude.

The heart of the system lay in leasing out convicts as laborers.[6] As an economic matter, governments and private capital profited handsomely. Indeed, at one point Alabama earned nearly 12 percent of its total annual revenue from the leasing of convicts to private enterprise. Two Mississippi sheriffs reported making between $20,000 and $30,000 each from the sale of black convicts to white planters in a single year. Measured in today's dollars, this would have been the equivalent of between $263,000 and $394,000. This was no anomaly: "revenues from the neo-slavery poured the equivalent of tens of millions of dollars into the treasuries of Alabama, Mississippi, Louisiana, Georgia, Florida, Texas, North Carolina, and South Carolina," concludes Douglas Blackmon in his 2009 Pulitzer Prize–winning exposé of the convict leasing system, *Slavery by Another Name*. Customers for convict labor ranged from plantations and regional industry to the great corporate titans of the age. In 1907, US Steel acquired ownership of a coal-mining interest that was then the largest client of the Alabama convict system. It quickly ramped up mining and the use of slave labor, paying one county $60,000 to acquire every prisoner arrested in 1908, and entering into similar contracts with 20 other counties in an effort to secure a steady supply of convict labor through at least 1912.

To give further context to the $60,000 paid by US Steel, consider the sliding rate Alabama charged for prisoners forced to work in dangerous coal mines. "First-class" prisoners were leased out for $18.50 a month, with the understanding that they would cut and load four tons of coal a day, or be subject to whipping. The weakest inmates, rated as "dead hands," were leased out for just $9 a month, and lashed if their subterranean struggle failed to produce a ton of coal—2,000 pounds—each day.[7] The term "dead hands" was tragically apt, as the prisoners' new masters faced a different economic calculus than under formal slavery. In slavery's antebellum form, humans as property were at least minimally protected because of their long-term financial value.[8] But under convict leasing, a man's value did not exceed what his employer paid the state monthly. If the laborer died in custody, the employer suffered only trivial financial inconvenience, as another convict could be readily procured at the same tariff. One former slave owner, lamenting slavery's demise as a more humane relationship, bemoaned convict leasing's brutal math: "Before the war, we owned the negroes . . . If a man had a good negro, he could afford to keep him. . . . But these convicts, we don't own 'em. One dies, get another."⁹ "One dies, get another," reports historian Eric Foner, became the working motto of the system's architects.¹⁰

Alabama state inspectors reported horrendous mortality rates in the mines: of the 684 forced laborers imprisoned at one mine in 1888 and 1889, over a third died.¹¹ In order to work the convicts to near-death, guards routinely employed extreme violence. Inspectors found that in one two-week period, 137 floggings were administered to the 165 forced laborers then at an Alabama mine. In addition to the whip, various apparatuses and techniques of torture helped to manufacture hell on earth. Included among these were "come-a-longs," steel bracelets attached to a prisoner's wrists and fastened to a cross bar such that a twisting of the bar drove the victim to his knees in excruciating pain; and the "pick shackle," a heavy, sharpened pick-head riveted upside down to an inmate's ankle, making it impossible to run or even walk normally, and often affixed for the duration of a prisoner's sentence. Blackmon reports that convict camp records are littered with notations regarding "amputations of feet and lower legs as a result of blood poisoning from the injuries caused by iron shackles abrading bare skin into raw, infected lesions." In addition, Blackmon documents the prevalence of sundry forms of water torture, from pinning a man down and pouring water on his face so as to stop his breathing, to repeatedly plunging laborers head first into water barrels and holding them there until their spasms subsided, then reviving them and repeating, forcing them to endure the terror of drowning over and over again. Destroyed by the hopelessness and pain of their Sisyphean situation, many men begged their wardens to kill them, while others, to reduce their economic value and so possibly gain their freedom, mutilated themselves by "slicing their heel strings, hacking off their hands, or gouging out their eyes."¹²

Convict leasing recreated a facsimile of slavery directly, with convict laborers held and exploited under the terror of the lash in fields, factories, and mines. But it also reconstituted pre-Civil War racial stratification by undergirding the rise of debt peonage and sharecropping across the rural South. Those men swallowed alive by the prisoner-leasing system were almost always "convicts" only as a thin, cruel subterfuge, arrested by self-serving sheriffs and tried before venal judges for trivial offenses. The system's ubiquity and caprice assured that virtually no African American man was safe unless under the protection and control of a white landowner or employer. If you wanted to be sure you would make it home from town—rather than being swept up, imprisoned under spurious charges, and sold into the convict lease system—you needed the surety provided by a powerful white man. Blacks went into sharecropping, a relationship itself akin to slavery, partly because they needed white bosses to protect them from the lethal convict labor system. The mortal threat of convict leasing and the chain gang subjugated African Americans to an agricultural peonage system at least until the mid-1940s.[13]

The convict leasing system did not truly end until World War II, when the federal government took note that enemy propagandists were contesting the global public relations battle by publicizing Southern horrors, whereupon the government finally exerted itself in earnest to end the renewed enslavement of African Americans.[14] Just how many blacks the convict slavery system ultimately ensnared is difficult to establish, but the scale seems astonishingly vast. In Alabama in 1927 alone, 27,701 men were arrested on misdemeanor charges and offered for sale by county sheriffs. In Blackmon's estimation, "roughly half of all African Americans—or 4.8 million—lived in the Black Belt region of the South in 1930, the great majority of whom were almost certainly trapped in some form of coerced labor."[15] Between circa 1870 and 1945, the manufactured connection between race and crime stood at the deadly core of white supremacy and racial exploitation in the South. When Nixon drew on this linkage in the late 1960s, he wasn't simply referencing a sociological fact about racial groups and crime rates; Nixon was investing new power into a fabricated fusion of blacks and criminality that had helped a revamped form of slavery survive the Civil War, and kept it current until just a couple of decades earlier.

■ THREE RACISMS

The terrors of convict leasing—and even the machinations of Richard Nixon—may seem located in the distant past, curious relics from a racist time but not so relevant to today. Yet convict leasing has much to teach us about our conceptions of racism, as well as about how racism operates in dog whistle politics. Currently, three understandings of racism predominate: hate, structural racism, and implicit bias. Each of these helps us understand racism, and more so when considered together. Yet none effectively explains the creation and persistence of convict leasing, or today's racial demoguery. As I will suggest after discussing these three prevailing conceptions, convict leasing and dog whistle politics are better explained in terms of strategic racism.

The racism-as-hate model. The most common understanding of racism emphasizes discrete acts of bigotry by malicious individuals. Under this version, racism is easy to spot and clearly reprehensible. In convict leasing, for example, the racist would be the ruddy-faced, morally stunted prison warden, spewing bilious racial epithets as he mock-drowns another struggling victim. Today's skinheads, aggressive young whites whose tattoos often shout Nazi claims of racial supremacy, provide another image of the prototypical, hate-motivated racist. Recently, the number of hate groups has been spiking, posing a vicious threat to society.[16]

This model has a deep intuitive resonance, but also a distancing dynamic that makes racism seem remote. When most people think about quintessential examples of racism, they think about the angry white mobs that attacked civil rights protesters in the 1950s and 1960s, or hooded Klansmen burning crosses to terrorize black families in the night. These archetypes seem readily explicable in terms of malevolence, and so buttress the racism-as-hate conception. But when used as the sole understanding of racism, the hate model makes racism seem common in the past and rare in the present, notwithstanding some hate-groups' contemporary resurgence. Because very few in society today scream racial epithets or threaten racial violence, racism seems extremely unusual in the present.

This distancing helps make the hate conception popular with broad swaths of the public, and also especially preferred among conservatives. For the public at large, racism-as-hate provides self-protecting clarity: if racists are like those in the 1950s who screamed at black school children and burned crosses, then most everyone can safely conclude that they, at least, are not racists. Hollywood understands this, and rarely depicts racism other than through caricatures of ignorant bigots excreting reprehensible opinions, sparing the audience from having to grapple with a complex view of racism that might implicate their own beliefs and behavior.

Conservatives, with the important assistance of the Supreme Court, also propagate this understanding of racism, as it undercuts claims that racial discrimination remains a major social problem. By linking racism to discrete acts stemming from malice, this conception makes contemporary discrimination almost impossible to prove because showing malice inevitably requires some statement of evil intent—and those who engage in racial discrimination today typically have the wit not to shout out their prejudices. With discrimination hard to prove, its very presence comes into question. Since conservatives on the Supreme Court adopted a malice conception of racism in 1979, when using this approach the Court has rejected every claim of discrimination against non-whites brought before it. Today, the constitutional law that supposedly protects minorities defines racism solely in terms of hate, and as a result this doctrine has not found any discrimination against minorities since Jimmy Carter sat in the White House.[17] This is more than a matter of doctrine, and more than a question for individual litigants; the Court's pronouncements, especially on socially contentious issues like race, help shape what passes as commonsense.

Structural racism. Another conception of racism emphasizes structures rather than individuals. Racism under this view is woven into society's fabric; more than the cruel warden, the convict lease system itself is seen to embody racism. The idea of structural racism, also known as institutional racism, entered the American vocabulary in the late civil rights era, and a definition from that time drives the meaning home:

> When white terrorists bomb a black church and kill five black children, that is an act of *individual racism*, widely deplored by most segments of the society. But when in that same city—Birmingham, Alabama—five hundred black babies die each year because of the lack of proper food, shelter and medical facilities, and thousands more are destroyed and maimed physically, emotionally and intellectually because of conditions of poverty and discrimination in the black community, that is a function of *institutional racism*.[18]

Institutional racism stresses how past mistreatment drives current inequalities. Up through the 1940s, a Southern society built around convict leasing and debt peonage may have trapped half of all African Americans. Meanwhile, many of the government programs arising in the 1930s and 1940s—efforts that contributed to the great boom in the American middle class—were effectively available to whites only. These racially stratified differences connect across generations to vast disparities today in the average wealth of white and black families. Whereas in 2009 the typical white family had a net worth of $113,149, this outstripped the figure for African American families by 20 to 1, with the average black family owning assets of only $5,677.[19] Or put this another way: for every dollar held by whites, blacks had a lonely nickel in their pocket.[20]

Where the hate model looks for bad actors, structural racism is much more focused on outcomes. At the extreme, the question of culpable individuals drops out, and the overriding concern becomes breaking down the structures of inequality that otherwise threaten to replicate themselves indefinitely. In its focus on results, institutional racism is often understood as a radical conception of racism, since it implies a moral obligation to actually change social structures. This radical quality stems from the implications, though, and not from the analysis itself. There's nothing especially revolutionary in suggesting that social dynamics frequently continue through inertia. Indeed, insofar as it eschews identifying contemporary culprits, a structural account sometimes can be politically safer than the hate model. Structural racism is racism without racists. All that said, precisely because institutional racism implies a need to change society, it was rejected long ago by conservatives, including those on the Supreme Court who repudiated this understanding of racism in the early 1970s.

Implicit bias. Today, unconscious bias constitutes the main rival to the focus on intentional animus. This theory is especially popular among critics of the Supreme Court and among liberals more generally. They stress that almost all of us draw on racial ideas at the implicit level, sorting those we meet and forming early judgments virtually automatically, long before our conscious minds have a chance to recognize, let alone object to, the errors. Evidence for the existence of implicit bias can be readily found—indeed, experienced—in the "Implicit Association Test," available online to anyone who wishes to take it. It uses tiny differences in how quickly one pairs words like white and good, and black and bad, to detect unconscious subscriptions to notions of white superiority and black inferiority.[21] Persons first taking the test typically find the results startling. Almost all of us, of whatever color, harbor implicit biases. This burgeoning science stands as a direct refutation of the Court's understanding of racism: it shows that racial discrimination often results from unconscious thought processes, and need not stem from intentional malice, or indeed any conscious purposes at all.

Despite its strength in challenging constitutional law's singular focus on purposeful malice, spotlighting implicit bias carries three interrelated risks. These are not mistakes with the theory, but rather, errors in how unconscious bias is commonly understood. The first is the fallacious sense that "race is hardwired into our reptilian brains," as a friend evocatively but erroneously insisted. The second is that everyone favors their own race and is biased toward other races. The final inaccuracy is to suppose that, since bias is unconscious and universal, there's little anyone can do.

Rather than refer to implicit bias, I prefer to highlight what I term commonsense racism. Like the implicit bias model, this conception of racism emphasizes its unconscious quality. But rather than focusing principally on how our minds work, commonsense racism stresses the origins of racial biases in our culture and social structures. It's true that we are "hardwired" to unconsciously assign meaning to perceived *differences*. But it's false that we're automatically programmed to think in terms of *race*. Rather, notions of race come from a shared culture steeped in racial stereotypes, as well as from material arrangements like segregated cities that make race a supremely salient social category. As the race scholar john powell explains, "the unconscious is largely social. It is the environment, including our social structures and cultural meanings, that both create the negative associations and uses them in priming" our psyches.[22] It's not race our minds naturally seek out, but difference generally. Thus the fact that race comes automatically to mind reflects not our nature but our society.

In turn, precisely because implicit racial biases reflect widespread cultural stereotypes and social structures, these biases track dominant white-over-nonwhite dynamics. It's not the case that each group favors its own and dislikes others. Rather, in general all members of our society, including racial minorities, are unconsciously predisposed to hold positive associations regarding whites and negative presumptions about minorities. Despite this, we are not helpless in the face of implicit bias. One immediate solution is to self-critically reflect on how taken-for-granted ideas about race might be influencing our judgments and actions. Research in this field makes it clear that purposeful attention to race is key to avoiding racial discrimination.[23] In addition, if racial thinking arises out of stereotypes and social structures, then changing these can reduce implicit bias. Even small alterations in our milieu can shift how often unconscious racial biases are triggered, and also, whether persons are routinely encouraged to counteract the possible operation of implicit biases in their thinking.

More than angry bigotry, commonsense racism explains much of the harm race does in our society. Because race infiltrates our minds so thoroughly, even persons deeply and genuinely committed to humane engagement with others often nevertheless draw upon pernicious racial stereotypes.[24] In turn, racism gains a large degree of social power from the actions of good people in thrall to racist beliefs. Reconsider convict leasing and debt peonage. These could wreak havoc for 70 years because they made sense, as a cultural matter. Most whites didn't wrestle with whether these practices were evil, as this question never rose that high into their consciousness. Instead, the settled ideas of whites as decent folks and blacks as dangerous work animals resolved for many, at the unconscious level, the moral rightness of convict leasing. Certainly, this devilish practice could not have continued without the broad acquiescence of the white population in the South. It was simply commonsense, for many whites, that the states' law enforcement machines should feed African Americans into the maw of a brutal system of oppression and exploitation that proceeded under the motto "one dies, get another."

These three conceptions of racism—hate, structural racism, and implicit bias or commonsense racism—provide useful lenses for examining the racial complexities of convict leasing. This abhorrent system was as an amalgam of hate-filled cruelty, deeply structured inequality from the slavery era that facilitated a new yet similar system of institutionalized exploitation, and unconscious racial biases that allowed many to turn a blind eye to a ghastly arrangement.

But there's something missing from this account. Convict leasing built up relatively quickly, in just a few years. Spite alone didn't do that. Hate didn't create new structures and rationales for the exploitation of black labor. Likewise, while unconscious notions of white superiority and black depravity no doubt played a role, convict leasing was not the product of anyone's id. Unconscious minds did not elaborate new criminal laws, nor devise a new form of chattel slavery even more lethal than its predecessor. Nor was convict leasing a mere continuation of past structures, unaided by contemporary actors. This was not inertia, but purposeful effort. Convict leasing constituted a carefully planned shift in the machinery of labor extraction. Southern elites systematically set about creating a new form of racial exploitation, building a system arguably more brutal, deadly, and dehumanizing than slavery itself. Today's dominant conceptions of racism do not give us a way to fathom this process. For that, we need a different understanding of racism, seeing it as sometimes cold and calculating.

■ STRATEGIC RACISM

Convict leasing functioned to protect the white financial interests jeopardized by slavery's end, and also was crafted to shore up white dominion over blacks in the new post-slavery world. The invention of the institution stemmed from the desire of dominant elements in society to secure their wealth, power, and status by creating a new form of slavery. The elaboration of convict leasing suggests purposeful action, not animated by hate, but instead propelled by conscious, intentional plotting. In this conception, racism emerges as the self-interested, strategic manipulation of racial antipathies. *Strategic racism refers to purposeful efforts to use racial animus as leverage to gain material wealth, political power, or heightened social standing.*[25]

This sort of racism may seem marginal, at least in the sense of being relatively rare—and so in its most calculating forms it may be. Nevertheless, the purposeful manipulation of racial ideas forms the poisonous core of racism. Indeed, this dynamic returns us to the very origins of race. How did racism first arise? Hate for different races cannot explain where racism comes from, for this would be entirely circular: racial hate cannot explain the origins of racial hate.[26] Instead, notions of race were invented, and racial hatred stimulated, to justify exploitation. In the context of colonial North America—one instance in a larger pattern of colonialism that produced the racial ideologies of the modern world—European migrants began to invent ideas about "racial differences" in order to justify their treatment of the indigenous populations on the Eastern seaboard as well as those from western Africa. These American and African populations were quite varied, organizing themselves into local nations and speaking multiple languages. At the beginning of the 1600s, before European settlement began in earnest and before the first Africans were brought to North America, the white, red, and black races did not exist. Within a century, though, these races were firmly established in cultural knowledge and social practice— with white supremacy providing a divine right to rule, and with red and black savagery justifying the expropriation of Native American land and the enslavement of African labor.[27]

For almost everyone, it is wrenching to encounter, let alone participate in, the level of intense suffering associated with driving persons from their homes or forcing people into bondage. If, however, we can convince ourselves that our victims are not like us—do not feel pain the way we do, are not intelligent and sensitive, indeed are indolent, degenerate, violent, and dangerous—then perhaps we're not doing so much harm after all; indeed, more than protecting ourselves, maybe we are helping the benighted others. And how much better, in terms of excusing our own self-interest, if it turns out that forces beyond anyone's control (and hence beyond our moral responsibility) doom these unfortunate others to subservience; if, say, God or nature fixed their insuperable character and determined their lot in life. Exploitation can be more easily justified if the exploited are placed within a fixed hierarchy—a natural or divine division of the population into the superior and inferior. Gender traditionally works this way, with basic biological distinctions supposedly justifying sharp demarcations in social roles. In different settings, caste, religion, language, ethnicity, and class, among others, all provide markers of difference sufficiently deep to justify appalling abuse. These various forms of differentiation work in discrete ways, but also share a fundamental similarity: they are the stories societies tell themselves to justify violent exploitation. In the United States, race provides such a core story, and strategic racists are the master narrators.

This is not to say that strategic racists stand completely outside the fictions they create. For however calculated their actions, racial entrepreneurs tend to reinvent existing racial ideas, rather than making them up whole cloth. Those justifying inequality do so from within already unequal societies, with extant beliefs that provide handy material for new uses. Even at the inception of racial ideology in North America, for instance, older notions of fixed differences, such as that between Christian and heathen, provided the raw materials that facilitated the evolution of distinctly modern racial ideas.[28] Likewise, in justifying convict leasing, strategic racists drew on existing ideas of racial difference created under slavery. Also, beyond drawing on available ideas, racial strategists stand within their own fictions because those seeking power typically will themselves to believe their own fabrications. Strategic racism almost always carries a strong element of self-delusion. But all that said, the principal point remains: strategic racism stands apart from other racisms insofar as its practitioners coldly set out to turn race to their advantage.

A last important point: because strategic racism is strategic, *it is not fundamentally about race.* The driving force behind strategic racism is not racial animus for its own sake or brutalizing nonwhites out of hate; it is the pursuit of power, money, and/or status. If other means of gaining these ends are ready at hand, calculating actors will use those instead of or in addition to race—just as dog whistle politicians today also often use gender, sexual orientation, and religion to whip up hysteria along those other lines too. Yes, provocateurs stimulate racial hatred intentionally, and yes they do tremendous damage to nonwhite communities. But strategic racists act out of avarice rather than animus. Their aim is to pursue their own self-interest; racism is merely a route to mammon, not an end in itself.

Dog Whistle Politics as Strategic Racism

Wallace, Goldwater, and Nixon constitute classic strategic racists. In the context of the times, they were all initially racial moderates. They may have harbored tainted beliefs, but racial animosity did not drive their actions. Instead, they concentrated hard, weighing and sifting, to figure out how they could most effectively gain votes. If a more promising route had been available, they would have taken it. But race seemed the most likely avenue, so each opted to harness racial divisions to their agenda of getting elected. This was not about racism, it was about winning. Also, they were not racially omniscient, moving instead within a settled framework of ideas about race that for the most part they took for granted. Even so, unlike most in society, these politicians thought long and deep about how to turn race to their advantage. We've previously defined strategic racism as purposeful efforts to use racial animosity as leverage to gain political power (or material wealth and social standing). By this definition, Wallace, Goldwater, and Nixon acted out of strategic racism.

This last sentence sparks an important clarification. I write interchangeably of "dog whistle politics" and "dog whistle racism." The first is a less freighted term. But the truth is, racial dog whistle politics *is* dog whistle racism. It is a strategic manipulation of racial ideas in pursuit of political power and (especially once big-money conservatives got behind the tactic) material wealth.

"Racism" is a heavily laden term, and its use is often discouraged. One objection is political: because the term is so divisive, referring to racism is supposedly counterproductive. Another is analytical: "racism" means too many different things to be helpful. When in the concluding chapter I turn to concrete steps for combating race-baiting, I'll pick up the political question of whether to use the term "racism" to describe dog whistle politics. Here, I want to argue that it is at least descriptively accurate.

The cold calculations behind racial demagoguery lack the heat of virulent racial hatred; lack the ubiquity of unconscious bias; and lack the inexorable inertia of institutional racism. And yet, perhaps more than any of these, strategic racism lies at racism's very heart. In pursuit of land and labor, power, wealth, and status, self-interested parties fashioned racial beliefs about "whites," "blacks," and "reds" in the first place. Repeatedly thereafter, strategic racists adapted racism to protect their advantages and to pursue additional interests. Especially in the face of challenges to racial hierarchy—the end of slavery, the repudiation of open white supremacy—strategic racists labored to remake old ideas into new forms capable of preserving or even enhancing their power. The ultimate goal was not racial terror for its own sake; it was instead money, control, and prestige. But the method chosen to pursue power nevertheless routinely reinvigorated racism. And as in the past, so too today: dog whistle demagogues reinvent racism for a new age, giving it renewed life, vigor, and staying power. Dog whistle racism is *racism*—indeed, it is racism's most poisonous core—because it legitimizes, energizes, and stimulates the entire destructive project of racial divisions.

To fully understand dog whistle politics, we have to start thinking about racism as sometimes strategic. A 2006 study found that, when given a list of 40 descriptive words, members of the public were most likely to use the following terms to describe a "racist": close-minded, opinionated, stubborn, and ignorant. Here are the words the public *least* associated with racists: calm, intelligent, and wealthy.[29] This needs to change. The stereotypes that tie minorities to crime don't simply reside in minds that are shuttered, uneducated, and cantankerous. They are believed by most, and more importantly, these falsehoods are purposefully manipulated by persons otherwise cool, smart, and rich. These stereotypes form part of a strategy: a weapon in the hands of dog whistle racists seeking votes and power. They were elevated after slavery to justify convict leasing, and reinvigorated after the civil rights movement to shatter the New Deal coalition.

We have learned to see racism in the spittle-laced epithets of the angry bigot. We must also learn to see racism in the coded racial entreaties promoted by calculating demagogues.

■ POLITICS AND RACIALIZED MASS INCARCERATION

This book stresses how racial appeals turn large segments of the voting public against liberal governance and thus wreck the broad middle class. Yet we should not ignore the especially severe damage done to communities of color. Again, this was not the aim, but it was the inevitable outcome. The constant warnings about undeserving and dangerous nonwhites inexorably evolved into competition among politicians over who could take the most punitive stand against minorities, whether cast as welfare cheats or criminals, illegal aliens or terrorists. The utterly predictable, terribly tragic result has been the devastation of black and brown lives. We can see just one example of this in the rise of racialized mass incarceration. While less lethal and exploitative than convict leasing, racialized mass incarceration shows that even today we are not so far from countenancing massive systems of racial brutality as we typically believe.

In 1970, when Nixon embraced the Southern strategy and began in earnest to connect nonwhites with the breakdown of law and order, the number of people in state and federal prisons serving at least one year behind bars stood at around 200,000. That number translated into about one out of every 1,000 Americans.[30] Compare that to the present: a recent study reports "the total adult inmate count at the beginning of 2008 stood at 2,319,258." This more than ten-fold leap reflects a dramatic surge in incarceration well beyond population growth. Today, more than one out of every 100 adults is behind bars.[31] This bears repeating: on any given day, out of a 100 adults in the United States, one is locked up. This incarceration rate, the highest in the world, exceeds the highest rate among European democracies by 500 percent.[32] The United States has 5 percent of the world's population, but holds 25 percent of the planet's prisoners.[33] Since the Southern strategy took hold, we have built up a massive carceral apparatus on a scale unprecedented in our history or among the world's nations.

This system of grossly excessive incarceration is closely tied to race. In 2008, among white men aged 18 years or older, 1 in 106 were behind bars. The comparable number for Latino men was 1 in 36; for black men, it was 1 in 15. For black men between the ages of 20 and 34, a sickening 1 in 9 were locked up in 2008.[34] Shifting from the rate of imprisonment within the population to the risk of incarceration faced by individuals over the course of their lives, by 1999 a black man born in the late 1960s had a one-in-five chance of having gone to prison for at least a year, while for men in that cohort who dropped out of high school, the risk of imprisonment surged to a staggering 59 percent.[35] This is not mass incarceration with no modifier; it is *race-based* mass incarceration, a system of putting especially black and brown men behind bars on an enormous scale. Michelle Alexander, author of a devastating exposé on racialized mass incarceration entitled *The New Jim Crow*, offers a heart-stopping bottom line: as of 2008, "more African-American men are in prison or jail, on probation or parole than were enslaved in 1850, before the Civil War began."[36]

What explains the rise of racialized mass incarceration? It's not racial differences in crime rates. To measure crime rates we must take into account poverty and age. Poverty correlates with criminal activity, both because those without resources are more likely to commit crimes, and also because the poor spend more of their hours in public spaces intensively policed by the state. Another factor associated with crime is youth, with young men in particular likely to engage in high-risk and anti-social behavior. Paying attention to these factors, when one compares crime rates across poor males in the high-crime ages of 15 to 18, it turns out that poor youth of color almost across the board are *less* likely to commit crimes than their white counterparts.[37] Poor white youths typically report committing more crimes of all sorts than do minorities. Still, this means that, because blacks and Latinos are disproportionately poor and young relative to the population as a whole, they are disproportionately involved in crime, and perhaps this modest disproportion—not in the propensity to commit crime, but in the likelihood of being poor and young—explains arrest and conviction patterns. It does not. Young men of color are far, far more likely than young white men to be swept into the maw of the American crime control system, even when taking into account youth and poverty.

So what drives mass incarceration? Recently, sociologists and political scientists studying the rise of mass incarceration have pointed to its origins in dog whistle politics and the use of crime as a proxy language for race.[38] This is not to finger Nixon as primarily responsible; he gave the race-crime frame national prominence, but others built on it. As we shall see, Ronald Reagan also campaigned using "crime" as code for dangerous nonwhites, and much more aggressively than Nixon, Reagan put the immense resources of the federal government behind his slogans. To fulfill his campaign promises to crack down on threatening minorities, Reagan transformed the federal criminal justice system. Under Reagan, the Department of Justice de-emphasized investigations of white collar crime—precisely the sort of sophisticated, inter-state crime that requires a well-funded national response. Instead, the Reagan administration made street crime its principal target, declaring a "War on Drugs." When announced, less than 2 percent of Americans thought drugs were a major problem. This shift in emphasis, though, allowed the Feds to go after those Reagan repeatedly portrayed as menacing society. During his first administration, anti-drug funds at the FBI surged from $38 million to $181 million, and the Drug Enforcement Agency's spending skyrocketed from $86 million to over $1 billion. Meanwhile, illustrating the full perversity of the effort, spending on health care for drug treatment plummeted, with the National Institute on Drug Abuse suffering a budget cut from $274 million to $57 million, and with anti-drug funds for the Department of Education slashed from $14 million to $3 million.

Yet this is not just a story of Republican perfidy. Once it became clear that campaigning to get tough on crime attracted votes, the Democrats also jumped on the bandwagon. We will see that Bill Clinton was especially aggressive in adopting dog whistle themes, including law and order. Clinton pushed "three strikes" laws that rapidly swelled the prison population; championed a $30 billion spending bill to build up federal and state police forces and prisons; and escalated Reagan's drug war beyond what anyone might have imagined possible a decade earlier.[39] Dog whistle politics contributed forcefully to racialized mass incarceration. Campaign slogans did not stay at rallies or remain in commercials; they quickly morphed into get-tough policies with real human consequences. Republicans may have started it, but Democrats soon joined them in dog whistle one-upmanship that over decades spawned the prison system we stagger under today.

SHATTERED LIVES

Return to one of the numerical points cited above, that the US incarceration rate exceeds the highest rate in Europe by 500 percent.[40] Imagine for a moment that absent the multi-decade political obsession with getting tough on crime, the United States would now be incarcerating people at the highest European rate, rather than five times that rate. This would suggest that perhaps four out of five persons that we put in prison today end up there as a result of dog whistle politics.

Now imagine yourself among those four out of five put behind bars so that politicians could prove their toughness on crime. Here's the briefest catalog of the wreckage of your life: Your connection with your family strained if not broken, your job gone, your housing gone. You're trapped in a cell, stripped of your dignity and privacy, given inadequate health care, deprived of meaningful opportunities for self improvement in prison—no classes, no skills training, no mental or behavioral counseling (this is punishment, remember, not rehabilitation, another devolution you can chalk up to racial politics). And when you come out, you find your life chances vastly diminished, your right to vote gone, no right to welfare to help you back to your feet or to catch you if you falter, locked out of government-supported housing and discriminated against when seeking a place to rent, disqualified for a student loan, and every time you apply for a job they ask about your criminal record and that provides a perfectly legal reason not to hire you.[41] And you're just one person. But we've done that to millions upon millions, and dramatically remade our society in the process.

One expert estimates that black men who have been incarcerated suffer a 42 percent reduction in expected lifetime earnings.[42] Another study puts the estimated loss in lifetime income of all offenders at a staggering $300 billion.[43] Meanwhile, the criminal system removes and returns inmates in concentrated patterns that hit the poorest minority neighborhoods particularly hard, imposing devastating economic losses on those communities least able to bear such loads.[44] With good reason the economist and race scholar Glenn Loury describes the crime control system as a "monstrous social machine that is grinding poor black communities to dust."[45] As we'll see more fully in the next chapter on Reagan and the new robber barons, dog whistle politics wrecks the whole middle class. Yet it lands its heaviest blows against those historically most oppressed by race, the nonwhite communities locked into crushing poverty all over the country.

3

The Wrecking Begins: Reagan

With Ronald Reagan, we retrieve the thread of plutocratic politics, showing how it went from the fringes in the 1960s, to think-tank respectability in the 1970s, and then into government policy in the 1980s. Reagan's success drives home how dog whistle racism wrecks the middle class: by helping to convince the middle class that government—and not concentrated wealth—is the greatest threat in their lives.

The rocket-quick rise of racial politics leveled off briefly in the 1970s, before shooting upward again. In good part because of racial appeals, the Republican Party had transformed the crushing defeat of Barry Goldwater into the overwhelming re-election of Richard Nixon. Then, in the 1976 presidential race, the defection toward the Republicans temporarily decelerated. Revulsion over corruption in the Nixon White House, revealed in the Watergate scandal, played a role. In addition, in an effort to distance himself from Nixon's dirty tricks, the Republican candidate and former Nixon vice president, Gerald Ford, refused to exploit coded racial appeals in his campaign. Not that this marked the disappearance of race-baiting; instead, it merely shifted to Ford's opponent, former Georgia governor Jimmy Carter. Carter was a racial moderate, and today he deservedly enjoys a reputation as a great humanitarian. Nevertheless, in the mid-1970s he knew that his political fortunes turned on his ability to attract Wallace voters in the South and the North as well. Campaigning in Indiana in April 1976, Carter forcefully opposed neighborhood integration:

> I have nothing against a community that's made up of people who are Polish or Czechoslovakian or French-Canadian, or who are blacks trying to maintain the ethnic purity of their neighborhoods. This is a natural inclination

on the part of the people. I don't think government ought to deliberately try to break down an ethnically oriented neighborhood by artificially injecting into it someone from another ethnic group just to create some form of integration.[1]

Carter adopted an emerging technique in the 1970s, hiding references to whites behind talk of ethnic subpopulations, and he also presented blacks as trying to preserve their own segregated neighborhoods. Notwithstanding these dissimulations, few could fail to understand that Carter was defending white efforts to oppose racial integration, and many liberals criticized Carter for doing so. Nixon, who had been loudly berated by Democrats when he announced that neighborhood integration was not in the national interest, surely appreciated the spectacle. As Carter, too, came under attack, he apologized for using the term "ethnic purity," but made a point of reiterating on national news that "the government shouldn't actively try to force changes in neighborhoods with their own ethnic character."[2]

Carter won the presidency in 1976 with 48 percent of the white vote, sharply better than the Democratic presidential candidate four years earlier who had pulled support from only 30 percent of white voters. But even with widespread revulsion at Nixon as well as Carter's own Southern strategy, Carter did not manage to carry the white vote nationally. It was his 90 percent support among African Americans, many still furious at Nixon's dog whistling, that put Carter over the top. In the mid-1970s, racial realignment in party affiliation had been temporarily slowed, not knocked down. Moreover, Carter's racial pandering—and Ford's principled failure—seemed to cement the political logic of race-baiting. In the 1980 campaign, Ronald Reagan would come out firing on racial issues, and would blast past Carter. Just 36 percent of whites, only slightly better than one in three, voted for Carter in 1980.

■ RONALD REAGAN

Why did Ronald Reagan do so well among white voters? Certainly elements beyond race contributed, including the faltering economy, foreign events (especially in Iran), the nation's mood, and the candidates' temperaments. But one indisputable factor was the return of aggressive race-baiting. A year after Reagan's victory, a key operative gave what was then an anonymous interview, and perhaps lulled by the anonymity, he offered an unusually candid response to a question about Reagan, the Southern strategy, and the drive to attract the "Wallace voter":

You start out in 1954 by saying, "Nigger, nigger, nigger." By 1968 you can't say "nigger"—that hurts you. Backfires. So you say stuff like forced busing, states' rights and all that stuff. You're getting so abstract now, you're talking about cutting taxes, and all these things you're talking about are totally economic things and a byproduct of them is, blacks get hurt worse than whites. And subconsciously maybe that is part of it. I'm not saying that. But I'm saying that if it is getting that abstract, and that coded, that we are doing away with the racial problem one way or the other. You follow me—because obviously sitting around saying, "We want to cut taxes and we want to cut this," is much more abstract than even the busing thing, and a hell of a lot more abstract than "Nigger, nigger." So anyway you look at it, race is coming on the back burner.[3]

This analysis was provided by a young Lee Atwater. Its significance is two fold: First, it offers an unvarnished account of Reagan's strategy. Second, it reveals the thinking of Atwater himself, someone whose career traced the rise of GOP dog whistle politics. A protégé of the pro-segregationist Strom Thurmond in South Carolina, the young Atwater held Richard Nixon as a personal hero, even describing Nixon's Southern strategy as "a blue print for everything I've done."[4] After assisting in Reagan's initial victory, Atwater became the political director of Reagan's 1984 campaign, the manager of George Bush's 1988 presidential campaign, and eventually the chair of the Republican National Committee. In all of these capacities, he drew on the quick sketch of dog whistle politics he had offered in 1981: from "nigger, nigger, nigger" to "states' rights" and "forced busing," and from there to "cutting taxes"—and linking all of these, "race . . . coming on the back burner."

When Reagan picked up the dog whistle in 1980, the continuity in technique nevertheless masked a crucial difference between him versus Wallace and Nixon. Those two had used racial appeals to get elected, yet their racially reactionary language did not match reactionary political positions. Political moderates, both became racial demagogues when it became clear that this would help win elections. Reagan was different. Unlike Wallace and Nixon, Reagan was not a moderate, but an old-time Goldwater conservative in both the ideological and racial senses, with his own intuitive grasp of the power of racial provocation. For Reagan, conservatism and racial resentment were inextricably fused.

In the early 1960s, Reagan was still a minor actor in Hollywood, but he was becoming increasingly active in conservative politics.[5] When Goldwater decided to run for president, Reagan emerged as a fierce partisan. Reagan's advocacy included a stock speech, given many times over, that drummed up support for Goldwater with overwrought balderdash such as the following: "We are faced with the most evil enemy mankind has known in his long climb from the swamp to the stars. There can be no security anywhere in the free world if there is no fiscal and economic stability within the United States. Those who ask us to trade our freedom for the soup kitchen of the welfare state are architects of a policy of accommodation."[6] Reagan's rightwing speechifying didn't save Goldwater, but it did earn Reagan a glowing reputation among Republican groups in California, which led to his being recruited to run for governor of California in 1966. During that campaign, he wed his fringe politics to early dog whistle themes, for instance excoriating welfare, calling for law and order, and opposing government efforts to promote neighborhood integration.[7] He also signaled blatant hostility toward civil rights, supporting a state ballot initiative to allow racial discrimination in the housing market, proclaiming: "If an individual wants to discriminate against Negroes or others in selling or renting his house, it is his right to do so."[8]

Reagan's race-baiting continued when he moved to national politics. After securing the Republican nomination in 1980, Reagan launched his official campaign at a county fair just outside Philadelphia, Mississippi, the town still notorious in the national imagination for the Klan lynching of civil rights volunteers James Chaney, Andrew Goodman, and Michael Schwerner 16 years earlier. Reagan selected the location on the advice of a local official, who had written to the Republican National Committee assuring them that the Neshoba County Fair was an ideal place for winning "George Wallace inclined voters."[9] Neshoba did not disappoint. The candidate arrived to a raucous crowd of perhaps 10,000 whites chanting "We want Reagan! We want Reagan!"—and he returned their fevered embrace by assuring them, "I believe in states' rights."[10] In 1984, Reagan came back, this time to endorse the neo-Confederate slogan "the South shall rise again."[11] As *New York Times* columnist Bob Herbert concludes, "Reagan may have been blessed with a Hollywood smile and an avuncular delivery, but he was elbow deep in the same old race-baiting Southern strategy of Goldwater and Nixon."[12]

Reagan also trumpeted his racial appeals in blasts against welfare cheats.[13] On the stump, Reagan repeatedly invoked a story of a "Chicago welfare queen" with "eighty names, thirty addresses, [and] twelve Social Security cards [who] is collecting veteran's benefits on four non-existing deceased husbands. She's got Medicaid, getting food stamps, and she is collecting welfare under each of her names. Her tax-free cash income is over $150,000."[14] Often, Reagan placed his mythical welfare queen behind the wheel of a Cadillac, tooling around in flashy splendor. Beyond propagating the stereotypical image of a lazy, larcenous black woman ripping off society's generosity without remorse, Reagan also implied another stereotype, this one about whites: they were the workers, the tax payers, the persons playing by the rules and struggling to make ends meet while brazen minorities partied with their hard-earned tax dollars. More directly placing the white voter in the story, Reagan frequently elicited supportive outrage by criticizing the food stamp program as helping "some young fellow ahead of you to buy a T-bone steak" while "you were waiting in line to buy hamburger." This was the toned-down version. When he first field-tested the message in the South, that "young fellow" was more particularly described as a "strapping young buck."[15] The epithet "buck" has long been used to conjure the threatening image of a physically powerful black man, often one who defies white authority and who lusts for white women. When Reagan used the term "strapping young buck," his whistle shifted dangerously toward the fully audible range. "Some young fellow" was less overtly racist and so carried less risk of censure, and worked just as well to provoke a sense of white victimization.

Voters heard Reagan's dog whistle. In 1980, "Reagan's racially coded rhetoric and strategy proved extraordinarily effective, as 22 percent of all Democrats defected from the party to vote for Reagan." Illustrating the power of race in the campaign, "the defection rate shot up to 34 percent among those Democrats who believed civil rights leaders were pushing too fast."[16] Among those who felt "the government should not make any special effort to help [blacks] because they should help themselves," 71 percent voted for Reagan.[17]

GOLDWATER'S REVENGE?

Today Reagan is a folk-hero of the right and center and is so widely popular that Barack Obama often feels obliged to invoke Reagan's name reverentially.[18] Why this obeisance to Reagan? At least partly it reflects a sense widely shared among liberals that the United States is historically and at heart a conservative country, requiring genuflection at the feet of conservative icons. For an example of this liberal belief in the country's bedrock conservatism, consider an essay published several weeks before the 2012 presidential election, when the portents indicated an uncertain Democratic victory. Editorialist Frank Rich argued that whether Obama won or lost, conservatism would triumph in the end: "This is a nation that loathes government and always has. Liberals should not be deluded: The Goldwater revolution will ultimately triumph, regardless of what happens in November."[19] Is Rich right? Was Reagan a first step away from the exceptional politics of the New Deal era and back toward a more fundamentally conservative America? Are we at root a conservative country, moving inexorably in the direction of Goldwater's repudiation of liberal governance?

The simplest way to answer this question may be to look at public attitudes toward government's role in solving major social problems. In 2009, the political scientists Benjamin Page and Lawrence Jacobs exhaustively reviewed survey data on American attitudes toward activist government, compiling the results in a book entitled *Class War? What Americans Really Think about Economic Inequality*. Here are some of their findings:

- 87 percent of the public agrees that government should spend whatever is necessary to ensure that all children have really good public schools they can go to.
- 67 percent agree that the government in Washington ought to see to it that everyone who wants to work can find a job.
- 66 percent agree that the Social Security system should ensure a minimum standard of living to all contributors.
- 73 percent agree it is the responsibility of the federal government to make sure all Americans have health care coverage.
- 68 percent agree that government must see that no one is without food, clothing, or shelter.
- 78 percent favor their own tax dollars being used to help pay for food stamps and other assistance for the poor.[20]

These hardly come across as the cold-hearted responses of a conservative polity wedded to Goldwaterite principles. Instead it is Lyndon Johnson's vision, not Goldwater's, that seems represented even today in the above opinions.

When it comes to the role of government in offering a helping hand and moderating capitalism, we are a fundamentally liberal country, one committed to the principle that we're all in this together. Is it plausible that, from Johnson's decisive triumph in 1964 to Nixon's landslide re-election in 1972, the United States did a sudden about-face regarding liberal government? I suspect rather that Nixon's win—and Reagan's, and that of the other conservative dog whistlers—more resembles Goldwater's peculiar victory in the Deep South. There, whites committed to the New Deal nevertheless allowed racial entreaties to bamboozle them into voting for an anti-New Deal candidate. Since 1972, we seem to have witnessed the Republicans proving out that when it comes to racial resentment, "the whole United States is Southern." Like Goldwater, dog whistlers seem to win more on the strength of racism than conservatism. We should not confuse current antagonism toward government with an enduring rightwing national zeitgeist. Instead, we should have confidence in the liberal "we're all in this together" ethos of the American people, even as we recognize the power of race to produce self-destructive voting patterns.

Here's another version of the same conversation, this one focused on explaining conservative dominance in the United States by highlighting why some voters are deeply conservative, while others are committed liberals. Scholars have offered various explanations, yet consistently these theories focus on individual attributes. Suggestions include personalities attracted to social domination; psychological preferences for order; differences in core values; and differences in moral intuitions.[21] I'm sympathetic to the insights offered as a way to understand individuals. Yet I remain skeptical of the larger project of explaining conservatism in individualistic terms. If in 1964 almost two out of three whites voted for a politician who embodied New Deal liberalism, in 2012 almost the same proportion of whites supported a candidate hostile to activist government. Or again, whereas since 1964 in every election a majority of whites has voted for the GOP, only rarely have more than one in ten African Americans done so. Are whites fundamentally different people now than they were in the 1960s? Is there a different distribution of personality types, psychological preferences, values, and moral intuitions among whites and blacks? Rather, it seems likely the principal explanations for conservatism today must be located in history, culture, and context. Yes, there are intriguing differences between individuals that help explain why some embrace and others repudiate dog whistle politics. But more important to understanding this phenomenon is the 50-year trajectory of dog whistle racism in US society.

■ FROM THE MARGINS

The peripheral rather than core character of conservatism in American society is made clear by returning to the 1960s to track old-time hostility to liberal government. This is important not simply as a historical exercise, but to understand exactly how anti-New Deal politics eventually went from marginal to mainstream.

THE JOHN BIRCH SOCIETY

The John Birch Society illustrates the extremism that once marked anti-liberal politics. This rabidly anti-communist group promulgated outlandish conspiracy theories, claiming for instance that the federal mandate to put fluoride in drinking water was part of a nefarious plot to brainwash the country.[22] With these sorts of ideas, the John Birch Society certainly seems like a worthy candidate for the dustbin of history, and so it would be, except that many of its views constitute today's normal politics.

Massachusetts candy manufacturer Robert Welch, powerful in business circles as a former director of the National Association of Manufacturers, founded the John Birch Society in 1958 to combat "communism" in American life. In a context in which actual domestic support for communism was virtually nil, "communism" in rightwing discourse primarily functioned as a hyperbolic catchall for everything that was supposedly wrong with a political establishment that had embraced the New Deal.[23]

Unsurprisingly, the 1964 election of Lyndon Johnson and his push to enact Great Society programs unhinged Welch and his JBS cohort, causing consternation bordering on apoplexy. In 1966, Welch published an essay entitled "The Truth in Time" to lay bare once and for all the depths of the conniving plot against a slumbering United States. Weaving together historical fact, paranoid fiction, and end-times phraseology, Welch began his essay with "the Illuminati," a secret society of would-be world rulers who supposedly fomented the French Revolution and eventually "coalesced into the Communist conspiracy as we know it today."[24] Arriving at the present nearly out of breath, both from the exertion of fabricating history and from the near-hysteria induced by his tale, Welch warned that "the one great job left for the Communists is the subjugation of the *people* of the United States." Welch then cataloged their dastardly "methods," and these capture the central themes of reactionary politics that have since emerged:

> the constant indoctrination of young and old alike, through our educational system, and through our communications and entertainment media, in a preference for "welfare" and "security" against responsibility and opportunity; making an ever larger and larger percentage of American industry, commerce, agriculture, education, and *individuals* accustomed to receiving, and dependent on, government checks; a constant increase in legislation, taxation, and bureaucracy, leading directly towards one hundred percent government; . . . the creation of riots and the semblance of revolution under the guise and excuse of promoting "civil rights"; . . . [and] destroying the power of local police forces to preserve law and order.[25]

The whole thing might be laughable, though it also provides a good description of the hobgoblins conjured by the right today. First, there's the supposed moral breakdown caused by the siren call of welfare and government-guaranteed economic security. No doubt Welch would have applauded Mitt Romney's dismissal of 47 percent of the country as "dependent upon government, who believe that they are victims, who believe the government has a responsibility to care for them [and who will never assume] personal responsibility and care for their lives."[26] Next, Welch shuddered at the prospect of a government-run economy, a specter repeatedly raised in the contemporary opposition to health care reform. Also, Welch bemoaned the collapse of "law and order," thus anticipating decades of racial pandering conducted in promises to get tough on crime. Finally, Welch saw a special menace from nonwhites, evidenced in his fear of riots and revolution under the excuse of promoting civil rights. Welch fiercely opposed integration, and his racial fears were widely shared in the Birch Society.[27] Today, of course, racial panic continues to rip through the right.

Heralding the "everything old is new again" politics of the right fringe, in 2007 the rightwing media personality Glenn Beck interviewed a JBS spokesperson, interjecting in the midst the conversation: "when I was growing up, the John Birch Society—I thought they were a bunch of nuts. But now . . . you guys are starting to make more and more sense to me."[28] Maybe this comment says more about the older Beck, who today is not especially known for his sanity. But it also reflects a core truth: in the 1960s, Birch Society discourse struck almost everyone—even the young Beck—as crazy talk. More than extreme, Welch's half-baked intellectualism made conservative ideas risible, fodder for a good guffaw but not the sort of stuff that anyone beyond the fringes of American politics would believe.

Understanding this, in 1965 conservative movement builder William F. Buckley tried to clear space for a more serious conservatism by denouncing Welch's views as "far removed from reality and common sense."[29] Buckley recognized the larger problem. In the battle of ideas about how best to organize society, the right had not only lost, it had no tenable arguments whatsoever. The intellectual and political class as a whole broadly agreed on the need to foster a system in which the government ensured that free enterprise served the overarching interests of democracy. While Republicans and Democrats disagreed on how best to structure market rules and social welfare provisions, there was nevertheless wide consensus regarding the probity of regulated capitalism. The John Birch Society, or the repudiated politics of candidates such as Barry Goldwater, simply provided no credible counterweight to this consensus. How would conservatives develop it?

The Powell Memorandum and the Rise of Conservative Think Tanks

As the 1960s came to a close, the right increasingly recognized the lack of credibility around conservatism. In the summer of 1971, the Chamber of Commerce asked Lewis Powell, former head of the American Bar Association and a prominent corporate lawyer from Virginia, to diagnose the anemic character of conservatism. Powell is better known today as a Supreme Court justice, for later that year Nixon appointed him to the Court, partly using the elevation of this Southern lawyer to signal the administration's opposition to civil rights.[30] Of more immediate concern here, though, is the memorandum Powell prepared for the Chamber of Commerce outlining what he perceived as the challenges to the "free enterprise system," and how it might be saved.

Powell's memorandum condemned assaults on business by the predictable rabble: "Communists, New Leftists, and other revolutionaries who would destroy the entire system, both political and economic."[31] More worrisome for Powell, though, was his sense that these attacks were supported by "perfectly respectable elements of society: from the college campus, the pulpit, the media, the intellectual and literary journals, the arts and sciences, and from politicians." Powell also sharply criticized American business for its "apathy and default," and was bewildered by the "extent to which the enterprise system tolerates, if not participates in, its own destruction." Powell thought he saw a pusillanimous mentality among corporate leaders. "The painfully sad truth is that business, including the boards of directors' and the top executives of corporations great and small and business organizations at all levels, often have responded—if at all—by appeasement, ineptitude and ignoring the problem."

Rallying his team with a last-down pep talk, Powell proposed vigorous and concerted corporate mobilization to fund and support an army of national organizations capable of generating conservative ideas and also of inserting them into the national conversation. Powell had in mind existing institutions, though he also urged the creation of new front groups. These organizations should make special efforts, Powell advised, in penetrating the major idea-generating sectors of American society: higher education, especially the social sciences; the media, especially television; and the court system. As to their methods, Powell advised creating stables of "scholars" who could generate material supporting free enterprise, and assembling corps of "speakers of the highest competency," ever ready to take to the airwaves. In the battle over the future of America, Powell advised corporations to manufacture their own beholden intelligentsia.[32]

Powell's memorandum almost immediately came to fruition. "Strident, melodramatic, and alarmist," the historian Kim Phillips-Fein reports, the memorandum "struck a nerve in the tense political world of the early 1970s, giving voice to sentiments that, no matter how extreme they might have seemed, were coming to sound like commonsense in the business world during those anxious years. Not all businessmen shared Powell's passions. But those who did began to act as a vanguard, organizing the giants of American industry."[33] The Powell memorandum inspired a flush of donations to already-established institutions, like the Chamber of Commerce and the American Enterprise Institute, and also encouraged the creation and funding of a raft of conservative think tanks, most notably the Heritage Foundation, the Manhattan Institute, and the Cato Institute.[34] As one example, according to a study of the radical right's origins, one strong Birch Society backer, Joseph Coors, the president of Coors Brewing Company, "poured millions of dollars into dozens of evangelical and New Right organizations and established a pattern for corporate funders: the Scaife, Smith Richardson, Olin, and Noble foundations; the Kraft, Nabisco, and Amway corporations, to name just a few."[35] After the early 1970s, money that had once funded fringe conspiracy theories now flowed into more respectable "think tanks."

At the time, existing think tanks offered non-partisan venues for research and policy debates, and their general reputation was positive. Looking for ways to produce and package conservative ideas, the think tank form and name served reactionary forces well: they would concoct their own research and stage their own debates under the umbrella of "think tanks," with their reassuring connotation of thoughtful neutrality. But rather than fostering wide-ranging inquiry, these new institutions were designed to pump out consistent messages supporting the priorities of their financial backers. In the world of conservative think tanks, apostasy became a firing offense for individuals, and also sufficient cause to defund organizations. In one recent example, the prominent conservative David Frum saw his salary vanish at the American Enterprise Institute after he criticized Congressional Republicans for vilifying Obama's health care bill.[36] As one critic quipped about these conservative think tanks, "they don't think; they justify."[37]

■ ACHIEVING MAINSTREAM LEGITIMACY

Rightwing think tanks found a perfect ally in Ronald Reagan, who combined an eminently likeable demeanor with a pitiless view of the poor and an ideologue's fervor for repealing the New Deal.[38] In 1980, ten days after Reagan won the presidency, the Heritage Foundation issued a 3,000-page, 20-volume report entitled *Mandate for Leadership*, specially written to serve as "a blueprint for the construction of a conservative government."[39] The new president distributed a version to every member of his cabinet, and by Heritage's estimate implemented two-thirds of its recommendations in the first year of his administration.[40] Reagan also spoke glowingly of AEI, arguing that "today, the most important American scholarship comes out of our think tanks—and none has been more influential than the American Enterprise Institute."[41] Reagan at once wrapped himself in the legitimacy of the new think tanks and simultaneously bolstered that very legitimacy, helping them launder propaganda into "the most important American scholarship." He did this not only by extolling their work, but also by adopting their agenda as his own.

Following *Mandate for Leadership's* main goal for the Reagan presidency, the administration moved aggressively to reduce taxes for the rich. Reagan slashed rates for corporations and individuals in the highest income brackets, with the cuts enacted in 1981 alone showering $164 billion on the corporate sector, at that point the most generous business tax reduction in the history of the nation.[42] Over the course of his presidency, Reagan lowered the top marginal tax rate on individuals from 70 percent to 28 percent.[43] As Hedrick Smith notes in *Who Stole the American Dream?*, "The windfall from his tax cuts for America's wealthiest 1 percent was massive—roughly $1 trillion in the 1980s and another $1 trillion each decade after that. The Forbes 400 Richest Americans, enriched by the Reagan tax cuts, tripled their net worth from 1978 to 1990."[44] Under Reagan's tax policies, the process of transferring wealth from the poor and the middle class to the rich and especially to the super-rich began with a vengeance.[45]

What convinced voters to rally behind Reagan's tax giveaways to the rich? More than anything else, it was Heritage's second principal goal that helped Reagan sell his tax cuts: gutting welfare. Limiting welfare had long been part of the plutocratic agenda, as cutting government spending on social services promised to reduce tax demands on the wealthy. Aided by dog whistle politics, however, curtailing welfare emerged as more than a goal; it also became a means of mobilizing a broad hostility toward government itself. This hostility in turn helped sell tax cuts: even if the cuts did not directly benefit the middle class, they nevertheless provided a means to lash out against the reviled liberal state.

LIBERTY, WELFARE, AND INTEGRATION

We can explain shifting perceptions of welfare in the twentieth century through three conceptions of liberty. The first is "liberty *from* government." This libertarian version stresses freedom from state coercion, and, more generally, negative freedom from external constraints. During the robber baron era of the late nineteenth and early twentieth centuries, the so-called "malefactors of great wealth" easily manipulated this conception of liberty to support their own agenda. These plutocrats, many having made their fortunes through government contracts and state-backed monopolies, cynically celebrated "rugged individualism" for the little guy, preaching that the freest man was the one solely responsible for himself. These sorts of arguments were mobilized to oppose unions, workplace safety rules, minimum wage laws, and financial support for the unemployed, the injured or disabled, and the elderly. Despite the rhetoric, however, there was little liberty in penury. During the Great Depression it became brutally apparent that genuine freedom depended on security in the face of market vicissitudes. The "rugged individual" shriveled up and blew away in the fierce winds of the Dust Bowl.

The negative conception of "liberty from" was thereafter supplemented by a positive version of "liberty *through* government." Under this New Deal version, government gave individuals the realistic power to make their own choices by tempering market abuses and liberating citizens from the dire constraints of need. In his last Sunday speech before his assassination, Martin Luther King, Jr., told the audience: "We hold these truths to be self-evident . . . that all men are endowed with the inalienable rights of life, liberty, and the pursuit of happiness." Then he continued: "But if a man does not have a job or income, he has neither life or liberty nor the possibility of the pursuit of happiness. He merely exists."[46] Positive liberty sees freedom not in the abstract, but in the concrete options realistically open to citizens. Thus, rather than seeing government as an enemy of liberty, New Deal liberalism came to see government as key to promoting liberty. The modern liberalism that arose with the New Deal still restricts government infringements on liberty in some areas, such as speech. But more fundamentally it promotes positive liberties by empowering government in other areas, for example in regulating the market and providing help to the needy.

A broad consensus arose around liberty through government; it suffered during the 1960s, however, as hostility to civil rights and integration increased. A new conception of liberty began to emerge: "freedom to exclude." Both earlier concepts of liberty had underlying racial subtexts, being largely restricted to whites. But freedom to exclude had an explicit racial message: it meant the liberty to exclude nonwhites from white neighborhoods, workplaces, and schools.

When Lyndon Johnson declared his War on Poverty, he extended the benefits of social welfare to nonwhites. In the process, this effort targeted segregation, for obviously poverty in nonwhite communities was deeply tied to racially closed workplaces, schools, and housing. As a result, welfare and integration became tightly linked, and hostility toward integration morphed into opposition to welfare. "The positive liberties [that the War on Poverty] extended to African Americans," notes Jill Quadagno, a scholar of race and welfare, "were viewed by the working class as infringement on their negative liberties, the liberty for trade unions to discriminate in the selection of apprentices and to control job training programs; the liberty to exclude minorities from representation in local politics; the liberty to maintain segregated neighborhoods."[47] To talk of rank racial discrimination in unions, politics, and housing in the language of a perceived infringement on liberty may seem strange. Yet for many, this is how they experienced integration. It was a social experiment being forced on them by government, and therefore a governmental infringement on their liberty to exclude.

Reagan's campaign against welfare helped make the case for tax cuts by successfully using social programs like welfare, and its implicit connection to integration, to convince voters that the real danger in their lives came from a looming, intrusive government. This idea that government was the primordial threat would have seemed silly in the decades immediately following the bitter experience of the Great Depression. But decades removed from that hardship—and after many whites had risen into the comfortable ranks of the middle class—government impingements on personal liberty came to seem the greater threat to the well-being of many. Like the earlier concept of liberty from government, freedom to exclude presented government as the problem, and thus, provided grounds for opposing liberalism and its vision of liberty through government. The rugged individual, hostile to government regulation of the market, died in the Great Depression; but after the civil rights movement, he rose from the grave as the "traditional individual," resentful of government efforts to force unwanted racial integration. Both figures, convinced that government rather than concentrated wealth posed the greatest threat to their vaunted liberty, proved willing to support the robber barons of their day.

Ironically, the very structure of New Deal aid facilitated the demonization of the activist state. Responding to the individualistic strain in American culture, New Dealers and their heirs purposefully sought to *hide* from many beneficiaries how government helped them. From the outset, for instance, Social Security's architects told recipients that these were "earned" benefits, rather than the stigmatized "welfare" given to the penurious. Similarly, many other wealth transfer programs have been structured as tax breaks, again cloaking the role of the activist state.[48] In the historian Molly Michelmore's evocative terms, the liberal reform agenda "enabled and encouraged the majority of citizens to define themselves as *taxpayers* with legitimate claims on the state not shared by *tax eaters* on the welfare rolls."[49] Liberals obfuscated the assistance provided by government—a calculated decision aimed at reducing opposition from a public steeped in norms of individual responsibility, though also communitarian values. The dissimulating design of the liberal state, perversely, eased the task of conservatives keen on stoking hostility toward liberal governance. Even if apocryphal, the oxymoronic Tea Party cry "Keep Government out of my Medicare!" epitomizes how anti-government sentiment can be mobilized more easily when the public fails to discern government's helping hand.

During the Reagan era, for the first time since the onset of the Great Depression, significant cultural space opened up to present government—rather than concentrated wealth—as the greatest threat to freedom faced by the middle class. In turn, massive tax cuts were sold as the appropriate way to restrain a looming, intrusive state. On one level, of course, the tax revolt of the 1980s was more precisely targeted towards preventing the transfer of resources to "them," the "undeserving poor," who were disproportionately people of color. More than this, though, opposition to taxes came to mean opposition to government meddling. The point is not that Reagan or other Republican administrations have reduced the size of government (on the contrary, they've repeatedly vastly expanded federal power and dramatically increased the national debt, not least through unsustainable tax giveaways to the rich). The point, rather, is that they *sold* tax cuts for the rich, and indeed the whole agenda of reduced regulation and slashed services, as an expression of hostility toward liberal government. The anti-tax insurgent Grover Norquist has been widely quoted as saying: "I'm not in favor of abolishing the government. I just want to shrink it down to the size where we can drown it in the bathtub." But what makes many voters sympathetic to the idea of extinguishing government in the first place? For many, this seething hostility toward government is rooted in racial narratives of freedom in jeopardy.

Affirmative Action

At the urging of the Heritage Foundation, the Reagan administration also used—indeed, created—affirmative action as a wedge issue.[50] Affirmative action emerged in the late 1960s out of efforts to directly foster integration in schools and workplaces, and while often the object of resentment, until the 1980s such programs nevertheless enjoyed broad support from a polity generally committed to fulfilling the civil rights goal of breaking down segregation. Reagan set out to not only roll back but politicize affirmative action, and to spearhead this effort he appointed William Bradford Reynolds to head the Civil Rights Division of the Justice Department. Reynolds, an Andover- and Yale-educated corporate lawyer, had no background in civil rights; instead, he was a fierce critic of affirmative action, which he saw as racial discrimination against innocent whites.[51] Under Reynolds, the Justice Department began highly public campaigns to oppose affirmative action, presenting numerous arguments to the Supreme Court that race-conscious remedies amounted to impermissible racism against whites.[52] It also sought to intervene in school desegregation cases, encouraging local school districts to contest court-ordered integration plans. The administration defended segregated school districts so aggressively, it caused Drew Days, who had headed the Department of Justice's civil rights efforts under Carter, to despair, "What they seek is no less than a relitigation of *Brown v. Board of Education*."[53]

Like Reagan's campaign against welfare, his broadsides against affirmative action constituted a form of dog whistle politics.[54] The ostensible issue wasn't minorities at all, but the supposedly simple principle of not discriminating for or against any individual. In 1984, when Reagan won re-election in a landslide, the GOP platform had a new plank on affirmative action: "We will resist efforts to replace equal rights with discriminatory quota systems and preferential treatment. Quotas are the most insidious form of discrimination: reverse discrimination against the innocent."[55] The document said nothing about race directly, but obviously "the innocent" meant innocent whites. Attacking affirmative action provided a way for the GOP to constantly force race—and the party's defense of white interests—into the national conversation.

Beyond generally pushing the idea of whites as victims, attacking affirmative action had a more particular payoff in how this issue intersected with class. The constant harping on welfare directed attention to nonwhites defined overwhelmingly as poor and dysfunctional. This pernicious imagery was challenged, though, by the growing number of nonwhites attending top schools, holding good jobs, and living in nice neighborhoods. Attacking affirmative action provided a way to paint even successful minorities as still representing a threat to whites, by portraying these minorities as "thriving in jobs that they had obtained, not through hard work or merit, but through affirmative action—jobs that under any fair system of competition would have rightfully gone to whites."[56] Closely related to this, the charge that liberalism gave elite minorities an unfair advantage created a racial spook with which to directly rattle those whites whose wealth typically shielded them from contact with the poor of any color. Railing against affirmative action provided a way to tell well-off whites that even they were at risk from the liberal obsession with integration: their jobs, and also their children's access to top colleges, were under assault from do-gooder liberals.

In 1984, Reagan easily won re-election, capturing the white vote by a factor of almost two to one. Blacks heard the dog whistle too. Over 90 percent voted against Reagan—not that it mattered to the Republicans, for as Kevin Phillips had noted, with the support of enough whites the Republicans could win with virtually no African American support.

■ LIBERALISM AS ALWAYS ABOUT RACE

In the wake of 1984's pummeling, the Michigan Democratic Party commissioned Stanley Greenberg, then a political scientist and later a preeminent Democratic pollster, to help it understand the mindset of the voters abandoning the party in droves. Greenberg placed race at the epicenter of the tectonic shift. First, Greenberg found that many whites conflated middle-class identity with white identity, and saw blacks as a threat to their middle-class status: "Blacks constitute the explanation for their vulnerability and for almost everything that has gone wrong in their lives; not being black is what constitutes being middle class; not living with blacks is what makes a neighborhood a decent place to live." Second, picking up on the administration's campaign against affirmative action as discrimination against whites, Greenberg found that many whites had come to understand *themselves* as victims of racial mistreatment. "Indeed, discrimination against whites has become a well-assimilated and ready explanation for their status, vulnerability and failures." How exactly did whites come to understand themselves as racial victims? We'll explore that question in the next chapter.

Here, the most important of Greenberg's findings is his third: Reagan Democrats increasingly extended their antipathy from nonwhites to government as a whole. "These white Democratic defectors express a profound distaste for blacks, a sentiment that pervades almost everything they think about government and politics. These sentiments have important implications for Democrats, as virtually all progressive symbols and themes have been redefined in racial and pejorative terms."[57] This last insight, that for Democratic defectors "virtually all progressive symbols and themes have been redefined in racial and pejorative terms," goes to the root of how dog whistle racism wrecks the middle class. Progressive politics in general—not liberal politics only as applied to nonwhites—was now despised by a large group of voters as a sop to minorities and an infringement on the rights of whites. We might object that liberalism has no inherent racial valence; it's not about helping groups on the basis of race, but rather out of concern for human dignity. The core insight of modern liberalism is powerfully simple: we all benefit from a society that provides for the economic security and wellbeing of each member, whatever the heartbreaks of life. True, this vision was originally restricted by race to primarily help whites, but this was a tragic distortion that undercut the universal potential of New Deal liberalism. Johnson's Great Society was not about injecting race into liberalism, it was about removing racism from it.

Once government sought to fold nonwhites into the "we" that together comprises a healthy society, however, many voters rebelled. Encouraged by the Republicans, whites came to view as racially tainted not just programs specifically aiding nonwhites but *the entire liberal agenda.* "In essence, the Democratic message by 1984 was viewed by one sector of the white electorate—a crucial sector in terms of presidential votes—through what might be called the prism of race: traditional liberal messages were passed through a racial filter . . . even when no explicitly racial content was intended."[58] Reagan used dog whistle references to welfare and affirmative action to color how Americans saw government overall. He succeeded so well that many voters came to "hear" race when liberals spoke, even when it wasn't invoked or intended. With regard to liberalism in general, we might say that a "reverse dog whistle" began to blow: progressives could not speak without many whites hearing refrains of racial betrayal.

What if liberals sought to backpedal, toward the tainted New Deal bargain that supported liberal policies primarily for whites? Would this remove the racial stain from liberalism? As it turns out, since the 1980s we have been regressing in exactly this way. A 2011 Congressional Budget Office report examining all of the social assistance distributed by the federal government—including the benefits from dozens of programs, from Social Security and Medicare, to unemployment insurance and school lunches—shows that in 1979, 54 percent of these resources went to the poorest fifth of households in America.[59] In contrast, in 2007 that figure had dropped to 36 percent. Another study extended that trend line, finding that "the poorest American households, the bottom fifth, received just 32 cents of every dollar of government benefits distributed in 2010."[60] Today, nearly 60 percent of government benefits instead go to those in the middle-income quintiles. In other words, government help to individuals is no longer for the poor. Now it's primarily for those in the middle-income brackets.

Because whites are overrepresented in higher income brackets, assistance skewed to the better off slants help disproportionately toward whites. Compounding this racial dynamic, even among the poor, white households receive an unequal share of government help. Remarking that "the distribution of benefits no longer aligns with the demography of poverty," the *New York Times* reports that "African-Americans, who make up 22 percent of the poor, receive 14 percent of government benefits." In contrast, "white non-Hispanics, who make up 42 percent of the poor, receive 69 percent of government benefits."[61] The New Deal practice of welfare primarily for whites is returning.

So has support for welfare and liberalism returned as well? Hardly. The racial attacks on welfare were never about facts, but rather about manipulated resentments. Consider a *New York Times* feature piece from 2012 reporting on the state of the safety net in the United States.[62] The article focused on residents of Chisago, a county northeast of Minneapolis, to shine a light on those who received government benefits yet resented the help:

> As more middle-class families like [that of Ki Gulbranson] land in the safety net in Chisago and similar communities, anger at the government has increased alongside. Many people say they are angry because the government is wasting money and giving money to people who do not deserve it. But more than that, they say they want to reduce the role of government in their own lives. They are frustrated that they need help, feel guilty for taking it and resent the government for providing it.

Gulbranson earned $39,000 a year working multiple jobs to make ends meet. He also supported the Tea Party and its promise to slash government benefits. The article used the disconnect between Gulbranson's need for government help and his regressive politics to illustrate the paradoxical anger at liberal government exhibited by many who receive aid. Yet the *Times* authors, like virtually all who note this paradox, did not attempt to explain it.

Perhaps a clue to the paradox's resolution can be found in the photos accompanying the story. These showed that almost all of the "middle-class families" featured in the article, like Gulbranson, were white. Much of the bitter anger about receiving government benefits stems from the way in which liberalism has been racialized and darkened. In the cultural commonsense created by rightwing race-baiting, lazy nonwhites abuse welfare, while hardworking whites pay for it. This is not the reality, of course, not when a disproportionate share of welfare benefits go to whites, and not when the underlying complaint trades on ugly racial stereotypes. But reality is beside the point. What matters is that many whites think this of welfare and welfare recipients. In turn, this racial imagery likely torments those who consider themselves white, middle class, and hardworking, when abruptly they find that now they too are welfare royalty.

Having internalized a demonized view of welfare recipients, they torture themselves when it turns out sometimes they too need help.

Conservatism once spread a message of rugged individuals and shameless moochers. This cruel story lost its purchase in the Great Depression, replaced by liberalism's redemptive story of occasional misfortune amid a society of worthy individuals. We all need a hand sometimes, modern liberalism avowed, thereby not only providing material assistance but removing some of the psychological sting of defeat or affliction. The conservative message seemed mean and petty, a gratuitous slap at the less fortunate spouted most loudly by the scions of great wealth. Nevertheless, this socially destructive message regained strength after the civil rights movement, when dog whistle racism recast the rugged as white, and the shameless as black. Now, the individual-or-moocher frame is back in vogue, even—to their personal distress—among many of those needing government help.

■ WRECKING THE MIDDLE CLASS

So how does dog whistle racism wreck the middle class? Racial demagoguery convinces many whites to think about government help in terms of race, and then to reject liberalism and the lessons of the New Deal in favor of the nostrums promoted by corporate titans and loaded insiders. We've already discussed massive tax giveaways to the very rich, attacks on welfare programs, and assaults on affirmative action. Other mechanisms from the 1980s included the hamstringing of labor, epitomized by Reagan's mass firing of air traffic controllers who went out on strike, a blow not just to that union but a clear signal of increasing governmental hostility toward organized labor. In addition, the middle class suffered from economic deregulation, particularly in the banking industry, which led to massive fraud in and the collapse of the savings and loan sector. In a harbinger of financial deregulation's effects following 2008, the ensuing economic meltdown slowed the economy and led to widespread unemployment that endured for years. Beyond economic deregulation, the Reagan administration also began a sustained campaign against environmental regulation, freeing large polluters from government oversight. Justifying this hands-off approach, Reagan infamously belittled the whole idea of controlling pollution by quipping that trees cause more pollution than automobiles.

The predictable results can be summarized in poverty statistics. From 1960 to 1970, as the New Deal expanded into the Great Society, the number of Americans in poverty declined from 40 million to under 25 million. During the 1970s, after the rise of dog whistle politics but before its full hijacking by rightwing oligarchs, the numbers in poverty remained steady. During the 1980s, as Reagan and then George H.W. Bush reigned, those in poverty soared to 35 million. At the end of Clinton's second term in 2000, those mired in poverty had fallen to just above 30 million. But following the Great Recession that marked the end George W. Bush's presidency, over 46 million Americans were in poverty.[63] That's an additional 16 million good folks pushed into the material and emotional hardship of destitution in just one decade.

This book's subtitle suggests that race-baiting wrecks the middle class, as indeed it does. This is not, however, to claim that the *purpose* behind racial demagoguery is to destroy average Americans—it is not. The point, for politicians such as Wallace and Nixon, was to get elected and re-elected. Simultaneously, big money came to see dog whistling as a way to promote policies that favored society's sultans. These policies are, roughly, the same policies advocated by the malefactors of great wealth during the era of the robber baron: low taxes, a minimal or non-existent social safety net, and corporate control over the regulation of industry. These were, of course, policies that voters had repudiated during the New Deal as well as in the sweeping defeat of Barry Goldwater. Through their newly muscled think tanks and aided by Ronald Reagan, however, the modern plutocrats reintroduced these prescriptions to the American public as a response to the excesses of the civil rights era. Their aim was not to wreck the middle class, but to convince average Americans to support policies that transferred wealth and power to the already extremely wealthy and powerful. Like the nonwhites injured by dog whistle racism, the middle class was not a target—just collateral damage.

4

The False Allure of Colorblindness

Why do so many whites respond to the dog whistle refrain that they, and not minorities, are today's most likely victims of racial discrimination? Colorblindness helps to legitimate the substance of dog whistle complaints because it promotes understandings of race and racism that obscure discrimination against nonwhites and magnify the ostensible mistreatment of whites.

"Is your baby racist?" The question blared from the cover of *Newsweek Magazine* in September 2009, eight months after the inauguration of the nation's first black president. The accompanying story reported on several recent studies showing that young children not only notice race, they repeat painful stereotypes. In one study, a researcher recruited roughly 100 families from Austin, Texas; all of the families were white, with children between the ages of five and seven. When the children were asked how many white people were "mean," they commonly answered "almost none." But when asked how many blacks were mean, many answered "some" or "a lot."[1] The thrust of the article seemed to be that children possess racial biases. However eye-catching the title, though, it pointed in the wrong direction—at infants and little children rather than adults. The core of the article focused on parenting strategies, and especially on the desire to raise children to be colorblind—to be blind to race. The parents were *not* teaching their children to be bigots. Instead, they were doing their utmost to teach their children to reject racism by studiously ignoring race. Yet, even in a liberal bastion like Austin, it wasn't working.

Today the dominant etiquette around race is colorblindness. It has a strong moral appeal, for it laudably envisions an ideal world in which race is no longer relevant to how we perceive or treat each other. It also has an intuitive practical appeal: to get beyond race, colorblindness urges, the best strategy is to immediately stop recognizing and talking about race. But it is especially as a strategy that colorblindness fails its liberal adherents. We cannot will ourselves to un-see something that we've already seen. In turn, refusing to talk about a powerful social reality doesn't make that reality go away, but it does leave confused thinking unchallenged, in ourselves and in others. The Austin children exemplify this. Differences in race—including physical variation and its connection to social position—resemble differences in gender: they are plainly visible to new minds eager to make sense of the world around them. When unexplained, however, children (and our unconscious minds) are left susceptible to the power of stereotypes. As the *Newsweek* authors conclude, "children see racial differences as much as they see the difference between pink and blue—but we tell kids that 'pink' means for girls and 'blue' is for boys. 'White' and 'black' are mysteries we leave them to figure out on their own."

We should also acknowledge that colorblindness has an additional appeal: it seems to provide a safe route through the minefield of race relations. Many whites are understandably nervous to talk about race at all, though especially in racially mixed company. What if they slip and say something that sounds ignorant, or worse, bigoted? Simply avoiding race altogether seems to offer a solution. Yet, those who adopt a colorblind strategy often come across as *more* racially hostile, not less. Refusing to acknowledge obvious social differences creates an impression of suppressed dislike, and studies have shown that whites who studiously avoid mentioning race even when it is clearly relevant are perceived as more bigoted.[2] Perhaps this contributed to how the Austin children came to interpret their parents' racial attitudes, after their parents tried so hard to suppress references to race. Asked "do your parents like black people," more than half either said "no, my parents don't like black people," or simply answered, "I don't know." The researchers remarked, "in this supposed race-free vacuum being created by parents, kids were left to improvise their own conclusions—many of which would be abhorrent to their parents."[3]

If colorblindness seems to backfire, is there something that *does* help our children—and us—navigate the dangerous shoals of race? Yes: talking openly about racial differences and what they might mean. Psychological research shows that cognitive biases in social judgment "can be controlled only through subsequent, deliberate 'mental correction' that takes group status squarely into account."[4] The Austin researchers reached a similar conclusion, for they urged parents to use in the racial context the express methods they employ to help children overcome gender stereotypes. "Parents are very comfortable talking to their children about gender, and they work very hard to counterprogram against boy-girl stereotypes. That ought to be our model for talking about race. The same way we remind our [children], 'Mommies can be doctors just like daddies,' we ought to be telling all children that doctors can be any skin color. It's not complicated what to say. It's only a matter of how often we reinforce it."[5] In other words, best practices in the area of race involve doing the opposite of what colorblindness seems to command. We must notice and talk about race, self-critically and carefully, in order to understand and attempt to set aside its power over our imaginations.

As the Austin families found out, colorblindness fails as a strategy for transcending race on an interpersonal level. It's bad advice for those genuinely endeavoring to eliminate racism from their lives.

It's also bad advice for those seeking to comprehend and respond to dog whistle politics. Dog whistling cannot be resisted by refusing to talk about race, for this only leaves constant racial insinuations unchallenged, operating in the background to panic many whites. Indeed, dog whistle racism is not only protected by colorblindness, it rests fundamentally on colorblind mythmaking.

Much more than a racial etiquette, colorblindness provides a powerful framework shaping how people think about race and racism, and in doing so it helps give credence to dog whistle themes. Part of the power of colorblindness comes from its liberal origins and its close association with civil rights heroes, a linkage conservatives constantly belabor. Beyond this, the potency of colorblindness comes from what it teaches about racial discrimination, lessons almost always gleaned at the level of commonsense. Under the umbrella of colorblindness, ideas regarding race and racism geared toward protecting the superior position of whites in society have evolved significantly since the civil rights era. After tracing the history and conservative hijacking of colorblindness, this chapter focuses on bringing to the surface the core stories colorblindness spins—about the end of discrimination against minorities, the blame they deserve for their inferior social positions, the innocence of contemporary whites, and their racial victimization. These narratives undergird dog whistle politics in its effort to portray nonwhites as threats and whites as imperiled.

■ COLORBLINDNESS: FROM RADICAL TO REACTIONARY

The term "colorblind" comes to us from Justice John Marshall Harlan's lone dissent in *Plessy v. Ferguson*, the 1896 case that announced the "separate but equal" standard that sanctioned racial segregation throughout society.[6] Louisiana had recently enacted a law requiring that black and white railroad passengers ride in separate cars; turning back a challenge to this law as naked racial discrimination, eight justices voted to uphold it, thereby ensuring decades of group debasement symbolized and fortified by legally enforced segregation. Harlan dissented and declared—in what amounted to aspiration rather than description—that "Our Constitution is color-blind, and neither knows nor tolerates classes among citizens."[7]

Today, conservative advocates of colorblindness use this term as a shorthand for their opposition to affirmative action. They contend that colorblindness means government should never take race into account, not even as a way to promote racial equality. In 2007, the conservative Supreme Court justices blocked public school districts from considering race when assigning pupils to schools, even when seeking to maintain hard-won integration. Justifying this rigid rule, Justice Clarence Thomas proclaimed himself "quite comfortable with the company I keep. My view of the Constitution is Justice Harlan's view in *Plessy*: 'Our Constitution is color-blind.' "[8]

Thomas' invocation of Harlan to oppose integration is misplaced. First, Harlan clearly never meant to proscribe *all* governmental uses of race. Rather, Harlan advocated colorblindness to limit excessive oppression, in the context of what he supposed would be the eternal reign of white supremacy. He began the very paragraph in which he invoked colorblindness as follows: "The white race deems itself to be the dominant race in this country. And so it is, in prestige, in achievements, in education, in wealth and in power. So, I doubt not, it will continue to be for all time."[9] Harlan approved of many government racial restrictions that codified what he perceived as the natural inferiority of blacks. Some years before *Plessy*, Harlan had voted to uphold an Alabama law forbidding interracial marriage.[10] And two years after *Plessy*, Harlan wrote an opinion supporting a whites-only high school.[11] Harlan's famous dissent was not a call that the country literally become blind to race; quite the contrary. Perceiving a world where racial hierarchy was fixed, Harlan interpreted the Constitution to allow society to mark boundaries around those naturally relegated to the bottom. Even so, unlike his brethren, he objected to extreme civic exclusion. Harlan opposed the segregated train cars at issue in *Plessy* because he felt they unfairly limited the capacity of blacks to participate in civil life and the marketplace, not because he opposed any governmental use of race, and certainly not because he thought, as contemporary colorblindness doctrine asserts, that the Constitution forbade state efforts to ameliorate racism.[12]

Notwithstanding Harlan's own limited conception of colorblindness, as the civil rights movement gathered steam in the 1940s, its leading lawyers seized on "colorblindness" to challenge Jim Crow. The phrase "Our Constitution is color-blind" carried important rhetorical force, for in its simple declarative form it seemed to command an immediate end to all government laws mandating racial segregation. Thurgood Marshall, as lead counsel for the NAACP Legal Defense Fund, repeatedly encouraged his colleagues to cite Harlan's famous aphorism. One lawyer recalled that the *Plessy* dissent was Marshall's "Bible to which he turned during his most depressed moments. . . . I do not believe we ever filed a major brief in the pre-*Brown* days in which a portion of that opinion was not quoted. Marshall's favorite quotation was, 'Our Constitution is color-blind.' . . . It became our basic creed."[13] Clarence Thomas uses "colorblindness" more in the manner of Thurgood Marshall than John Harlan, as an argument against *all* government uses of race. Yet there is a crucial difference: Marshall did so when states overwhelmingly used race to humiliate and exclude; Thomas does so now that government virtually only employs race to remedy centuries of racism.

In 1954, the Supreme Court in *Brown v. Board of Education* overturned *Plessy* and formally ended school segregation. Notably, though, the justices did *not* adopt a colorblind bar on all government uses of race. Adopting strict colorblindness would have battered apart the entire edifice of segregation laws at once. The Supreme Court preferred to dismantle segregation "with all deliberate speed."[14] Put bluntly, this reflected a decision to temporize: the Court feared taking on too much too rapidly. It particularly sought to avoid abruptly declaring unconstitutional the emotional core of white supremacy—the ban on interracial marriage. Just after *Brown*, the Court used a procedural feint to avoid deciding a miscegenation case.[15] Only piecemeal and over time did the Court extend *Brown* to completely outlaw segregation, waiting over 13 years before it finally knocked down laws banning marriage between whites and persons of different races in *Loving v. Virginia*.[16]

Ironically, while the Court initially eschewed colorblind reasoning in order to protect segregation from too sudden an assault, over time the decision not to flatly prohibit government distinctions based on race came to seem wise for the goals of racial justice. By the mid-1960s, it was clear that through state subterfuge and social convention, racial segregation readily continued even absent laws expressly mandating it. As late as 1965, 11 years after school segregation was declared unconstitutional, fewer than 1 in 100 black students in the South attended schools formerly white by law, and the number of whites in predominantly black schools was infinitesimally small.[17] Though absolute colorblindness had been their watchword for decades, in the late 1960s civil rights lawyers dropped this demand. Instead, they began to stress the necessity of actively taking race into account to promote meaningful integration. This meant more than getting the Court to move faster than "with all deliberate speed." It meant actively pursuing integration through measures that used race as a tool, including through race-conscious placements of students, teachers, and administrators, and through the race-conscious allocation of resources.

Race-conscious efforts to promote integration reflected a basic insight about racial inequality: outlawing mistreatment was a step in the right direction, but by itself would not significantly correct settled disadvantage. Martin Luther King, Jr., expressed this idea using the metaphor of a foot race. In his 1964 book *Why We Can't Wait*, King lamented:

> whenever the issue of compensatory or preferential treatment for the Negro is raised, some of our friends recoil in horror. The Negro should be granted equality, they agree; but he should ask for nothing more. On the surface, this appears reasonable, but it is not realistic. For it is obvious that if a man is entered at the starting line in a race three hundred years after another man, the first would have to perform some impossible feat in order to catch up with his fellow runner.[18]

For King, and for the civil rights movement more generally, the goal was not merely to end formal segregation, but to break the deep connection between race and disadvantage. Simply declaring segregation laws illegal would not make African Americans "equal" in the eyes of a society steeped in degrading views of nonwhites. Nor would the end of formal segregation by itself equip a people hobbled by centuries of oppression to singlehandedly overcome the economic legacy of racism, especially in a society still accustomed to reserving the best jobs, neighborhoods, and schools for whites. Widespread acceptance of the supposed inferiority of blacks and the concrete realities of a stratified society combined to limit the life chances of those glibly declared "equal" and "free" the moment Jim Crow laws were struck down. As King recognized, true equality would be a long-term, arduous process. In this effort, policies and programs that used race as a basis for planning, for the distribution of resources and contracts, and for the allocation of spots in universities and workplaces, provided the most direct way to begin the process of social repair.

THE RISE OF CONSERVATIVE COLORBLINDNESS

Brown's command to end segregation provoked fervent opposition in the South, including political posturing by demagogic politicians like George Wallace and race riots by whites—and it also engendered a conservative reworking of colorblindness. Marshall himself had worried that colorblindness had an Achilles heel. While a colorblind ruling had the potential to overturn at once all segregation laws, it seemed to require no more than an end to such laws, not actual integration.[19] For the government to be technically colorblind, it need do nothing more than avoid direct references to race in its laws. This insight was scarcely lost on the recalcitrant South. A federal district court in South Carolina articulated a colorblind argument against integration as early as 1955: "The Constitution . . . does not require integration. It merely forbids discrimination. It does not forbid such segregation as occurs as the result of voluntary action. It merely forbids the use of governmental power to enforce segregation."[20] From here, it was but a short logical jump to the contention that colorblindness *prohibited* race-conscious integration measures. In 1965, the same court approvingly quoted the conclusion that "the Constitution is color-blind; it should no more be violated to attempt integration than to preserve segregation."[21] Thus by 1965, a conservative form of colorblindness had emerged: according to the newest friends of the theory, the Constitution forbade any state use of race, whether to segregate or—and this was the real agenda—to integrate.

Among these new proponents of colorblindness was Barry Goldwater. In October 1964, Goldwater was preparing to give his first full address to the nation on civil rights. He had been campaigning in the South on the strength of his vote against the 1964 Civil Rights Act, and now he faced a high-wire routine: On the one hand, he needed the votes of defiant whites and could not risk jeopardizing their support. On the other, he could not afford to come off as a redneck cowboy before the nation as a whole. Goldwater struck a balance: he would stick to his opposition to integration, but would dress it up in a tuxedo and give it a haircut. He decided to deliver his remarks at a $100-a-plate fund-raiser, anticipating that the well-heeled assembly would avoid awkward outbursts supporting segregation.

To costume his position, Goldwater sought assistance trimming his language, enlisting a Phoenix lawyer named William Rehnquist to help write the speech.[22] Rehnquist was an outspoken critic of civil rights, with a track record going back to *Brown* itself. When that case was first argued, Rehnquist had been a law clerk to one of the justices hearing it, and had written a memo urging that segregation be upheld, averring that "*Plessy v. Ferguson* was right and should be re-affirmed."[23] But in the decade since, Rehnquist had moderated his language, and by 1964 he couched his opposition to civil rights as support for property rights (that is, the right of property owners to discriminate racially), making him an ideal choice to help Goldwater recalibrate his message. Entitled "Civil

Rights and the Common Good," the talk reprised the property rights argument, but also took another rhetorical turn, masterfully co-opting the language of civil rights to oppose integration as a moral evil. "It has been well-said that the Constitution is color-blind," Goldwater began, before according that hallowed phrase its perverse new meaning: "And so it is just as wrong to compel children to attend certain schools for the sake of so-called integration as for the sake of segregation."[24] His audience knew what he meant: government should not use race to impose integration on unwilling whites. Despite their polished cuff links and pearls, the crowd roared approval, "letting loose a hail of wolf whistles and throaty cries that raised the roof."[25]

When this reactionary version of colorblindness first reached the Supreme Court, it met unequivocal rejection. By this time, the Court included Thurgood Marshall, who had been appointed by Lyndon Johnson. In 1971, a unanimous Court overturned a North Carolina law requiring "color blind" school assignments, deeming it merely the latest stratagem to avoid integration. Seeing through this cynical maneuver, the Court warned against laws that "control school assignment plans by directing that they be 'color blind'; that requirement, against the background of segregation, would render illusory the promise of *Brown v. Board of Education*." The Court explained, "Just as the race of students must be considered in determining whether a constitutional violation has occurred, so also must race be considered in formulating a remedy. To forbid, at this stage, all assignments made on the basis of race would deprive school authorities of the one tool absolutely essential to fulfillment of their constitutional obligation to eliminate existing dual school systems."[26]

This stand against reactionary colorblindness did not hold. Nixon appointed four justices to the Court. We've now met two. The first was Lewis Powell, the author of the memorandum urging corporations to create their own indebted intelligentsia. The second was William Rehnquist, the *Plessy* supporter and Goldwater speechwriter—and, it bears adding, Ronald Reagan's eventual choice to serve as Chief Justice, a post he held from 1986 until his death in 2005. These appointments sharply changed the Court's political composition, especially with regard to civil rights. By 1978, now on the losing side, Justice Marshall found himself urging his new colleagues to reject race-blindness as a bar on affirmative action: "It is because of a legacy of unequal treatment that we now must permit the institutions of this society *to give consideration to race* in making decisions about who will hold the positions of influence, affluence, and prestige in America."[27] Marshall did not prevail, either for colorblindness as a NAACP lawyer fighting segregation, or against it as a Supreme Court justice seeking to protect an essential means of promoting integration. Instead, over the last few decades conservative justices have steered the Court toward a colorblind vision in which, as we see next, racism against minorities is over while racism against whites is rampant.

In the late 1960s, a structural conception of racism began to take hold, briefly influencing equality law. For instance, this view gained national prominence in 1968 when the National Advisory Commission on Civil Disorders published what became popularly known as the Kerner Report. Seeking to explain the devastating riots marching across the country, from Los Angeles in 1965, to Chicago in 1966, to Newark in 1967, the report famously warned that the United States was "moving toward two societies, one black, one white—separate and unequal." Buttressing this claim, the report detailed the punishing reality confronting African Americans, compiling over 500 pages of evidence on the extreme material hardships of overt discrimination, segregated and inferior schooling, inadequate housing, lack of access to health care, systemic police violence, and labor market exclusion. More than simply painting the harrowing circumstances confronting blacks, the report identified its root cause not in blacks themselves but in American racial dynamics. Focusing particularly on the ghetto, the report stated on its first page that "segregation and poverty have created in the racial ghetto a destructive environment totally unknown to most white Americans. . . . White institutions created it, white institutions maintain it, and white society condones it."[28]

This conception of structural racism began to penetrate the legal field, for instance with a key decision in 1971 holding that outcomes, not just intentions, mattered in cases challenging discrimination. In *Griggs v. Duke Power*, a large Southern employer had long expressly restricted blacks to menial work, organizing its workforce to ensure that no black would earn as much as the lowest-paid white employee. After Congress enacted the 1964 Civil Rights Act forbidding racial discrimination in employment, the company complied only nominally, adopting hiring requirements that on their face no longer referred to race, but that effectively preserved the established racial hierarchy. Still, the company's new procedures were technically neutral, and this challenged the courts to look behind the surface at actual social patterns, including outcomes. In *Griggs*, the Supreme Court found the company liable for discrimination, warning that "good intent or absence of discriminatory intent does not redeem employment procedures or testing mechanisms that operate as 'built-in headwinds' for minority groups."[29] By condemning "built-in headwinds," the decision seemed to herald a concern with structural discrimination in addition to express exclusion and naked bigotry.

As it turned out, *Griggs* represented the high-water mark for antidiscrimination law. Over the remainder of the decade, conservatives on the Court, including Powell and Rehnquist, chipped away at the standard for proving discrimination against nonwhites. By 1979, the Court had embraced the "racism as hate" model we continue to struggle under today, demanding proof of malice on the part of a culpable actor.[30] This bar is almost insurmountable. Absent a recorded use of a racial epithet or an in-court confession, malice is virtually impossible to prove. For instance, in a 1987 death penalty case the Court weighed a Georgia system that was 22 times more likely to impose capital punishment on an African American convicted of murdering a white versus a black victim.[31] The Court deemed this stark racial disparity irrelevant. It also dismissed as immaterial that this statistical pattern strongly correlated with social practices of white-over-black hierarchy stretching back to slavery. Refusing to even engage this evidence, the conservatives on the Court stubbornly maintained that the sole measure of racism was proof of malice, and then they upheld Georgia's death penalty machinery. Under the Court's approach to discrimination against nonwhites, only a bullheaded bigot who publicly vows to harm minorities should worry; no one else need fret. Since the Supreme Court adopted the malice test in 1979, it has never found discrimination against nonwhites under that approach, not even once.[32] As far as the Court is concerned, racism against nonwhites must involve proclaimed animus, and that has all but disappeared.

What, then, of supposed discrimination against whites? In 1977 the Court for the first time fully considered a challenge to race-conscious affirmative action when it weighed the legality of New York's decision to create a majority-nonwhite voting district. The Court applied its developing intentional harm rule. Then, saying it could discern "no racial slur or stigma with respect to whites or any other race," the Court easily upheld this corrective use of race.[33] The constitutional law seemed clear: all allegations of racial discrimination, whether against nonwhites or whites, would have to meet the same test of intentional harm. But this rule had an unfortunate consequence, at least from the conservative justices' point of view: it readily upheld affirmative action plans. After all, such efforts were designed to remedy racism rather than to oppress whites. If there were incidental harms, these were akin to the ancillary harms that accompany virtually every regulation—matters for legislators to weigh, but far from the sort of purposeful group oppression that the Court demanded nonwhites prove in order to show unconstitutional discrimination.

The next year in *University of California v. Bakke*, Justice Lewis Powell changed the rules. He concluded that in affirmative action cases, intentions did not matter. It was irrelevant, he said, whether a program was motivated by malice or benevolence. Paralleling the Southern use of colorblindness to oppose integration, Powell instead insisted that the constitutional harm occurred the moment that government took express notice of race.[34] After *Bakke*, the constitutional law around racial discrimination bifurcated. If the state expressly mentioned race—common almost exclusively in affirmative action programs—then the Court would review the legislation with extreme skepticism, in virtually every case overturning the challenged program. If, however, the government avoided any direct invocation of race—the new normal in discrimination cases—then the Court would demand proof of malice, an insuperable hurdle. A reactionary form of colorblindness became king: quick to condemn all corrective uses of race, but blind to racial discrimination against minorities.

■ COLORBLINDNESS, RACE, AND RACISM

The contemporary constitutional law on race is a disaster, and yet colorblindness likely does far more damage to the country politically than it does legally, for colorblind conceptions of race and racism bolster dog whistle politics. To fully grasp how so requires a sense of how colorblindness defines race and racism, and this in turn necessitates reviewing how these core concepts continue to evolve.

NATURE OR SOCIETY?

As Harlan's casual endorsement of white supremacy demonstrates, through the nineteenth century the belief in white superiority was pervasive, even among those opposed to dominant forms of racial oppression. During this era, "race" was understood to reflect nature and/or divine command, not human practices. Moreover—and this will be especially important to our discussion of reactionary colorblindness and dog whistle politics—from the outset, race was believed to involve both physical differences *and* distinctions in culture, behavior, and ability. Consider slurs common when Harlan wrote, like "lazy nigger," "dirty Mexican," or "sneaky Chink." These vile terms inseparably conjoined biology and behavior: physical distinctions supposedly corresponded to innate behavioral and cultural deficiencies. Indeed, as a way to justify inequality, race did its most destructive work by emphasizing temperament and ability, rather than mere differences in integument. More than skin pigment, it was nonwhite laziness, filthiness, and mendacity—and, correspondingly, white industry, hygiene, and honesty—that supposedly explained inferior and superior positions in society.

Related to the belief that races reflected divine intention or the natural order, the notion of "racism" was literally unknown at the time. At the core of that concept is a sense of moral censure: racism is unjust. But beliefs in innate racial inequality could not be perceived as morally evil until they were first seen as factually wrong. This was impossible to imagine for persons steeped in the belief that racial hierarchy was natural or divinely ordained. Thus Harlan could not see his own views about the permanent superiority of whites as racism. For him, racial inequality was simply an obvious fact of life.

As the nineteenth century closed, however, the settled ideas regarding race began to founder. In part, the developing break with supremacist beliefs reflected increasing problems with racial categories. In North America, groups like white, black, and red had long sufficed. They made sense in terms of a supposed division of humans according to the world's continents. More fundamentally, they fulfilled the social need for which they were created: to justify slavery and the usurpation of Native American lands. But the nineteenth century brought Americans into increasing contact with a world full of various peoples, and the inability to fit everyone into formerly self-evident categories began to draw the whole operation into question. Where did persons from the Indian subcontinent belong, or from the Middle East or Polynesia? Also, while it was evident that people looked different, did sharp boundaries actually exist? Obviously, reproductive isolation played a large role in shaping human features: population groups in close contact often developed shared appearances, while those further apart bore less resemblance. Didn't these shifts occur gradually, for instance as one moved across the Eurasian landmass, and not in the clean lines suggested by the sharp division between white and yellow? Such conundrums began to push anthropologists toward skepticism that the world's myriad people divided neatly into the few overarching racial groups that dominated the popular imagination.

Beyond the categorical problem, a more fundamental attack on race arose, one that challenged the assumed link between biology and character. At the close of the nineteenth century, social scientists like Franz Boas and W.E.B. Du Bois increasingly labored to repudiate the supposedly innate connection between physical differences and individual or group capacity. Attempting to separate the two, they argued that race amounted only to superficial physical differences. As to evident inequalities in group condition—the dominance of whites in every social sphere, and the degraded condition of most nonwhites—they argued that *social practices* led to such divergences. In other words, they reversed the causal story: rather than inherent differences producing unequal social positions, these insurgent race critics claimed that social custom created the observed differences between groups.

By the mid-twentieth century, these ideas came to define liberal understandings of race. Gunnar Myrdal's *An American Dilemma*, published in 1944 to widespread acclaim, marked this ascendance. Myrdal argued that race amounted to superficial physical differences such as "skin color," and had little or nothing to do with intelligence, morals, culture, or behavior. Instead, he laid inequalities between the races directly at the feet of social organization, and more specifically, the power of whites over blacks: "Practically all the economic, social, and political power is held by whites. . . . It is thus the white majority group that naturally determines the Negro's 'place.' All our attempts to reach scientific explanations of why the Negroes are what they are and why they live as they do have regularly led to determinants on the white side of the race line."[35] (One could hear the Kerner Commission drawing on this insight when it later wrote of the ghetto, "white institutions created it, white institutions maintain it, and white society condones it.")

Breaking the fictional connection between biology and group position created room for the widespread emergence of the idea that racial practices were unjust and immoral. In other words, ground began opening for the popular acceptance of a notion of "racism." Meanwhile, at mid-century strong impetus in this direction came from Europe and Asia, where the United States was confronting fascist nations that made racial supremacy central to their propaganda, and that also took racist logic to horrific extremes. In a way that whites had not previously appreciated when the violent subjugation of darker-skinned non-Europeans was involved, the utter dehumanization and mass extermination of Jews in Europe discredited ideas of racial supremacy. The suddenly obvious evil of brutalizing people because of pretended racial differences led to the introduction of a new word into the popular vocabulary of the United States: "racism." George Fredrickson, in his history of that phenomenon, concludes that "the word 'racism' first came into common usage in the 1930s when a new word was required to describe the theories on which the Nazis based their persecution of the Jews." Or more pithily: "Hitler gave racism a bad name."[36]

RACE AS BLOOD, RACISM AS "DIFFERENT TREATMENT"

Conservative colorblindness today draws upon, but also betrays, the liberal understandings of race and racism from the mid-twentieth century. It draws upon liberal race theory by conceptualizing race as only a superficial physical characteristic. But it betrays liberal thinking on race by rejecting the deep *social* connection between race and group differences. Boas, Du Bois, and Myrdal were not arguing that race was exclusively a matter of skin color and nothing more. They were rebutting the idea that the evident differences between groups— the wealth and power held by many whites, and the misery many nonwhites endured—reflected innate dispositions. Race *did* connect to group position and individual capacity, they argued, but as a result of social practices, not biology. Colorblindness today jettisons this key insight, that social dynamics give race tremendous salience in the lives of individuals and the trajectories of communities. Instead, it simplistically insists that race is only a matter of superficial differences, an idiosyncratic tic like blood type that has no bearing on the dimensions of individual lives or group situations.

Consider Justice Antonin Scalia's argument against affirmative action, made while still a law professor: "I owe no man anything, nor he me," Scalia protested, "because of the blood that flows in our veins."[37] "Blood" is a powerful metaphor with important liberal antecedents, for instance in the aphorisms that we all bleed the same, or that everyone's blood is the same color. Used in this way, references to blood emphasize our shared humanity. Scalia proceeds differently. He presents affirmative action as a racial debt ostensibly owed by whites, and objects that it's wrong to hold whites indebted merely because of biology. But no individual or group is held responsible on the basis of biology. Rather, social practices tied to race place racial groups in different relationships to affirmative action. If whites are not directly aided under affirmative action programs, it's because of their social position, not their hemoglobin. As used by Scalia, blood is not an endorsement of our shared humanity so much as a way to posit the complete independence of each individual from the social history around race. References to blood or skin color become techniques for neatly disjointing race from social context and instead portraying race as simply an accident of nature, a distinctive birthmark with no bearing on any particular individual's lived circumstances, nor any connection to hundreds of years of social dynamics. Race-as-blood denies context and history.

This is more than an analytic error; it is a political strategy that undergirds attacks on affirmative action. First, race-as-blood undercuts the liberal arguments for using race to promote integration. Affirmative action seeks to promote integration, which in turn is designed to combat negative stereotypes and to foster interracial solidarity. It also aspires to compensate groups that have long suffered exclusion from schools, neighborhoods, unions, and employment opportunities. Race-conscious remedies also respond to present structural discrimination and implicit bias, forcing the consideration of race in circumstances where racial disadvantage may be operating. Finally, affirmative action aims to break down structures of inequality that through inertia are otherwise likely to continue into the future. Each of these rationales, though, turns on the connection between race and social practices. Colorblindness denies this connection, discrediting justifications for race-conscious remedies by insisting that race has no relationship whatsoever to social patterns. Then, having shorn affirmative action of its basic rationales, conservatives ridicule it as no more than an effort to assemble a pleasing color palette. It is thus that Clarence Thomas mocks affirmative action as "racial aesthetics," jeering universities for seeking "a certain appearance, from the shape of the desks and tables in its classrooms to the color of the students sitting at them."[38] By reducing race to blood and thus defining it as strictly and superficially biological, racial reactionaries do not engage so much as sidestep the core arguments supporting affirmative action as a mechanism to correct destructive social hierarchies.

Next, race-as-blood redefines affirmative action as racism against whites. By divorcing race from social context, conservatives can describe racism as merely treating someone *differently* on the basis of race. Racism need not involve abuse or subordination, for the socially irrelevant character of blood suggests that *any* differential treatment is morally wrong. Colorblindness shifts the harm of racism from degradation, exclusion, and exploitation, to being treated differently on the basis of a socially irrelevant characteristic—no matter how benign the motive. Expressing this startling view, Thomas argues that "government-sponsored racial discrimination based on *benign* prejudice is just as noxious as discrimination inspired by *malicious* prejudice. In each instance, it is racial discrimination pure and simple."[39] Is affirmative action the same thing as Jim Crow segregation? Or the internment of Japanese Americans during World War II? Or Native American genocide? Of course not. Racism's harm lies in dehumanization and violence, not in mere differentiation, and certainly not in racial distinctions made in order to repair racism's painful legacies. The "different treatment" produced by affirmative action lies a chasm apart from the racial violence of segregation, internment, or genocide. Yet by defining race as a superficial characteristic and racism as any use of race, colorblindness misrepresents affirmative action as the moral equivalent of racial oppression.

For however nonsensical, the colorblind conflation of affirmative action and racism has tremendous rhetorical punch. Partly, the power of colorblindness stems from the resonance of the rhetoric itself. Because colorblindness has strong liberal roots, icons of racial justice can be found extolling colorblind ideals. Examples include not only Thurgood Marshall, but Martin Luther King, Jr. His exhortation that people be judged not "by the color of their skin but by the content of their character" is a favorite among conservatives. Obviously when heralding Marshall and King, today's colorblind partisans neglect to mention that these heroes argued strongly *for* race-conscious remedies. Likewise, conservatives fail to admit that the colorblindness of today does not descend directly from the sanctified civil rights era, but from the unrepentant South, which deployed colorblindness to fight integration tooth and nail. Despite these omissions, or rather because of them, colorblindness has strong appeal insofar as it *sounds* racially enlightened, not racially reactionary.

Beyond this, the popularity of colorblindness stems from casting whites as victims of racism, and from its practical implications in preserving the racial status quo. As Goldwater recognized, like states' rights, colorblindness is a dog whistle. It invokes a higher principle, yet also communicates sympathy for supposedly imperiled whites. The lofty goal behind colorblindness, we are continually reassured, is racial justice. But in practice, just as with states' rights, colorblindness translates into opposition to integration. There are some well-meaning liberals who continue to cling to colorblindness out of loyalty to a utopian vision of a raceless society. But for most fans of colorblindness, its attraction lies in that it sounds fair—even as it fosters the impression that discrimination against whites is rampant, and works assiduously to defeat policies actually geared to achieving integration.

■ ETHNICITY, CULTURE, AND BEHAVIOR

Depicting race as mere skin color helps present affirmative action as racism against whites, but it also leaves racial conservatives in several binds. First, how can they explain what we see all round us? Our society is obviously stratified by race. Look at our ghettoes and barrios—or the halls of Congress and the nation's boardrooms. Clearly something must explain white dominance, but what? Maybe continued inequalities reflect some lingering vestige of racism, which in turn implies a social and specifically governmental duty to respond. This produces the second bind: if racism does remain a problem, how can conservatives object to remedying it? More particularly, while they have an argument that affirmative action is itself racist, how can they attack traditional liberal solutions to inequality, such as welfare, job training, housing, education, and the like? What makes these efforts futile, or even unfair to whites? Finally and most importantly to dog whistle politics, how can conservatives talk about race—about why minorities pose a looming threat and how whites are imperiled—if race is just a matter of skin color? If race is solely a matter of pigment, there's no reason for whites to fear minorities. After all, aren't we all the same? Race-as-blood helps bolster some conservative arguments, but it also strongly undercuts others.

Colorblindness answers by opportunistically switching to another under-standing of race, frequently dropping race-as-blood to talk about racial groups as *ethnicities marked by distinct cultures*. To be clear, conservatives do not ex-pressly equate ethnicity and race; indeed, when pushed, they revert to the notion that race is only a matter of superficial biology, and so, deny that racial groups can be defined by distinct cultures. Yet that is only when challenged; otherwise, conservatives routinely employ ethnic terms as a coded way to talk about racial groups and their supposedly incompatible behaviors and beliefs.

Partly because conservatives deny that race is anything more than blood yet constantly use an ethnic vocabulary to discuss group cultures, the popu-lar imagination often confuses race and ethnicity. More focused attention to their relationship shows how, today, the notion of ethnic difference is central to modern racism. Ethnicity provides a basis for blaming minorities for their infe-rior positions, since it faults their supposedly defective cultures; simultaneously, it exonerates whites, since racism is no longer to blame for inequality. This in turn answers the question of government help: such assistance is futile because only nonwhites can reform their inferior cultures and self-defeating behaviors. Finally, the ethnic turn promotes a new culture talk that surreptitiously resur-rects old stereotypes, allowing conservatives to reinvigorate a pernicious aspect of racism: contentions about fundamental differences in behavior and culture between innocent whites and threatening nonwhites.

ETHNICITY

The concept of ethnicity originated in the early twentieth century, when it arose as a means of erasing racial differences among whites.[40] From its inception, even as "white" developed in contradistinction to black and red, persons of European descent in North America commonly divided themselves along racial lines, with strong beliefs about racial characteristics and racial failings. Slurs like Hun, Mick, Pollack, Wop, and Kike recall this phenomenon. During the 1920s, University of Chicago sociologist Robert Park began to challenge this narrative. He used the concept of cultural pluralism, rather than natural difference, to promote a conception of race that stressed the gradual assimilation of diverse groups.[41] Under his view, all immigrant groups followed a similar trajectory from exclu-sion, clannishness, and poverty, to eventual full inclusion, assimilation, and material success. Park's theories soon spread beyond the academy and helped shape popular conceptions of group integration into American society, buttressing the idea of America as a great melting pot. In turn, when World War II demonstrated the horrors of anti-Semitism, this encouraged the adoption in the United States of an ethnic vocabulary that sharply distinguished between race as biology and ethnicity as culture.[42] Most persons of European descent increasingly came to see themselves as a racially undifferentiated people—that is, as simply white—though also as members of groups defined by local folkways. The verities surrounding fundamental racial differences gave way to new truths that instead saw only trivial ethnic differences, with all of the various European sub-groups supposedly sharing a single racial identity as white, as well as similar histories of struggle and eventual success on America's shores.[43]

What had been "races" supposedly divided by deep natural differences now became "ethnicities" distinguished only by cultural diversity. This was an advance toward racial egalitarianism, for it erased racial hierarchy among persons of European descent. But it did not transcend race, for undergirding the notion of ethnic equality was the powerful assumption of a shared white racial identity. Ethnicity in the 1940s and 1950s did not cross the color line, but instead operated as a way to foster solidarity among whites.

Nevertheless, as the civil rights movement gathered force in the 1960s, an ethnic vocabulary and more generally a notion of groups defined by distinctive cultures was available as a way to reconceptualize racial dynamics. An extension of ethnicity across the color line might have been a felicitous development, for instance if society had come to see nonwhites in terms of cultural variety and a shared humanity. Instead, though, when ethnicity eventually was applied to nonwhites, it changed form and became another way of explaining unbridgeable difference. Where supremacist conceptions of race attributed minority failings to nature, ethnic conceptions would link virtually the same faults to their culture. Ethnicity ultimately replaced nature with culture, but otherwise left the stereotypes explaining minority inferiority largely untouched.

BLAMING MINORITIES

Nathan Glazer and Daniel Patrick Moynihan—the former destined to spend decades at a post at Harvard writing on race and public policy, the latter to become a Democratic Senator from New York famed for his expertise on welfare—helped instigate this ethnic retooling as applied to nonwhites. In 1963, Glazer and Moynihan published a history of New York City, *Beyond the Melting Pot: The Negroes, Puerto Ricans, Jews, Italians, and Irish of New York City*.[44] This volume effectively laid the groundwork for contemporary reactionary conceptions of race in the United States, including arguments that nothing should be done to alleviate racial inequality. As evident in the subtitle, Glazer and Moynihan pushed ethnicity across the color line: ethnicity would explain not only the New York histories and contemporary positions of Jews, Italians, and the Irish, but also blacks and Puerto Ricans.[45] Rather than extend to racial minorities the presumption that they possessed valuable cultures, however, Glazer and Moynihan used ethnicity to locate in their cultures the ultimate source of those groups' social failure.

Consider their explanation for why minority children (unlike earlier white immigrant students) failed to learn in New York's schools:

> There is little question where the major part of the answer must be found: in the home and family and community. . . . It is there that the heritage of two hundred years of slavery and a hundred years of discrimination is concentrated; and it is there that we find the serious obstacles to the ability to make use of a free educational system to advance into higher occupations and to eliminate the massive social problems that afflict colored Americans in the city.[46]

Glazer and Moynihan acknowledged the destructive legacy of past racism in distorting the cultures of nonwhite groups. This was an important concession, but one that only half followed the liberal insight from mid-century that tied the situation of nonwhites to past *and present* social practices. Politically, acknowledging the harmful effects of past discrimination was costless, for the most pressing questions centered on present causes of poverty and marginalization, and what that implied for social policy.

In their focus on the present, Glazer and Moynihan largely dropped structural impediments from their analysis. Rather, in "major part" they directed attention to "the home and family and community" for the immediate causes of the inferior educational, social, and material position of racial minorities. Glazer and Moynihan especially emphasized the destructive consequences that flowed from "broken homes," as when:

> the mother is forced to work (as the Negro mother so often is), when the father is incapable of contributing support (as the Negro father so often is), when fathers and mothers refuse to accept responsibility for and resent their children, as Negro parents, overwhelmed by difficulties, so often do, and when the family situation, instead of being clear-cut and with defined roles and responsibility, is left vague and ambiguous (as it so often is in Negro families).[47]

This quote from Glazer and Moynihan on the pathologies of the black family may trigger a sense of familiarity. These remarks anticipated by just a couple of years Moynihan's more widely known conclusions regarding blacks and welfare policy, conclusions that ultimately led him, as an official in the Nixon administration, to recommend a policy toward nonwhites of "benign neglect."

Two years after publishing *Beyond the Melting Pot*, Moynihan drew on ethnicity when he published a major paper that would become known as the *Moynihan Report*. Moynihan framed the report around the civil rights movement's increasing demands for equality. These demands, he warned, could not be met because of failings in the black community itself. Moynihan's deepest concern was the black family. It was the "Negro family," Moynihan asserted, that "is the fundamental source of the weakness of the Negro community at the present time." Dysfunction in the black family originated in racism and structural subordination, Moynihan acknowledged, but he argued that group dynamics within the black community perpetuated black misery without any external help from white racism. "At this point," Moynihan concluded, "the present tangle of pathology is capable of perpetuating itself without assistance from the white world."[48]

Moynihan's report shoved attention away from the structural components of racism into a bitter, poisonous fight over the health of black family life. The next year, Moynihan waded back into the melee with an article that made crystal clear his normative position: "a community that allows a large number of young men to grow up in broken families, dominated by women, never acquiring any stable relationship to male authority, never acquiring any set of rational expectations about the future—that community asks for and gets chaos. Crime, violence, unrest, disorder . . . that is not only to be expected, but they are very near to inevitable. And it is richly deserved."[49] Chaos in the black community, Moynihan opined, stemmed from its cultural failings. As to crime, violence, unrest, and disorder, the community got what it richly deserved. Race, and more particularly race as it intersected with gender roles, was once again the prime culprit explaining the failure of minorities.

It is important to emphasize how reactionary this position was. At least since Teddy Roosevelt, prominent progressives had been arguing that forces beyond individual control all too often trapped the poor and the marginalized, and that society had an obligation to remedy to the extent possible these limiting structures to ensure that everyone had a fair shot. This liberal ideal became the dominant political consensus after the brutal experience of the Depression, spurring the salving programs of the New Deal. Given racism's history, this sense of misfortune beyond personal control, in turn implying the need for government assistance, should have applied with particular force to nonwhite communities. But in Moynihan's analysis, it did not. For Moynihan to argue that blacks were the authors of their own failure would seem, in today's world, uncharitable and mean-spirited, something closer to what Newt Gingrich might say. In the mid-1960s, it was earthshaking, for it repudiated the liberal consensus upon which the modern state was predicated.

In this sense, the connection between Moynihan and Gingrich isn't merely a faint echoing. Rather, Moynihan's use of culture to blame blacks and to argue that government is powerless to remedy poverty was subsequently carefully cultivated by conservative thinkers, including Charles Murray, Dinesh D'Souza, and Myron Magnet.[50] They molded the story, downplaying the destructive effects of past racism, and adding the accusation that liberal programs themselves create cultural pathologies in nonwhite communities. The core point, though, endured: minority culture, not racism, explains nonwhite poverty and makes government assistance futile. This has now germinated into a broad political consensus, especially though not exclusively among Republicans.

Whites believed in structural remedies when they saw the poor as people like themselves, folks sometimes trapped by larger forces or bad breaks. They shifted to a belief in personal failings when they began to see the poor as nonwhites fundamentally unlike themselves. Today, conservatives like Gingrich seek to both stoke and exploit the conviction that the poor choose their fate. Pursuing the Republican nomination in 2012, Gingrich argued that laws limiting work by young children, a cornerstone of Teddy Roosevelt's 1910 Square Deal, should be repealed. He explained: "Really poor children in really poor neighborhoods have no habits of working and have nobody around them who works. So they literally have no habit of showing up on Monday. They have no habit of staying all day. They have no habit of 'I do this and you give me cash' unless it's illegal."[51]

The imagery here is Moynihan's, of black children raised in pathologically dysfunctional households that guarantee generation after generation of black poverty. As legal scholar Dorothy Roberts observes, "the powerful Western image of childhood innocence does not seem to benefit Black children. Black children are born guilty. They are potential menaces—criminals, crackheads, and welfare mothers waiting to happen."[52] Gingrich trades on this imagery, even as he purports to describe poor children in general. And his point is that government cannot help, not even when it seeks to protect young children from the hardship of work. Let them sell their labor in the market for whatever they can get, he advises, for individual effort, even by children, is the only way out of poverty. The discredited laissez-faire ideology of the early twentieth century has come storming back.

To be perfectly clear, the problem is *not* that Moynihan, Gingrich, and others dare to talk about culture. Daily conditions of life inevitably shape ways of living, lessons often imparted to the next generation. Thus, it was not that Moynihan completely erred in the basic claim that larger social practices damaged black family life (Gingrich's fact-challenged claims are another matter). Scholars focused on the black community such as E. Franklin Frazier and Kenneth Clark had already said as much decades before.[53] Prominent civil rights leaders such as Martin Luther King, Jr., also lamented the harm done to black families. Indeed, today critiques of personal failings intertwined with outrage over structural disadvantage continue to form staples of black political thought.[54] Again, the problem lay not in mentioning culture and behavior. Rather, the grievous error lay in installing cultural pathology as *the root cause* of continued nonwhite failure, often to the complete exclusion of structural factors.

Compare Moynihan's conclusion that social legislation could not succeed with the analysis urged by Martin Luther King, Jr. He, too, offered a despairing portrait of the "shattering blows on the Negro family [that] have made it fragile, deprived and often psychopathic," a description nearly as negative as Moynihan's. Yet King offered this prescription:

> The most optimistic element revealed in this review of the Negro family's experience is that the causes for its present crisis are culturally and socially induced. What man has torn down, he can rebuild. At the root of the difficulty in Negro life is pervasive and persistent want. To grow from within the Negro needs only fair opportunity for jobs, education, housing and access to culture. To be strengthened from the outside requires protection from the grim exploitation that has haunted [the community] for 300 years.[55]

King's solution, offered in the winter of 1965, was access to jobs, education, and housing, coupled with freedom from further exploitation. King's hope lay in addressing the structural components of white racism, not in placing a national spotlight on the damaged black family. Ethnicity has been shaped into a reactionary ideology not merely through a focus on group cultures, but because it uses arguments about defective cultures to utterly displace any attention to ongoing dynamics of racial subordination. Ultimately, in conservative hands, race presented as ethnicity faults minorities for their own situation, thereby undercutting arguments for liberal repair.

EXONERATING AND CELEBRATING WHITES

Furthering the sense that minorities could only blame themselves, ethnicity also erased "whites" as a dominant group. Ostensibly, there existed instead only a welter of ethnic minorities—Irish, Italians, Jews, Poles, and so on—many of which themselves had earlier suffered discrimination. Justice Powell used this argument to attack affirmative action, questioning whether there even existed a white race: "the white 'majority' itself is composed of various minority groups, most of which can lay claim to a history of prior discrimination at the hands of the State and private individuals. Not all of these groups can receive preferential treatment and corresponding judicial tolerance of distinctions drawn in terms of race and nationality, for then the only 'majority' left would be a new minority of white Anglo-Saxon Protestants."[56] Far from being dominant, Powell presented the white group as comprised of various vulnerable minorities, each of which labored under "a history of prior discrimination at the hands of the State and private individuals." Ethnicity even converted the most elite whites into racial victims, with WASPs becoming America's most vulnerable potential victim, as the only group ineligible to claim affirmative action. America's elite now turned out to be just another marginalized group. If whites did not exist, how could they be responsible for racial inequality?

Beyond disaggregating whites into vulnerable minorities, ethnicity also provided a means by which whites could celebrate their white identities and segregated neighborhoods. Where this had recently represented reviled manifestations of white supremacy, now it reflected laudable expressions of ethnic pride.[57] Like the blacks, Latinos, and Asians clamoring to be seen in a positive light, theoretically the Italians, Irish, and Poles were merely expressing group pride in their distinctive ethnic origins. Yet treacherous notions of white superiority were inextricably mixed in. Especially after their virtual disappearance in the 1950s, the revival of European ethnic identities in the 1970s connected intimately to white reactions to the civil rights era.[58] Nor were racially astute politicians slow to adopt the new vocabulary. Recall Jimmy Carter's racial pandering, when he spoke out forcefully against government efforts to promote neighborhood integration: "I have nothing against a community that's made up of people who are Polish or Czechoslovakian or French-Canadian, or who are blacks trying to maintain the ethnic purity of their neighborhoods," Carter said. "This is a natural inclination on the part of the people."[59] Disfavored expressions of white supremacy reemerged as worthy ethnic pride—not only as the moral equivalent of black efforts to rescue a stigmatized identity, but also as a legitimate basis for resisting integration.

DOG WHISTLING AROUND CULTURE AND BEHAVIOR

The turn to ethnicity in the late 1960s and early 1970s as a substitute language for race helped fuel dog whistle politics. Ethnicity told a story of groups either defeated or elevated by their own cultures. Dog whistle politicians embraced the ethnic fiction, amplifying themes of deviant nonwhite behavior and white innocence. The narratives promoted alike by the ethnic turn and racial demagogues—a lack of work ethic, a preference for welfare, a propensity toward crime, or their opposites—reinvigorated racial stereotypes, giving them renewed life in explaining why minorities lagged behind whites. These stereotypes might have faded as society addressed racism. Instead, they became the staples of political discourse, repeated ad nauseam by politicians, think tanks, and media.

Precisely because ethnicity encouraged talk of group differences in culture and behavior, it kept alive a potent aspect of racial ideology, narratives of fundamental differences in capacity that supposedly explained group hierarchy. Ethnicity avoided what seemed central about race, its claims about differences rooted in nature. But in practice, direct references to nature mattered surprisingly little. Even absent this, racial narratives had tremendous social and political potency simply by emphasizing the racist commonsense that groups were divided by differences in habits, temperament, and ability rooted in the groups themselves. Ethnicity helped keep racism vibrant by preserving its core—the stories whites told about their essential superiority, and the tales they repeated about fundamentally inferior nonwhites. Racial demagogues could drop direct references to biology and racial groups, and still stir racial passions. Ethnicity helped establish a commonsense framework in which discussions of dysfunctional culture and menacing behavior were readily understood as describing the essential identity of nonwhites.

Yet racial demagogues did more than resurrect old stereotypes; they altered them in ways that combined assaults on nonwhites with attacks on liberalism. Shaped by the coded language of *conservative* dog whistle politics, racial stereotypes increasingly connected ideas of minority inferiority with rightwing political narratives. This dynamic was so powerful that it ultimately contributed to a marked evolution in the forms taken by racial prejudice. Today, the most powerful racial stereotypes—the ones most generally credited and in widest circulation—dovetail precisely with dog whistle narratives jointly attacking minorities and liberalism.

Already in 1971, social psychologists studying racism began describing an evolution from "old-style" endorsements of white supremacy to new forms of prejudice that linked the failings of blacks to deficient cultures, especially to their refusal to adopt conservative precepts of rugged individualism.[60] Support for bans on interracial marriage and restrictions mandating whites-only neighborhoods slipped, but endorsements of more abstract statements like "Negroes who receive welfare could get along without it if they tried" and "the streets aren't safe these days without a policeman around" surged.[61] By the mid-1990s, a strong consensus existed among social science researchers that racial prejudice had changed. Scholars remarked that "a new form of prejudice has come to prominence, one that is preoccupied with matters of moral character, informed by the virtues associated with the traditions of individualism. At its center are the contentions that blacks do not try hard enough to overcome the difficulties they face and that they take what they have not earned."[62] Harvard sociologist Lawrence Bobo's term for this new prejudice, "laissez-faire racism," highlights the close connection between present forms of racial resentment and the resurgence of an anti-government ideology.[63]

In accord with the stories spun by dog whistle politicians, many whites have come to believe that they prosper because they possess the values, orientations, and work ethic needed by the self-making individual in a capitalist society. In contrast, they have come to suppose that nonwhites, lacking these attributes, slip to the bottom, handicapped by their inferior cultures and pushed down by the market's invisible hand, where they remain, beyond the responsibility, or even ability, of government to help. Today's most powerful stereotypes blame minority culture in a manner tied closely to conservative myths of rugged individualism.

We can see the strong connection between group stereotypes and dog whistle themes in a recent survey on racial prejudice undertaken by social psychologists. The survey found that during Obama's first four years in office, the percentage of Democrats expressing prejudiced views about blacks remained steady at just over 30 percent—still a discouragingly high proportion.[64] It also found that the number of Republicans expressing anti-black prejudice increased significantly over those years, going from 71 percent to 79 percent, which is to say, to roughly four out of five. Beyond these high numbers, though, focus on the precise questions in the survey. To measure prejudice, the study asked respondents whether they agreed or disagreed with statements like:

- Over the past few years, Blacks have gotten more economically than they deserve.
- It's really a matter of some people just not trying hard enough; if Blacks would only try harder, they could be just as well off as whites.
- Irish, Italians, Jewish, and other minorities overcame prejudice and worked their way up. Blacks should do the same without special favors.[65]

While these statements reference race directly, they also track major themes in dog whistle politics: the notion that blacks receive more than they deserve; the stereotype of laziness; the use of an ethnic conception of race to blame blacks for their own failings.

Bucking the trend of seeing these sentiments as reflecting a modern form of prejudice, a few scholars have objected that instead survey questions such as these—which have been in use since the 1970s—measure a confounded mixture of racial sentiment and policy attitudes. These critics insist that because prejudice and policy are interwoven, it's impossible to know to what extent prejudice alone continues.[66] But this misses the point: the confluence of racial prejudice and conservative politics *is* the new racism. It's a product of almost a half-century of ethnic discourse and coded race-baiting that has remade racism into a set of ideas jointly demonizing nonwhite culture and activist government. These ethnic-racial-political stereotypes have become staples of modern racial discourse, and now seem like self-evident truths to a staggering four out of five Republicans. It is now virtually commonsense, at least among the GOP faithful, that minorities fail, and they succeed, as rugged individuals.

■ WHITES AS VICTIMS

In a 2011 poll, more than half of whites thought that discrimination against their race was "as big a problem" as the mistreatment of nonwhites. Among Republicans and Tea Party members, nearly two out of three sympathized with this view of whites as racial victims. Among those who "most trust Fox news," the number stepped even higher.[67] Colorblindness lies at the heart of the contemporary belief held by many whites that they are the true racial victims in US society today. Let's reprise what colorblindness tells them:

- *Race* is just a matter of blood, and has no connection to past or present social practices.
- *Racism* means being treated differently on the basis of race. Since affirmative action treats whites differently because of race, it constitutes racism. Thurgood Marshall and Martin Luther King, Jr., agree. On the other hand, there is little racism against minorities today: witness the absence of proven malice.
- *Ethnicity* shows that whites do not exist as a dominant group, but only as ethnic minorities with just as much right as other minorities to protect their own group interests.

- *Group cultures* differ, and it's not racist to acknowledge that white ethnics have succeeded, and nonwhite groups have failed, on the basis of differences in group capacity and behavior. Moreover, since groups are the masters of their own fate, it is futile (in addition to being racist) for government to give some groups special handouts.

When laid out this way, it's no surprise that Reagan and other political leaders since have embraced colorblindness. It sounds liberal yet works like a racial cudgel, denying that there's discrimination against minorities, elevating whites as racial victims, justifying white superiority, and facilitating dog whistle racial appeals that emphasize culture and comportment.

And one more thing: colorblindness also protects dog whistle race-baiting against charges of racism. Even though conservatives repeatedly use an ethnic vocabulary, they always hold in reserve the colorblind insistence that race is just a matter of blood. This provides a stock defense of dog whistling, for it allows politicians to demagogue culture and behavior, while insisting that they cannot possibly be engaged in racial pandering because they have not directly referenced biology. In the next race chapter, Chapter Six, we will examine at length how colorblindness facilitated the rise of new ways of communicating and defending racism. Before then, however, we turn to consider important evolutions in dog whistle politics since the 1990s.

5

Shifting the Tune: Clinton and W.

The early story of dog whistle politics focuses on Republicans and African Americans. After briefly considering George H.W. Bush, this chapter uses Bill Clinton to show that Democrats have also adopted coded racial appeals. It then moves to the presidency of George W. Bush to explore important evolutions regarding which groups serve as racial targets. After 2001, racial demagogues increasingly emphasized supposed threats from Arab Muslims as terrorists and Latinos as illegal aliens.

Through the spring and summer of the 1988 presidential campaign, George H.W. Bush, Reagan's vice president, was behind in the polls. Bush lacked Reagan's easy charisma, but bore the burdens of that administration's failures, including the collapse of the savings and loan sector and a shaky economy. Also contributing to his lackluster support, Bush initially rejected Wallace-Nixon-Reagan-style race-baiting. Long allied with the more socially moderate Northeast strand of the Republican Party, that sort of despicable racial opportunism offended the values of old-line Republicans like Bush. Nevertheless, as Bush found himself lagging in the polls, at one point trailing by 17 percent, Gerald Ford's shadow grew stronger, reminding Bush of another moderate Republican who had rejected the dog whistle and suffered at the ballot box. Meanwhile, his campaign manager, Reagan henchman Lee Atwater, was intimately familiar with racial demagoguery. With Atwater's reassurances that he had plotted a racial route to victory, Bush ultimately turned to race to save his flagging candidacy.

The Bush campaign injected race into the contest through the persona of Willie Horton.[1] A convicted murderer who escaped while released on weekend furlough, Horton subsequently invaded a home in which he stabbed and bound a man and raped his fiancée. The Democratic presidential candidate, Michael

Dukakis, bore tangential responsibility for Horton's escape, for as a governor he had vetoed a measure that would have made convicted murderers ineligible for furloughs. But more pertinently from Atwater's point of view, Horton was black and his victims were white. The image of a black man breaking into a home and raping a white woman conjured the hoariest of racist narratives: the vile and violent black rapist victimizing white purity. The Horton case thus played directly into the dog whistle depiction of blacks as depraved criminals and law-abiding whites as their innocent victims. At a meeting with Republican operatives in mid-summer, Atwater chortled at the prospect of the coming media frenzy: "They were going to 'strip the bark off the little bastard [Dukakis],' he promised. 'For all I know,' he added sarcastically, 'Willie Horton . . . may end up to be Dukakis' running mate.' "[2] Another Bush aide said at the time, "Willie Horton has star quality. Willie's going to be politically furloughed to terrorize again. It's a wonderful mix of liberalism and a big black rapist."[3]

Atwater choreographed an elaborate roll-out of the Horton assault against Dukakis. He began by surreptitiously directing journalists to the issue, in the hope of creating seemingly independent interest in the case, and also solicited campaign ads by nominally separate political action groups. The effort was sensitive because it traded on explosive racial insinuations and risked coming across as a scurrilous racial attack. In true dog whistle style, the most effective Willie Horton ad never mentioned race at all. Instead, it showed a grainy mug shot of Horton, clearly black, staring blankly into the camera. Over this image, a disembodied voice declared, "Dukakis not only opposed the death penalty, he allowed first-degree murderers to have weekend passes from prison. One was Willie Horton, who murdered a boy in a robbery, stabbing him 19 times." The image then shifted to show Horton under arrest by a white police officer. "Despite a life sentence, Horton received 10 weekend passes from prison. Horton fled, kidnapped a young couple, stabbing the man and repeatedly raping his girlfriend." As each horrendous element of the crime was narrated, one by one the indictments flashed under Horton's photo: "Kidnapping." "Stabbing." "Raping." Finally, the voice intoned: "Weekend prison passes: Dukakis on Crime." The production values were deliberately terrible, making the ad "the political equivalent of a supermarket tabloid, emphasizing the personal and the sensational."[4]

The commercial hit its mark with deadly accuracy. From lagging his opponent, Bush gained ground and took the lead. Over the month when the Horton furor reached its crescendo, 12 percent of the electorate switched its allegiance from Dukakis to Bush. "No campaign ever turns on one issue," a historian observed, before adding, "but no one—*no one*—who followed the [1988]

Stills from the Willie Horton campaign commercial, including his mug shot and a photo of his arrest captioned with his crimes, but with no express mention of race. "Weekend Passes," 1988

campaign believes George Bush had any more devastating ally than the homicidal black rapist Willie Horton."[5]

■ BILL CLINTON

Despite pulling off a win in 1988, Bush lost his re-election campaign in 1992. Many factors contributed to Bush's 1992 collapse. Conservatives were dismayed that Bush had reneged on campaign promises by cooperating with Democrats to raise taxes. Divisive cultural politics, off-putting to moderates, also erupted at the 1992 Republican National Convention, including a galvanizing moment when conservative stalwart Pat Buchanan declared: "There is a religious war going on in our country for the soul of America. It is a cultural war, as critical to the kind of nation we will one day be as was the Cold War itself." Bush was also seriously undercut by the third-party candidacy of billionaire conservative Ross Perot. But beyond these factors, it is also true that Bush faced a formidable opponent in Bill Clinton. Where does Bill Clinton fit in the narrative arc of dog whistle politics?

Taking a page from Jimmy Carter, Clinton emphasized his Southern heritage, as well as the Tennessee origins of his running mate, Al Gore, in his bid for the presidency. Clinton also drew inspiration from Lyndon Johnson, who hailed from Texas, one of the original states of the Southern confederacy. In 1964, Johnson had campaigned throughout the South as an economic populist, cautioning voters not to be distracted by race-baiting. In a New Orleans campaign speech, Johnson had warned, "All they ever hear at election time is 'Negro, Negro, Negro!' The kind of speech they should have been hearing is about the economy and what a great future we could have in the South if we just meet our economic problems."[6] Like Johnson, Clinton urged white voters to focus on class rather than race. When he announced he was seeking the presidential nomination, Clinton echoed and amplified Johnson's warning, identifying race-baiting as a national dynamic:

> For twelve years, Republicans have tried to divide us—race against race—so we get mad at each other and not at them. They want us to look at each other across a racial divide so we don't turn and look to the White House and ask, Why are all of our incomes going down? Why are all of us losing jobs? Why are we losing our future?[7]

Clinton thus hoped to refocus the attention of racially resentful whites onto the economy.

But undoubtedly aware that Johnson's populist message had failed in the South, and convinced of the national reach of race-baiting, Clinton did not depend on an economic message alone; rather, he decided to engage in his own racial pandering. Clinton thus campaigned as a "New Democrat": one resistant to black concerns, tough on crime, and hostile to welfare.[8] The New Democrats heeded the decades-old advice of Democratic pollsters Scammon and Wattenberg, who in 1970 had urged the party to jettison its "pro-black stance." Clinton also seemed to be listening to Thomas and Mary Edsall, whose book *Chain Reaction* came out in 1991. As the authors of the most comprehensive critique of the Southern strategy to date, the Edsalls regarded further racial backlash as virtually inevitable unless the Democrats distanced themselves from African Americans and recalibrated their politics to endorse limiting welfare and ratcheting up the war on crime.[9]

During the 1992 campaign, Clinton engaged in several bits of political theater to demonstrate that he was not beholden to African American interests. In one especially tragic act, Clinton maneuvered to insulate himself against a Willie Horton-style attack, though at the cost of a human life. Mid-campaign, Clinton flew back to Arkansas to oversee the execution of a mentally impaired black individual, Ricky Ray Rector. Rector had killed a man in a fight that broke out at a dance. Despondent at the prospect of arrest, Rector shot and killed the police officer who came to his home, and then attempted suicide by shooting himself in the head. He survived, but with profound brain damage. The surgeon who performed Rector's life-saving surgery reported that the operation had been "a classic prefrontal lobotomy" that had left Rector "totally incompetent" to assist any attorney who took his case.

Rector's execution raised the troubling question of whether it was moral to execute someone incapable of understanding what was happening to him or why it was happening. According to the prison's death-watch log, Rector spent his final days as he had for most of his ten years in prison, "howling and barking like a dog" in his T-shirt, boxer shorts, and socks. And, as he always did, Rector put aside the dessert from his final meal to finish later—presumably to be enjoyed after his execution.[10] Clinton refused to grant a last-minute pardon, ensuring that Rector would be executed. After Rector was dead, Clinton reputedly concluded, "I can be nicked a lot, but no one can say I'm soft on crime."[11]

Another bit of theater involved insulting Jesse Jackson. Republicans had long recruited new voters by linking various Democratic candidates to Jackson, a preacher and civil rights leader turned Democratic Party activist who emerged as a favorite target of racial caricatures. Clinton accepted an invitation to speak at a convening hosted by Jackson, and then to the dismay of the assembled audience used the occasion to upbraid a young rap artist, Sister Souljah, for heated comments about the recent riots in Los Angeles as well as racially offensive lyrics.[12] The intended audience was not in the room, but rather were the white voters whom Clinton hoped would see him "standing up" to blacks by pushing away rather than embracing the Reverend and his supporters. Jackson himself recognized he had been played. Referring to himself in the third person, he explained that Clinton "was actually talking to the TV audience. He was not talking to the people who were there. He was using the people who were there as a platform to spread his message . . . purely to appeal to conservative whites by containing Jackson and isolating Jackson."[13] Indeed, Clinton spent the summer sparring with Jackson, stoking the issue and playing up the schism. Clinton knew his audience. "What Clinton got out of the Sista Souljah affair were votes, particularly the votes of the so-called Reagan Democrats like the North Philadelphia electrician who said 'the day he told off that fucking Jackson is the day he got [mine].' "[14]

Clinton's pandering to dog whistle sensibilities extended well beyond the campaign trail. In fact, he made them a centerpiece of his administration's accomplishments. As president he endorsed a federal Three Strikes law dramatically expanding the nation's incarcerated population; he funneled a further $30 billion into Reagan's "war on crime"; and he vastly increased the number of federal offenses subject to capital punishment. As Michelle Alexander reports in *The New Jim Crow*, "the Clinton administration's 'tough on crime' policies resulted in the largest increases in federal and state prison inmates of any president in American history."[15] Playing to the other core theme of dog whistle racism, Clinton also oversaw a massive restructuring of welfare that dramatically reduced the numbers receiving benefits—some, because they transitioned to jobs, but many others because of new limits. Among the changes, Clinton ended Aid to Families with Dependent Children, a welfare program for impoverished children that had been a staple of the New Deal approach since 1936, but which the right had trashed in racist terms for encouraging poor black women to have children out of wedlock.[16] Clinton replaced this program with block grants to states, traditionally the price Southern Democrats had exacted in other areas of welfare to make sure little aid went to African Americans. There's no doubt that Clinton was under pressure from conservatives in Congress to gut welfare. Yet there's also no question that Clinton, in the face of such pressure, publicly postured as someone who would, as he promised in his first State of the Union address, "end welfare as we know it."[17] Here again we see dog whistle politics as a strategy—perhaps eagerly embraced, perhaps reluctantly adopted, but a strategy nonetheless.[18]

After 12 years of Reagan and Bush, the election of a Democrat did not mark the end of dog whistle politics so much as its bipartisan normalization. Bill Clinton won the presidency partly because he too was willing to campaign—and govern—in dog whistle terms. Today, dog whistle racism provides the terrain on which almost all politicians, Republican and Democratic alike, compete for white allegiance. Notice how, in the 2012 contest between Obama and Romney, both sides invoked Clinton's accomplishments and methods.

Mitt Romney took a page from Clinton when he needled a black audience to build credibility with a white one. When Romney addressed the NAACP national convention in the summer of 2012, he made a point of saying he would cut "Obamacare," using a politically charged label for the Affordable Health Care Act that was virtually guaranteed to draw a sharp response from the largely black audience. Indeed, the audience immediately reacted with boos, and this rebuke in turn became the media's focus in covering the event. "I think it was a calculated move on his part to get booed at the NAACP convention," House Democratic Leader Nancy Pelosi remarked.[19] "The speech sounded like it was designed not for the audience in the room, but for those in Republican living rooms," Charles Blow opined.[20] Hinting that he knew full well what he was doing, Romney later admitted in an interview with Fox News that he had anticipated being booed. "I think we expected that, of course," he explained. "Romney's press staff was bragging about getting booed," complained one Democratic analyst, who further noted that Romney's press secretary widely disseminated multiple news stories about the incident.[21] It's an ironic form of flattery when Republicans imitate the racial pandering techniques of Democrats, and all the more so when the Democratic model is not from the 1960s but the 1990s.

Meanwhile, Obama also occasionally seems to stage his own Sister Souljah moments, lecturing black audiences on "taking responsibility" in a way seemingly calculated to appeal to white audiences primed to view blacks as irresponsible.[22] More directly, though, Obama drew on Clinton himself. At the 2012 Democratic National Convention, the Obama campaign shunted Joe Biden aside, giving the time typically allotted to the vice president to Clinton. Perhaps they did so simply because of Clinton's popularity; but precisely whom Clinton was most popular with could not have escaped the administration's attention. As the *New York Times* noted, "Mr. Clinton may be most valuable because of his credibility with a voting constituency that Mr. Obama has struggled with, working-class whites. 'There is no Democrat who is more trusted than President Clinton by white working-class voters for having their interests at heart and being on their side.'"[23] Left unremarked was how Clinton achieved his special rapport with "white working-class voters."

Clinton's connection with working-class whites was something his wife also sought to capitalize on in her own political campaign. In her 2008 match-up against Obama for the Democratic nomination, Hillary Clinton claimed that her white working-class support made her a stronger presidential contender. In that contest's waning days, Clinton used race to make a last ditch argument that she was more electable than Obama: "I have a much broader base to build a winning coalition on," she explained in an interview, citing a recent poll that she said "found how Sen. Obama's support among working, hard-working Americans, white Americans, is weakening again, and how whites in both [Indiana and North Carolina] who had not completed college were supporting me."[24] Clinton's equation of "hard-working Americans" with "white Americans" struck many as a form of intentional dog whistling.[25] Perhaps it was, though maybe this linkage was merely an unconscious slip, even if one that revealed the cultural power of the stereotypes contrasting supposedly hardworking whites and lazy blacks. What was no mistake was Clinton's insistence that race gave her an edge. Pushed to clarify her remarks, Clinton insisted that "these are the people you have to win if you're a Democrat in sufficient numbers to actually win the election. Everybody knows that."[26] If indeed Hillary Clinton is the Democratic nominee for president in 2016, we should expect her to be quite clear-eyed about the importance of whiteness to her electability, and we should not be too surprised if, like her husband before her, dog whistle politics forms part of her strategy.

THE FIRST BLACK PRESIDENT

The image of Bill Clinton as a purposeful dog whistler lies in tension with the popular conception of him as the country's "first black president." When Toni Morrison coined that description in 1998, she did not mean that Clinton's concern for the black community made him an honorary African American; rather, she argued that many aspects of Clinton's biography connected to stereo-types of blackness. "White skin notwithstanding," Morrison wrote, "Clinton displays almost every trope of blackness: single-parent household, born poor, working-class, saxophone-playing, McDonald's-and-junk-food-loving boy from Arkansas."[27] Nevertheless, her evocative label escaped the bounds of the meaning she first gave it, and now is commonly used to cast Clinton as a special friend of blacks, someone deeply comfortable around them and centrally concerned with their well-being. Indeed, when Barack Obama first entered the presidential cam-paign in 2007 against Hillary Clinton—and by extension against her husband—some prominent African American politicians, such as civil rights icon John Lewis, had more confidence in the Clintons' loyalty to the black community than in Obama's.[28]

Clinton's popularity within the black community points toward important differences in his version of dog whistle racism. Ever since Southern strategy architect Kevin Phillips made clear that the GOP could win without black support, Republicans have largely engaged in racial demagoguery smugly in-different to alienating African Americans. The only limit on their disdain for blacks has been the fear of offending whites who pride themselves on being racially fair.[29] Otherwise, Republicans typically disregard blacks except as a dis-posable foil for racial posturing.

For Clinton, and for Democrats in general, the black vote was not so much disdained as taken for granted.[30] The black community could be pushed away and even slapped down a bit, the Democrats calculated, without seriously jeop-ardizing African American electoral support. After all, the reasoning went, where could they go? Yet there was a risk: they might stay home rather than go to the polls. Thus the Democrats tended to strike a balance. For white au-diences, Clinton would moderately disparage blacks, yet would avoid the ex-treme tones sounded in the Willie Horton campaign or in references to "welfare queens." For black audiences, he would adopt a different tactic, employing a distinct sort of dog whistle: coded appeals to the black community designed to fly under most whites' radar. The object here was to reassure African Americans that the Democratic Party valued them, but without letting Reagan Demo-crats hear. One instance of this was Clinton's saxophone performance on the Arsenio Hall show, a late-night TV show with a black host. Falling far short of championing the black community, this was nevertheless sufficient to garner Clinton widespread support among African Americans. As race scholar Randall Kennedy points out, "socialized to expect hostility or indifference, many blacks are unduly impressed when politicians show them even minimal respect, let alone affection. For merely treating blacks as peers (even as he simultaneously endorsed laws that crippled black communities), Bill Clinton was fondly adopted by some African Americans as an honorary 'brother.' "[31]

WAS CLINTON A RACIST?

Bill Clinton is a hero to many liberals, so it's worth pausing to ask whether "the first black president" was a racist. If the term means only someone motivated by racial hatred, the answer is clearly no. There's every reason to believe that Clinton despised white supremacist-style racism and regarded blacks as worthy of the esteem and empathy of equals. There are stirring stories, for instance, of a young Clinton's efforts to help blacks in Washington, DC, displaced by the rioting in the wake of Martin Luther King, Jr.'s assassination, and of his friendships with African American peers while a law student at Yale.[32] Nor should we ignore the close relationship Clinton maintained with Vernon Jordan, an African American confidant sometimes referred to as the president's "First Friend."[33] Contrast this, for example, with the racism exhibited by Richard Nixon, whose secret White House tape recordings are littered with racist statements, such as when he told his personal secretary that African Americans would become productive citizens in perhaps 500 years and then only after they were "inbred."[34]

The starkly divergent racial views held by Clinton and Nixon reinforces an important point: the "racism" in dog whistle racism does not refer to individual bias, it refers to a willingness to manipulate racial animus in pursuit of power. When a dispute erupted about Ronald Reagan's racial pandering, his defenders cried foul, insisting he was no bigot. Economist and political commentator Paul Krugman offered this succinct rejoinder: "So what? We're talking about his political strategy. His personal beliefs are irrelevant."[35] Just so with Clinton: he understood the political advantage in race-baiting and chose to use it. It may have violated Clinton's values; indeed, he was likely deeply troubled by the perceived need to racially pander. Whatever the case, though, Clinton bit down on that whistle and blew. At root, the "racism" in dog whistle racism is the "strategy" in the Southern strategy; the racism lies in provoking racial animosities in order to gain votes and power. Under this definition, Bill Clinton was as deft a dog whistle racist as Wallace, Nixon, or Reagan before him.

DEMOCRATS AND PLUTOCRATS

Just as Clinton's race-baiting differed from his predecessors', so too did his economic policies. For instance, Clinton reversed the most egregious giveaways to the very rich, raising taxes on the top 1 percent of taxpayers and increasing the top marginal rate by almost a third, from 31 percent to 40 percent. As with

Wallace, for Clinton dog whistle politics was a route to electoral success, not a Trojan horse for the policy preferences of plutocrats. Partly through his willingness to raise some taxes on the very wealthy, Clinton managed to balance the federal budget during his years in office, and also helped steward the longest period of sustained peacetime economic growth in the history of the country.[36] But to be perfectly clear, Clinton was far from an economic populist. Instead, and importantly, his presidency marked a critical shift in Democratic priorities away from a concern with workers and toward a politics more indebted to Wall Street. As a New Democrat, Clinton distanced himself not only from nonwhites but also from another traditional Democratic constituency, organized labor. At the same time, the Democrats increasingly sought to appeal to big business, favoring policies like financial deregulation and economic globalization from which the largest financial titans and corporations profited most. Remarks Kim Phillips-Fein, a historian who chronicles the long-term assault on the New Deal, "as President, Bill Clinton accomplished much of what Reagan could not: the dismantling of welfare, the deregulation of Wall Street, the expansion of free trade."[37] These were not separate achievements, but part of a collective policy shift away from New Deal liberalism.

Race-baiting provided the sugar coating that convinced whites to elect conservative Republicans, and when the Democrats set out to compete on the same basis, they inevitably adopted not only some of the GOP's racial politics but parts of its economic agenda as well. The more they embraced dog whistle themes of threatening minorities spoiled by activist government, the more they committed to hostility toward liberalism. A bit of damning praise indicates this rightward shift: in 1995 Barry Goldwater wrote to the Republican Speaker of the House, Newt Gingrich, to say of Clinton, "he's a Democrat, but I do admire him, I think he's doing a good job."[38] Clinton was not Reagan or Bush, but he nevertheless presided over a sharp rightward lurch in Democratic priorities, one from which the party has yet to recover. (Barack Obama too espouses policies that more closely resemble those once associated with Republicans rather than Democrats. After his re-election, Obama acknowledged this relative conservatism: "The truth of the matter is that my policies are so mainstream that if I had set the same policies that I had back in the 1980s, I would be considered a moderate Republican."[39]) Dog whistle politics has pulled the whole political establishment away from liberalism; yes, Republicans more than Democrats, but both parties nonetheless have turned away from protecting the middle class.

■ BEYOND BLACK AND WHITE

Originating in the 1960s, dog whistle politics featured racial demagoguery targeting various minorities, but particularly emphasized fears regarding African Americans. As the United States became more multi-racial, however, and as the Democrats demonstrated they too could win the presidency through dog whistle appeals, some doubts developed among Republicans about the wisdom of continuing to make race central to their identity. Then came the horrific attacks of September 11, 2001, and as in so many other areas, the country changed direction. For its part, dog whistle racism surged anew, though with much of its hysterical focus shifting from African Americans to brown immigrants, both Muslim and Mexican.

George W. Bush

When George W. Bush ran for president in 2000, his background as the governor of Texas gave him experience with a tripartite racial system involving whites and also large black and Mexican American populations. Looking toward national office from Austin, Texas, in the late 1990s, the advantages of using dog whistle racism seemed to be waning. The Democrats had proven under Bill Clinton that they could blow that whistle too, and also, the demographic math was changing. A leading GOP strategist calculated in 1964 that Republicans could thrive as the white man's party because "this isn't South Africa. The white man outnumbers the Negro 9 to 1 in this country." But the overwhelming numerical superiority that existed in 1964 had substantially faded by 2000. Bush's main campaign strategist, Karl Rove, was leery of continuing with aggressive racial demagoguery. For Rove, the route to electoral success lay through a recalibrated message of "compassionate conservatism" that aimed to bring in political moderates as well as a modicum of support from nonwhites, especially Hispanics.[40]

The 2000 election was razor close, ultimately ending up in the Supreme Court where the conservative justices maneuvered to give Bush the victory.[41] The very closeness of the election suggested, however, that no votes could be spared, and when the returns were tabulated, it was clear that Bush's strategy of toning down the racism and reaching out to nonwhites had helped. Indeed, he won 21 percent of the nonwhite vote. During the early months of his presidency, Bush seemed to internalize the lesson that minority votes mattered. For instance, in the summer of 2001, just months into office, Bush lent the prestige of the presidency to the developing campaign against racial profiling by the police. Coming out firmly against profiling, Bush gave a national press conference in which he vowed, "We will end it in America."[42] Far from demonizing nonwhites, Bush seemed to be constructing a public stance validating the claim that rampant discrimination remained a national problem.

Bush's initial election and the early months of his presidency are instructive for those wondering when and how dog whistle racism might fade from presidential politics. The Bush campaign seems to suggest that, if nothing else, demography will supply an eventual cure. Yet there is reason to be skeptical. First, Bush may have come out against profiling, but he also returned to billionaire politics, which continued to need racial cover. For instance, with help from the Heritage Foundation, Bush pushed through one of the biggest tax cuts for the wealthy ever enacted. In 2001, Heritage helped sell Bush's tax cuts with the bold prediction that they would lead to economic growth sufficient to pay off the national debt by 2010.[43] In 2007, with the budget deficit ballooning to historic highs, Heritage reversed course and looked to dog whistle appeals to cover up how wrong they and the Bush administration had been. Now they claimed that it was "entitlement spending" that was dwarfing the "projected large revenue increases" that the tax cuts had supposedly generated.[44] According to the rightwing narrative coming out of Heritage, the deficit was not the result of a massive transfer of wealth to the rich but of government social aid programs. Hesitancy regarding dog whistle politics may have increased, but oligarchy-friendly policies continued to need the cover provided by racial narratives about out of control liberal programs.

In addition, Bush's success among nonwhites should be parsed more carefully. While Bush enjoyed the support of one in five minorities, that support came overwhelmingly from Latinos. Bush won 35 percent of the Hispanic vote in 2000 and a remarkable 45 percent in 2004.[45] GOP strategists chalked this support up to a conservative strand within segments of the Hispanic population, and this indeed may have contributed. We will return to GOP efforts to lure Latino votes in the final chapter. For now, suffice it to say that there is nevertheless good reason to worry that outreach to certain segments within the Latino community may not herald the end so much as the recalibration of racial appeals.

Shifting attention from Latinos to African Americans also suggests dog whistle politics will continue. Bush gained the support of only 9 percent and then 11 percent of black voters in 2000 and 2004, respectively. Even as he endeavored to reach out to Latinos, Bush did little to seek support in the black community. On the contrary, the administration aggressively resurrected Reagan's war on affirmative action, and packed the Department of Justice with GOP partisans anxious to slow down civil rights enforcement.[46] Anticipating

Bush's campaign, in the late 1990s the conservative political activist Ralph Reed predicted that "you're going to see a new Republican party that is still primarily white and that is fiscally and morally conservative, but that also is attempting to project an image of racial tolerance and moderation."[47] It's tempting to read his remarks literally: the planned GOP makeover was to be one of "image" and not substance. In any event, if the GOP experimented with easing dog whistle politics in the run-up to 2000 and just beyond, it did so only tepidly.

THE ARAB MUSLIM THREAT

The politics around race changed decisively after 9/11. Anti-immigrant sentiment had been at a slow boil in the United States since the mid-1980s, mainly focused on the increasing numbers of nonwhite immigrants from Latin America and Asia. Regarding Muslims, the 1970s oil crisis, the occupation of the American embassy in Iran, and a smattering of attacks in the 1990s had created the figment of a threatening Middle Eastern figure, but this shadow flickered ominously only at the periphery of America's racial imagination—until 9/11. The shock, rage, and desire for revenge that followed the surreal, slow-motion collapse of the World Trade Center towers stoked that simmer into a seething fury.

Predictably, some members of the public reacted with racial rage, and in the first few days after the attacks the president spoke out against hate crimes. Over the course of his administration, Bush also sought to temper anti-Arab prejudice that might alienate Middle Eastern war allies.

Nevertheless, in important respects the Bush administration built its response to 9/11 around racial appeals. Almost immediately, to demonstrate its resolve to "do something" about the attacks, US Attorney General John Ashcroft initiated a highly public dragnet, launching much publicized detentions and "investigatory interviews" of young men from Middle Eastern or Islamic countries who had entered the country in the previous two years. The opposite of Bush's pledge to end racial profiling, this was profiling as public spectacle, a publicity campaign built around profiling geared to salve the nation's thirst for action against a newly reviled group.[48]

One of the young men detained was Javaid Iqbal, a Pakistani citizen who was in the United States without authorization, working as a cable television installer on Long Island when he was picked up in the immediate wake of 9/11.[49] Iqbal alleges that while in detention in Brooklyn, "jailors 'kicked him in the stomach, punched him in the face, and dragged him across' his cell without justification; subjected him to serial strip and body-cavity searches when he posed no safety risk to himself or others; and refused to let him and other Muslims pray because there would be 'no prayers for terrorists.'"⁵⁰ Iqbal later sued Ashcroft over the abuse as well as the decision to conduct a dragnet against "Arab Muslim men." In a five-four decision, the conservative Supreme Court justices rejected Iqbal's claim at the pleading stage, denying him even the chance to prove his allegations at trial. They reasoned that the government had good reason for what it had done, and that alone precluded the possibility of bigotry tainting its actions:

> The September 11 attacks were perpetrated by 19 Arab Muslim hijackers who counted themselves members in good standing of al Qaeda, an Islamic fundamentalist group. Al Qaeda was headed by another Arab Muslim—Osama bin Laden—and composed in large part of his Arab Muslim disciples. It should come as no surprise that a legitimate policy directing law enforcement to arrest and detain individuals because of their suspected link to the attacks would produce a disparate, incidental impact on Arab Muslims.⁵¹

This "legitimate" explanation, the Court ruled, logically eliminated the possible existence of the malice it otherwise required Iqbal to prove to show racial discrimination.

Yet Iqbal was not complaining about an "incidental impact" on persons like himself; he was protesting against the purposeful targeting of all young men perceived to be Arab Muslim, one that in its physical violence and abuse of power seemed fueled at least partly by racial and religious vitriol. Moreover, the existence of a legitimate reason to look at persons from the Middle East hardly precluded the possibility that illegitimate impulses also operated. On the contrary, racial mistreatment often arises out of mixed motives. The detentions might have been motivated by a sense that they would help protect the country, but they were likely *also* animated by a racially tainted suspicion of all persons thought to be Arab Muslim—even if, like Iqbal, they were instead from Pakistan. Indeed, it's probable that these two reasons were inseparable: the conviction that mass detentions would protect the country almost certainly flowed from racial suspicions of Arab Muslims.

When Bush's Department of Justice responded to 9/11 by engaging in racially targeted interrogations and dragnets of Arab Muslims rather than individualized investigations and removals, it strongly contributed to the impression that the United States faced a *racial* threat rather than merely an extremist one. That threat ostensibly came from a new racial spook, the "Arab Muslim." As the *Iqbal* decision demonstrates, that category now operates as commonsense, with the seeming solidity of the group stemming from its inseparable association with Osama bin Laden. The 9/11 mastermind provides the archetype for this racial phantasm, for it is his visage that the public conjures when imagining the racial enemy. Yet when pressed, the Arab Muslim category bends and folds. There are, to be sure, Arabs who practice Islam, but the term seeks to join together two identities that are remarkably complex, Arab and Muslim. As a social category in the United States, "Arab Muslim" gains it most solid meaning from its construction as a threatening racial group.[52]

Nevertheless, obfuscating this racial dynamic, the targeting of Arab Muslims was often advanced in coded terms. In 2006, on the fifth anniversary of the hijackings, Bush set before the nation a Manichean vision of good versus evil:

> Since the horror of 9/11, we've learned a great deal about the enemy. We have learned that they are evil and kill without mercy, but not without purpose. We have learned that they form a global network of extremists who are driven by a perverted vision of Islam—a totalitarian ideology that hates freedom, rejects tolerance and despises all dissent. And we have learned that their goal is to build a radical Islamic empire where women are prisoners in their homes, men are beaten for missing prayer meetings, and terrorists have a safe haven to plan and launch attacks on America and other civilized nations. The war against this enemy is more than a military conflict. It is the decisive ideological struggle of the 21st century, and the calling of our generation. . . . This struggle has been called a clash of civilizations. In truth, it is a struggle for civilization. We are fighting to maintain the way of life enjoyed by free nations.[53]

With language like this, Bush helped cement the culturally potent image of US society locked in mortal combat with Arab Muslims. True, Bush was careful to cabin his remarks in terms of extremists and "a perverted vision of Islam," but the global terms in which he framed his analysis belied such fine distinctions. Bush transmuted our attackers from particular individuals and small factions of extremists into a whole civilization bent on our deaths and on the destruction of our way of life.

Even so, however, the reductive ugliness of Bush's analysis did not descend to old-fashioned racism. Rather, it was operating more in the register of a dog whistle, a way to advance a basically racial message while still maintaining plausible deniability. By deemphasizing biology and focusing instead on religion—on values and beliefs, rather than on physical essences—Bush could claim he was only criticizing a religion, or even more narrowly, the perversion of a religion. Whereas those engaging in open racism used racist epithets and direct references to biology to impugn this group, Bush was more careful, using religion and also behavior as a cover.[54] His speech—like the virulent opposition to mosque-building in the United States and the xenophobic ranting about sharia—was decidedly a form of racial demagoguery, hidden, however transparently, behind references to religious differences.

The Bush administration's initial public round-up campaign wasn't dog whistle politics in the normal sense of pandering for votes. But it was a political response built around a coded use of race: it endeavored to satisfy the urge for action and indeed revenge by showing that the administration was aggressively pursuing sinister nonwhites, yet while using religion and geography rather than race to identify those supposedly menacing the public. Moreover, after its initial use to justify domestic round ups, the administration expanded the Arab Muslim threat to legitimize war. The transformation of those who perpetrated the 9/11 attacks into a generic, implacable Middle Eastern foe helped Bush rally the nation for a war against Iraq initiated on fraudulent claims. Perhaps here more than anywhere else, a subliminal racial message proved key to the administration's aims. Yes, hyped weapons of mass destruction helped hoodwink the public. But even more fundamentally, it was the construction of an Arab Muslim threat that duped the majority of Americans into believing that Saddam Hussein and Iraq were deeply connected to Osama bin Laden and Al Qaeda. In turn, the racial and religious bigotry that justified the war also gravely tainted its conduct. Practices ranging from extraordinary rendition to torture could only have occurred at a state-sanctioned level, accompanied by broad public acquiescence, in the presence of widespread racist views about the nation's foes. Ultimately, the Bush administration defined itself and indeed the whole country in terms of a global confrontation with an Arab Muslim enemy, a confrontation widely perceived as a racial and religious clash. Yet as presented publicly, religion and geography helped thinly obscure the racial element, allowing Bush to garner support for his actions on the basis of coded racial appeals.

THE "ILLEGAL ALIEN" THREAT

If religious conflict provided a microscopically thin veneer of legitimacy to dog whistle attacks on Arab Muslims, cultural conflict played that same role with respect to the "illegal alien" threat. While this boogeyman has been decades in the making, it currently operates with a potency that rivals or exceeds the racial scapegoating of African Americans. Here, too, the 9/11 hijackings fanned the flames of xenophobia to new heights. Especially on the country's southern border, the War on Terror became a war on migrants.[55]

Throughout the twentieth century, the increasing presence of Latinos had been a cause for anxiety among some whites as well as a basis for political pandering, principally in the Southwest though occasionally across the country. After 2001, however, an old frame gained new urgency: the sense that Hispanics imperiled national security. In the 1980s, Ronald Reagan had warned that migrant workers from Mexico, as well as war refugees from Central America, constituted a potentially traitorous group in the nation's midst.[56] To many, this suggestion seemed farcical. After 2001, though, hysteria concerning national security made alarm about invaders from abroad seem well-warranted, thus creating a new opening for indicting Latinos as a menace to the country. This sense of crisis was also exaggerated for many by major demographic changes, as the Latino population grew to become the largest minority group in the United States, and also, as Hispanics increasingly moved into regions where they had not previously had a strong presence. During the Bush II presidency, even as the White House kept some distance from the most extreme expressions of racial panic around Latinos, many Republicans searched for electoral gold in warnings about the Hispanic threat.

Consonant with dog whistle techniques, conservatives publicly avoided the old racial language of spics, greasers, and wetbacks, and talked instead in the purportedly race-neutral language of cultural conflict. Consider Pat Buchanan, speaking in 2006: "If we do not get control of our borders and stop this greatest invasion in history, I see the dissolution of the U.S. and the loss of the American Southwest—culturally and linguistically, not politically—to Mexico. It could become a part of Mexico in the way that Kosovo is now a part of Albania."[57] Or observe the more erudite version, offered by Samuel Huntington, a Harvard professor of political science, in the pages of the establishment journal *Foreign Policy*: "The persistent inflow of Hispanic immigrants threatens to divide the United States into two peoples, two cultures, and two languages. Unlike past immigrant groups, Mexicans and other Latinos have not assimilated into mainstream U.S. culture, forming instead their own political and linguistic enclaves—from Los Angeles to Miami—and rejecting the Anglo-Protestant values that built the American dream."[58] Both Buchanan and Huntington show coded racial appeals at work: avoiding the language of race, they draw on the ethnic turn in conservative racial discourse to emphasize a potentially country-killing clash of cultures.

Beyond culture, those stirring dread around Latinos also frequently targeted behavior, in particular the act of migrating to the United States without lawful authorization. In a 2005 memo, Frank Luntz, a leading Republican wordsmith, offered some thoughts about immigration under the heading "Words that

Work"—work, that is, to get Republicans elected. Luntz encouraged Republicans to hammer key themes: "Let's talk about the facts behind illegal immigrants. They do commit crimes. They are more likely to drive uninsured. More likely to clog up hospital waiting rooms. More likely to be involved in anti-social behavior because they have learned that breaking the law brings more benefit to them than abiding by it."[59]

Not just politicians learned to use this language; from the Supreme Court bench, Justice Antonin Scalia proved a quick study. Criticizing a decision curtailing Arizona's effort to harass undocumented immigrants, Scalia wrote: "Arizona bears the brunt of the country's illegal immigration problem. Its citizens feel themselves under siege by large numbers of illegal immigrants who invade their property, strain their social services, and even place their lives in jeopardy."[60]

As always, the propaganda deviated from the reality. First, it bears mention that "illegal" is a misnomer: crossing into or remaining in the United States without proper authorization is not a crime, but rather a civil matter. Thus, contrary to Scalia's preference, the Court majority eschewed the term "illegal alien," noting that "as a general rule, it is not a crime for a removable alien to remain present in the United States."[61]

On the more fundamental question of assimilation, scholars recognize that today's immigrants from Latin America (and also from Asia), no different from the generations of European immigrants before them, are "being successfully incorporated into American society"; indeed, studies find "great continuities between the experiences of earlier European immigrants and current, predominantly non-European immigrants."[62] Moreover, the notion that crossing the border without authorization generates a pervasive disdain for the law is demonstrably false. Research shows that undocumented immigrants from Latin America commit far fewer depredations, not far more, than citizens.[63] Evidence shows too that undocumented immigrants are far less likely than others to use expensive social services, including hospital emergency rooms. Indeed, unauthorized immigrants pay considerably more in taxes—typically through payroll withholding—than they receive in social services. Because much of this goes to the federal government, this may be small comfort for states with large immigrant populations, but problems in the federal-state distribution of tax money paid by undocumented immigrants is a far cry from the falsehood that such migrants do not pull their weight in tax payments.

Notwithstanding its departure from reality, the "illegal alien" rhetoric is highly popular with racial demagogues. Stressing illegality provides a way to seed racial fears without directly referencing race. Scapegoating unauthorized immigrants carries a façade of neutrality insofar as it purports to refer to all persons present in the United States without proper authorization. Ostensibly, this would include the German citizen here on a tourist visa who takes a job, or the Canadian who enters as a visitor but decides to live in Aspen indefinitely. Yet these are not the faces that come to mind when the term is bandied about. Rather, the usual suspects—the unavoidable suspects when Tea Party patriots spit out the phrase at rallies on the southern border—are undocumented immigrants from Latin America, especially Mexico. Indeed, often it seems the term is not limited to immigrants at all, but rather expresses an alarm that applies to almost all persons of Latino descent, most of whom are US citizens.[64] By constantly drumming on the crises posed by "illegals," the right fuels a racial frenzy but can deny its intention to do any such thing.

THE DEMOCRATS FOLLOW

In the Democratic response to race-baiting around immigration, one sees a trajectory distressingly similar to that which produced racialized mass incarceration. As the Republicans agitated voters with dire warnings of "illegals," Democrats responded by adopting the same discourse, and often by offering their own draconian policies. Again, the Clinton administration led the way. Clinton met furor over immigration by dramatically increasing appropriations for border security and promising to crack down on "illegal aliens."[65] Yet reflecting how the scapegoating of undocumented immigrants connected to broader animosity toward brown-skinned immigrants in general, in 1996 Clinton signed a series of laws targeting immigrants lawfully present in the country. These laws vastly expanded grounds for the deportation of lawful immigrants; created powers of "expedited exclusion" for immigrants who had ever crossed the border illegally, even if they subsequently achieved lawful status; and stripped lawfully present non-citizens of many federal benefits.

The Obama administration has continued the hard line against immigration. In 2010, the Immigration and Customs Enforcement agency removed roughly 400,000 persons in one year alone, higher than the highest totals ever achieved by the Bush administration.[66] Virtually all of the immigrants who were deported in 2010—an astounding 97 percent—were Hispanic, a number highly disproportionate to the share of Latinos among all undocumented immigrants in the United States.[67] As of July 2012, the Obama administration had expelled 1.4 million undocumented immigrants, at a rate 1.5 times greater than the Bush administration.[68] Obama appeared to have listened to Democratic strategists who concluded in 2008 that the party needed to take a "tougher" tone when discussing immigration reform.[69] The rationale was to show that the Democrats were serious about enforcement, hoping to trade this off against eventual immigration reform. During Obama's first administration, however, this calculus produced record levels of toughness and no reform whatsoever. Only after the 2012 election, when Republicans decided that they needed some Latino votes, did a genuine possibility of reform open up. Prior to that, the harsh Democratic crackdown on Latin American migrants purchased very little at a terribly high price in human misery.

* * *

Before we leave this chapter, let me use a personal story to connect the targeting of Latinos with a larger point about dog whistle racism. We have been principally focused on the claim that it wrecks the middle class; again, as with racialized mass incarceration, we should not forget that dog whistle racism takes a particularly devastating toll on those it racially demeans. We might see this in the hundreds of thousands of persons deported every year—a wrenching process that tears apart families and causes enormous emotional devastation. But sometimes the numbers are so large, and the social distance so vast, we cannot see the damage politicians do in our names. In such circumstances, perhaps a simple story, even one from the margins of the calamity, can help bring into focus the human toll.

In 2011 I taught a seminar on Arizona's anti-immigrant legislation. This was a small seminar, and unbeknownst to me until well into the semester, one of my students was undocumented. She was much like the others: smart, passionate about social justice, and outraged by the blatant racial demagoguery of Arizona's leaders, but also temperamentally cool, rational, and restrained, perfectly exhibiting the professional deportment law schools seek to inculcate. Each week she came to class, and together the whole group observed Arizona from the academic stratosphere: surveying the history of Mexican immigration; studying theories of racism; parsing the mutating forms of racial discourse. Midway through the semester, though, she broke down. In the midst of tears, trauma, and pain, she choked out her personal connection to the subject matter, how she was actually one of "them." Her shattered façade jolted the class, and myself, out of academic detachment.

In the immediacy of her grief and distress, I was reminded of a profound truth. I had let slip from my analysis the most basic and human of facts: people were being hurt. All the hate and fear stoked by racial provocateurs wasn't just wafting away, a putrid miasma gradually dissipating into the air harmlessly. The hostility was penetrating peoples' hearts, wearying and wounding their souls. As she sobbed and shared stories of her family, her siblings, the people she loved and their pain and stress, and as her fellow students rushed to console her, I sat there muttering reassuring words but really just dumbfounded by a simple point, an insight that can too easily be lost in the midst of academic critique: when demagogues use offensive caricatures to inflame passions, they are demonizing *people*. Dog whistle politics turns people's lives into nightmares. People just like us. People whose heights of joy and depths of pain are no less real than our own, even as their humanity is rendered invisible by slurs about their behavior and culture. In our inability to recognize their humanity, we as a nation have lost part of our own.

6

Getting Away with Racism

A transparently racist statement can spell the end of a political career, so how do politicians get away with racial pandering? Dog whistling has long followed a standard choreography of punch, parry, and kick that tracks moves associated with colorblindness. More recently, rightwing politics has also sought cover by pushing nonwhite faces to the fore.

In the final month of the 2008 presidential campaign, a newsletter distributed by a local California Republican group claimed that if Obama was elected his image would appear on food stamps, instead of on dollar bills like other presidents. The broadside featured a phony $10 bill, now relabeled as "Ten Dollars Obama Bucks" in seals on each corner. In the middle, superimposed on the body of a donkey, was Obama's face, eyes twinkling and with a wide grin. Above that, the mock bill read "United States Food Stamps." Rounding out the racial parody, on the left there was a bucket of Kentucky Fried Chicken and a slab of ribs; on the right, a pitcher of Kool Aid and a large slice of watermelon.[1]

In the swirl of controversy that erupted, the group's president, Diane Fedele, accepted responsibility for circulating the cartoon, which she had received in a number of chain e-mails before she decided to reprint it, and she was quick to apologize: "I absolutely apologize to anyone who was offended. That clearly wasn't my attempt." She was, nevertheless, just a little befuddled by the outrage.

In what way could this be construed as racist, she wondered? Nothing about the imagery suggested race, she explained, as fried chicken and ribs, Kool Aid and watermelon were "just food." "I didn't see it the way that it's being taken. I never connected," she said. "It was just food to me. It didn't mean anything else." Fedele also said she was making no effort to connect Obama to welfare,

"It was just food to me. It didn't mean anything else," said the president of a local Republican group in denying that the cartoon, which she reproduced in the group's newsletter, had anything to do with race. © Tim Kastelein

or to food stamps in particular. Yet her text introducing the cartoon said, "If elected, what bill would he be on????? Food Stamps, what else!"

What, then, was the intent behind circulating the cartoon? Fedele claimed she meant to criticize Obama—ironically, for nothing less than injecting race into the presidential campaign. Over the summer Obama had warned an audience in Springfield, Missouri, that John McCain's campaign might stoop to scare tactics, charging: "Nobody really thinks that Bush or McCain have a real answer for the challenges we face, so what they're going to try to do is make you scared of me. You know, he's not patriotic enough. He's got a funny name. You know, he doesn't look like all those other presidents on those dollar bills. You know, he's risky."[2]

Fedele was incensed. "I thought his statement was outrageous and uncalled for and inappropriate and everything else I can think to call it." According to a local reporter, Fedele circulated the cartoon "to criticize Obama for saying over the summer that he doesn't look like the presidents whose images are on dollar bills. She said she didn't think it was appropriate for him to draw attention to his race."

Fedele also had a trump to play. How could she be a racist, she wondered, if she had once supported a black presidential candidate? "She said she doesn't think in racist terms, pointing out she once supported Republican Alan Keyes, an African-American who previously ran for president."

One more detail deserves to be mentioned before we step back to assess this contretemps. The cartoon's original creator was a liberal blogger who held a minor position with the Minnesota Democratic Party and who planned to vote for Obama. He created the cartoon and posted it on his website "to lampoon

Republicans who are afraid of government welfare programs and fearful of a Democratic president. He said that 'there's some people that are never going to get it.'" He was more right than he knew, as apparently many of those he sought to lampoon instead embraced and circulated his cartoon as a biting impeachment of Obama.

■ RACE IS EVERYWHERE AND NOWHERE

Even as late as the 1950s, it was commonplace for racial epithets to lace public discourse. Debates carried out on newspaper pages spoke regularly in terms we now regard as derogatory, and politicians routinely employed racial slurs. For instance, in November 1953 the *New York Times* ran a headline that blared "WETBACK INFLUX NEAR THE RECORD; October Figure Second Highest in History—Crime Follows the Illegal Immigrants."[3] Stimulated by and in turn fueling such fear-mongering, in 1954 the Eisenhower administration launched a mass expulsion campaign forthrightly called "Operation Wetback." Slurs like "wetback" are now entirely absent from public discourse—or rather, almost entirely, as Republican senator Don Young demonstrated in 2013.[4] Young's reminiscences about the golden days when his family "used to hire 50 to 60 wetbacks to pick tomatoes" notwithstanding, today even direct references to race make relatively few appearances. Yet as we've seen, race has hardly disappeared from politics. The once pervasive use of epithets has morphed into the coded transmission of racial messages through references to culture, behavior, and class. We live in a political milieu saturated with ugly racial innuendo.

But if so, why is there so little pushback from liberals? Why is racial pandering allowed to continue virtually unchallenged? As we've seen, partly the answer is that some liberals have themselves adopted dog whistle politics, whether out of sympathy to the underlying stereotypes or as a step toward getting Democrats elected. Beyond this, however, with assistance from colorblindness, conservative race-talk has adopted several strikingly effective strategies to insulate constant race-baiting.

Punch, Parry, Kick

The Obama Bucks controversy crossed the line into forbidden territory. Just as with Ronald Reagan when he first referred to the stereotypical food-stamp recipient as a "strapping young buck" before switching to the more ambiguous "some young fellow," Fedele's reprinted cartoon was too transparently racial.

Even the chair of the California Republican Party conceded Fedele had sinned, saying "any material that invokes issues related to race is absolutely unacceptable," and adding that the cartoon "inspires nothing but divisiveness and hostility and has absolutely no place in this election, or any public discourse."[5]

If overly exuberant, however, Fedele was in other respects simply practicing the rhetorical punch, parry, and kick of dog whistle racial jujitsu. Here are the basic moves: (1) punch racism into the conversation through references to culture, behavior, and class; (2) parry claims of race-baiting by insisting that absent a direct reference to biology or the use of a racial epithet, there can be no racism; (3) kick up the racial attack by calling any critics the *real* racists for mentioning race and thereby "playing the race card."

Punch. The punch is dog whistle's coded race-talk. In Fedele's case, it lay in circulating a caricature of a grinning Obama visually linked to food stamps as well as to victuals stereotypically beloved by African Americans. Here was the "happy coon" from the era of black face minstrelsy, grinning in childish delight over fried chicken and watermelon showered on him by the foolish largess of welfare. *This buffoon could soon be president*, the cartoon chided.

More generally, recall the various bugaboos politicians have mobilized the country against: criminals, welfare cheats, Arab Muslim terrorists, and illegal aliens. All of these invoke a new demonology that looks remarkably like the old one: nonwhites threatening the nation. On one level, the terms have changed: the menace arises from defective cultures and reprehensible behavior, rather than from these as they directly link to biology, as in the past. But the core dynamic remains: punch race into the conversation at every possible turn by bombarding white society with messages about the need to rally together. The colorblind invocation of ethnicity as a coded language for race is indispensable here. It is ethnicity, after all, that facilitates constant insinuations about fundamental group differences.

Parry. Dog whistlers then parry any resulting outrage by playing dumb, refusing to see the supposed connection between their comments and race. This too is pure dog whistle theater. A dog whistle is a *coded* racial appeal—one core point of the code being to foster deniability. The explicit racial appeal of yesteryear now invites political suicide. Dog whistle politics trades instead in studied ambiguity, where the lack of a smoking-gun racial epithet allows for proclamations of innocence. Fedele mimics this defense brilliantly when she says "it was just food to me. It didn't mean anything else." Fedele didn't use a slur or directly refer to race; she didn't say "coons like watermelon." So how could this be about race? It was just a watermelon—and some fried chicken, ribs, and Kool Aid.

Also reprising these basic jujitsu moves, consider Newt Gingrich's repeated besmirching of Obama as "the most successful food stamp president in American history."[6] In January 2012, during a Republican primary debate, Fox News political analyst Juan Williams challenged Gingrich on this and other racially provocative remarks, asking, "Can't you see this is viewed, at a minimum, as insulting to all Americans, but particularly to black Americans?" "No, I don't see that," Gingrich huffed. When Williams refused to be put off and repeated the question, the audience booed. Then they cheered when Gingrich bombastically retorted, "First of all, Juan, the fact is that more people have been put on food stamps under Barack Obama than any other president in history."[7] Set aside that food stamp use was at an all time high because of economic calamity rather than the president's policies. Focus instead on Gingrich's rhetorical steps. First, like Reagan and Fedele and countless others, he used references to food stamps to push the poison of race into the public's veins. Then, when challenged, he reacted with studied indignation—he was shocked, just shocked that anyone would see race in his comments. But of course the barbed point of those three words—food stamp president—was to link Obama to indolent blacks on welfare, and to communicate that Gingrich would stand with hardworking whites who earn paychecks. "How do I know this is true?" asked the novelist Walter Moseley after making a similar argument. "Because Mr. Gingrich is a political poet and good political poets always have their finger on the jugular vein of the nation. Mr. Gingrich has told me in three words that the battle line will be drawn by fear-stoked hatred."[8]

Or recall the "Obama Phone Lady," the gesticulating, overweight, visibly poor black woman shouting her support for Obama in a video that went viral in the months before the 2012 election. Filmed at an Obama rally in Ohio, the woman explained her enthusiasm for the president in terms of his ability to deliver goods to the poor. "Everybody in Cleveland, low minorities, got Obama phones. . . . Keep Obama in president, you know! He gave us a phone, he's gonna do more," she yells—and race-baiters loved her for providing a powerful caricature of the black Democratic voter. The video was posted to YouTube by a conservative activist in late September 2012, and within ten days had been viewed over four million times—aided by being featured on the conservative Drudge Report website and by Rush Limbaugh replaying the soundtrack on an endless loop on his radio program.

Yet when criticized for racial pandering, the right responded with incredulity. Said the person who posted the video: "I have no idea how it could be construed as racist because it's simply a woman speaking for herself."[9] Said another defender, "the above video is hilarious. It is representative of a group of Obama voters who feel entitled to handouts from government. It does not matter what the color of the speaker is. . . . Conservatives should not have to shy away from such amusing examples of entitlement mentality simply because the particular proponent of that mentality happens to be black."[10] As Elspeth Reeve correctly retorted in *The Atlantic Wire*, "The point of the video—and the reason Drudge and Limbaugh hyped it—is to say, this is what Obama voters look like: black, poor, stupid, and after your money. The video's subject wasn't picked out because she 'happens to be black,' she was picked out *because* she is black"—or more precisely, because she seemed to embody so many stereotypical attributes of blackness. Reeve continued: "This video, if placed in a Romney ad, would make George H.W. Bush's 1988 Willie Horton ad look subtle by comparison: the other guy is supported by scary black people, vote Republican!"[11] Yet by mid-October, the video was indeed featured in a Tea Party-supported ad running in three predominantly white Ohio counties.[12]

How could these provocateurs insist with a straight face that footage of an impoverished black woman as well as jabs about food stamps, stereotypical food stuffs, and entitlement mentalities had nothing to do with race? What made this at all plausible? It's colorblindness that provides crucial cover. Colorblindness allows conservatives to insist that race means blood and nothing more, so that references to culture and behavior cannot be about race. And it's colorblindness that promotes the claim that racism only exists when someone confesses to malice or uses an epithet, so that coded speech is never racism so long as it remains in code. Here then is the essence of the parry: the colorblind avowal that nothing but biology is race and that racism cannot be present until someone utters the wrong term. This is word magic at its most potent: say food stamps and entitlement mentality, and racism is nowhere to be seen; say black and suddenly racism springs into being. Colorblindness transforms the absence of any express reference to race into a broad shield against every charge of racism. As long as dog whistle demagogues stick to racial euphemisms, colorblindness defends them against every charge of racial pandering.

Conservatives now apply the colorblind rule that racism requires the use of an epithet to all rightwing discourse, with one further restriction: if a slur is used it must be electronically recorded, or it never happened. In the spring of 2010, multiple witnesses, including congressional representatives, reported that someone in a Tea Party crowd called Congressman John Lewis a "nigger."[13] According to the right, though, this testimony was not sufficient to establish what actually happened; rather, conservative partisans demanded electronic proof—a video or at least an audio recording. Absent that, allegations of racial attacks amounted only to self-serving and indeed "racist" propaganda. According to a rightwing website, "these radical liars will stop at nothing to ram their socialist agenda down America's throat. And, the state-run media will report their racist filth without question."[14]

Kick. Beyond the repeated punch and parry, dog whistle politics almost invariably launches a stinging counterattack. This is the kick: when accused of racism, turn the tables and accuse your accuser of injecting race into the conversation. The retort to John Lewis's allegation of racist abuse was, in keeping with the standard playbook, to label this charge "racist filth." Or return to Fedele. Charged with racial provocation, she followed the dog whistle script and claimed that she was merely responding to Obama's egregious racial pandering. Recall that she explained her cartoon as a response to Obama's having mentioned that Republicans might try to scare voters by pointing out that "he doesn't look like all those other presidents on those dollar bills."

In complaining that Obama outrageously inserted race into the conversation, Fedele followed the McCain camp, which went after Obama as a racial opportunist for implying that the GOP might stoop to scaring voters about race. Obama's warning was hardly far-fetched. Beyond the long history of dog whistling, the 2008 campaign itself was so saturated in racial ugliness—with vice-presidential candidate Sarah Palin accusing Obama of "palling around with terrorists" and campaign crowds yelling "kill him!"—that the *New York Times* editorial page eventually castigated the McCain campaign for "race-baiting and xenophobia."[15] Nevertheless, McCain's people fumed about Obama's summertime warning. A day after Obama's remarks, McCain's campaign charged that "Barack Obama has played the race card, and he played it from the bottom of the deck," adding "it's divisive, negative, shameful and wrong."[16] On the *Today* show, McCain campaign manager Rick Davis indignantly insisted "we are not going to let anybody paint John McCain, who has fought his entire life for equal rights for everyone, to be able to be painted as racist."[17]

When the McCain camp went on the racial offensive, how did Obama's team respond? Backpedaling furiously, Obama campaign strategist David Axelrod initially adopted the techniques of the right. Axelrod employed his own parry, responding implausibly that Obama's remarks about presidents on dollar bills had nothing to do with race. Obama, Axelrod claimed, was simply referencing "his status as a young, relative newcomer to Washington politics." Then he kicked back, charging that "race became an issue only when the McCain campaign cast a racial slant on Obama's remarks." Axelrod could play the same rhetorical game, denying Obama had invoked race and claiming to be offended by the very insinuation. Or perhaps this wasn't precisely the same game: not an effort to introduce and then avoid race, so much as an effort to recover from an unscripted slip. Obama probably never intended to mention race in the first place, and once he did, he calculated it was smarter politics to retreat than be dragged into a conversation about race that would only heighten doubts about his own racial identity. Be that as it may, the bottom line is that the Republican kick forced Obama off-balance, prompting him to withdraw his caution to expect race-baiting. Accepting the rightwing frame that Obama's remarks offensively cast McCain as a bigot, Axelrod was quick to clarify on national television that "Barack Obama never called John McCain a racist."[18]

Note how the dog whistle kick parallels the colorblind attack on affirmative action. Under colorblind constitutional law, racism has become any use of race, making "racists" out of those who use affirmative action to foster integration. In conservative discourse, meanwhile, the corollary practice is to malign as racial bombthrowers those who protest continuing racial injustices. Ostensibly, the real racists are those who publicly critique the on-going centrality of race in American society.

This claim that the critics of racial pandering are the real racists has a pedigree going back to the original dog whistle politician himself, George Wallace. As Wallace put it while on the hunt for angry white voters in 1968, "you know who the biggest bigots in the world are—they're the ones who call others bigots." He caviled, "Well, it's a sad day in the country when you can't talk about law and order unless they want to call you a racist."[19] According to Wallace's logic, protesting racial pandering makes you the biggest bigot in the world—and, presumably, pulling a fire alarm means you set the fire, while dialing 911 means you committed the crime.

Routed by these attacks, most progressives have stopped talking about race and racism, lest they be accused of being "the biggest bigots in the world." Like colorblindness, dog whistling is both a form of race talk and a way to ensure silence about race. Among conservatives it facilitates a constant din of racial insinuation couched in references to culture and behavior, while insisting there's no racism without an epithet or a direct mention of race. And among liberals it enforces a cowed silence, kicking up the racial conflict by accusing any critics of opportunistically injecting race into the conversation.

"I Guess I'm a Racist"

When Obama briefly referenced race as one of the ways that the GOP might try to scare voters, in addition to the typical "race card" retort, the McCain camp also struck back with the charge that Obama had sought to "paint John McCain . . . as racist."[20] This assailment deserves a bit more attention.

The claim to have been slandered as a racist frequently crops up on the right in response to liberal efforts to focus on troubling racial dynamics, and there may be a fair level of cynical strategizing at work in such conservative carping. By translating the claim that race continues to play a distorting role in American life into a narrow indictment of mean-spirited bigotry, conservatives are more able to easily dismiss the allegation as absurd. The invented charge of being a closet Klan member is readily repudiated. In addition, because the charge of being a racist is freighted with social opprobrium, alleging they have been so charged allows conservatives to cast themselves as unfairly maligned victims. The claim to have been called a racist sucks all the air out of the room, ending any substantive conversation; the only thing left is for the race critic to apologize and to deny that she intended to call anyone a racist. In short, for conservatives, alleging that they've been called a racist is good strategy.

But what about the emotional affect that often accompanies this particular defensive kick? Typically, those claiming to have been denoted racists exude outrage or distress. The imagined accusation, their emotions communicate, has wounded them personally, deeply bruising their sense of themselves. McCain's spokesperson reacted angrily, not only rejecting the non-charge but vigorously defending McCain as someone who "fought his entire life for equal rights for everyone," as if McCain's whole career had been smeared. Or consider the pained dismay communicated by actors in an ad opposing health care reform. The ad featured perhaps a dozen adults, mostly white and seemingly middle class, including one young woman with a toddler, looking directly into the camera to confess "I guess I'm a racist."[21] The ad interspersed these aggrieved confessions with text and a voice-over repeating the allegation made by some outspoken liberals, including Jesse Jackson and Jimmy Carter, that race likely informed some of the opposition to Obama's health care overhaul. These actors were signaling their antagonism to health care reform—and also to the charge that in politics race matters—by facetiously taking upon themselves the "racist" label. Yet when they intoned "I guess I'm a racist," their demeanor communicated not satire but heart sickness.

It's impossible to know whether, coming from a politician's camp or an anti-health care ad, these intonations of wounded feelings were genuine or feigned. Even if the latter, though, they nevertheless track a real sense of distress among many conservatives, including many Tea Party members, who feel that they have been unfairly vilified as racists. Sometimes allegations of having been called a racist constitute a strategic retort, but often they reflect a deeply felt wound.

Some greet this sort of defensiveness as a sign of progress. *At least we've arrived at a place where whites worry about being racists*, they say. But hair-trigger defensiveness is not a sign of forward movement. On the contrary, it reflects a pattern as old as racism. Racial ideas perpetually adapt to reassure members of the dominant group that, however unjust the social arrangements and whatever the attendant violence, they are good and decent folks. Thus, at virtually every historical juncture, challenges to existing racial structures—whether it be slavery 150 years ago or the inhumanity of racialized mass incarceration today—have often been received as personal affronts. Even in eras now recognized as unquestionably racist, most whites accepted the racial status quo as normal and moral, and internalized challenges to racial injustice as assaults on their integrity. Thus, that whites should continue to feel defensive today should not be taken to indicate racial progress.

In 1965, the novelist James Baldwin explored white defensiveness in an essay entitled "White Man's Guilt."[22] Baldwin started by noting how his color seemed to impede human connection with many whites. They saw his color first, and reacting to that, feared an indictment over their own racial position. "And to have to deal with such people can be unutterably exhausting," Baldwin wrote, "for they, with a really dazzling ingenuity, a tireless agility, are perpetually defending themselves against charges which one, disagreeable mirror though one may be, has not really, for the moment, made." Baldwin lamented that white defensiveness against possible charges of racism frequently skewed any possible relationship, repeatedly forcing him into exhausting gymnastics meant to reassure whites of their innocence. Just so with contemporary claims of wounded feelings at having been, supposedly, called a "racist." The actual charge of racial malice is almost never made. And yet, racial justice advocates are time after time pushed to provide exoneration from the fictional accusation of personal bigotry.

But this is only half the dynamic, and indeed, not the important half. Baldwin wrote that he did not need to level any charges, for the proof of white responsibility for racial oppression was everywhere in society. "The record is there for all to read. It resounds all over the world. It might as well be written in the sky. One wishes that Americans—white Americans—would read, for their own sakes, this record and stop defending themselves against it. Only then will they be enabled to change their lives." The imagined allegation against which many whites aggressively defend themselves today is of personal bigotry. The social indictment written in the sky is rather of a shared responsibility for race's continued distorting power.

Baldwin's words go to the larger impact generated when many whites feel implicated as racists. One dynamic is the forced exoneration. But the deeper result is to forestall desperately needed conversations about race in society. Claims to have been personally attacked take productive conversations about current racial patterns and collapse them into a stultifying ventilation of wounded feelings. It shifts attention from racial dynamics that hurt everyone, and focuses our eyes instead on the bruised egos of those whites who feel themselves personally targeted whenever the conversation turns to race. The imagined charge is of small-minded bigotry. The actual charge, written across society—including, importantly, in the racial politics of the GOP—is that race in various forms continues to harm us all. Histrionic distress about supposedly having been called a racist impedes recognizing the truth about race's continued harmful power.

■ RIGHTWING AFFIRMATIVE ACTION

In addition to the typical punch, parry, and kick of colorblind rhetoric, the local GOP leader behind the Obama Bucks episode also employed another defensive move increasingly typical of conservative race-talk: hiding behind a minority. She couldn't possibly be racist, Fedele explained, since she had once supported a black conservative for president—namely Alan Keyes, famous among other reasons for opposing sanctions against apartheid South Africa and for filing suit in 2008 to force Obama to prove his US citizenship.[23] Under a rightwing verion of affirmative action, conservatives push forward nonwhite spokespersons as a shield against accusations of racism.

After attending a Tea Party rally in 2010, *New York Times* columnist Charles Blow commented wryly on this tactic, noting the "diversity" on the stage, where the black, Asian, and Hispanic speakers looked like "a bizarre spoof of a 1980s Benetton ad," all while addressing a crowd that was overwhelmingly white. While the Asian speaker upheld God as the Tea Party's leader, the other two emphasized Tea Party themes treacherously connected to race. The black orator denounced Democrats for crying racism; the Latino excoriated welfare. Indisputably, their racial identities granted superficial legitimacy to their messages— if black and brown people thought this, perfunctory logic seemed to suggest, it could not be racially problematic. "It was a farce," Blow interjected, well aware that the Tea Party was almost all white, and dismayed by the apparent cynicism behind the composition of the podium.[24] Amid the strategies of the new racism, a key symbolic move is to find nonwhites willing to espouse, or at least provide cover for, dog whistle views.

CLINT BOLICK

One of the pioneers of this tactic is Clint Bolick, a central figure in the right-wing legal movement who played an important role in promoting Supreme Court Justice Clarence Thomas, himself an exemplar of this strategy. Their entwined careers epitomize how efforts to modernize dog whistle politics extends to putting nonwhite voices forward. Their duet also strongly reconfirms that such politics aim fundamentally to roll back the New Deal state.

Bolick cut his teeth in the first generation of conservative legal think tanks before moving into government during the Reagan administration, first at the Equal Employment Opportunity Commission and then in the civil rights division of the Department of Justice.[25] Reagan's decision to install rabid foes of civil rights in positions of authority over civil rights followed the Heritage Foundation's recommendation to pack targeted agencies with ideologues disposed to undercut their missions. Emboldened by his experience dismantling civil rights, Bolick stepped out of government at the end of Reagan's presidency and dedicated himself to developing updated forms of rightwing advocacy. He contributed as a theorist, writing books that outlined strategies for a conservative counterrevolution with a new face, and also as an institution builder putting those plans into practice.

Illustrating the interweaving of race and big-money politics, in 1990 Bolick published a strategy book entitled *Unfinished Business* that called for recasting anti-government ideology in the language of civil rights. In what he termed "the original civil rights vision," Bolick argued that "an individual's ability to participate in the free market system is the best possible way to promote justice." For Bolick, the defining case of the post-Civil War era was not *Plessy*, blessing segregation, but the *Slaughter-House Cases*, a Supreme Court decision that upheld the right of Louisiana to regulate abattoirs, and thereby confirmed the power of government to regulate the marketplace. "As a long-range strategy," he wrote, "we should establish as our ultimate objective the reversal of the *Slaughter-House Cases*." The audacity of this position is hard to overstate. Not only would it effectively repeal the New Deal, it would undo all of the twentieth-century reforms intended to curb market abuses and prevent great concentrations of power. It is no accident that *Unfinished Business* quoted approvingly from Herbert Spencer, a late-nineteenth century figure renowned for his pitiless endorsement of Social Darwinism, the philosophy of "the survival of the fittest" applied to human society.[26] Spencer argued against public education, health and safety regulations, and welfare, convinced that these programs artificially buoyed individuals destined to fail, to the long-term detriment of society.[27] This is the view Bolick endorsed when he envisioned civil rights as "permeated by the spirit of laissez-faire, with individual autonomy elevated to a moral absolute."[28] For Bolick, true civil rights lay in the nineteenth century vision of liberty from government, not in New Deal liberalism, and certainly not in government protections against racial discrimination or other market-place abuses that interfered with the prime directive of maximum freedom for the powerful to do what they please.

This was not, of course, a vision likely to win many adherents among the middle class, a fact that Bolick recognized fully. *Unfinished Business* was writ-ten more as an internal movement manifesto than as a public broadside, and its contribution came in outlining the long-range goal as well as in sketching strategies for getting there. Beyond gussying up robber baron interests as a civil rights issue, Bolick advocated two other interrelated innovations: pursuing change through the courts; and putting nonwhite faces at the fore. Regarding the former, Bolick explained that courts should be preferred because democrati-cally elected majorities would never vote for the regressive counterrevolution he had in mind.[29] We typically trust courts to enforce civil rights to protect power-less groups. Bolick instead urged using a bastardized version of civil rights to protect society's most wealthy against democratic rule. Bolick's 1990 theorizing provides an early indication of the right's long-range strategy to use the courts to war against liberalism. Exemplifying the fruition of this plan, the conservatives on the Court today make this the most conservative Supreme Court—and the most friendly toward big business—in a century.[30]

Bolick also advocated that nonwhites should be pushed forward as "sympathetic plaintiffs." As between "a white firefighter who loses a promotion because of a racial quota" and "a black schoolchild who is turned away from a magnet school in order to preserve racial balance," Bolick favored building a case around the latter.[31] Bolick worried that the aggrieved white might be seen negatively, whereas representing a black schoolchild gave credence to the charade that the right was supporting, rather than opposing, civil rights.[32] The president of another conservative legal group explained Bolick's reasoning more nakedly: Bolick's group "will never bring a reverse discrimination case on behalf of a white plaintiff," he observed. "It's an article of faith. . . . The reason for this is they don't want to be portrayed in the press as representing disgruntled white people. They want always to be representing racial minorities in these kinds of cases. That's a press strategy that drives their legal strategy."[33] From behind the distracting façade of black schoolchildren and other nonwhite plaintiffs, Bolick has made a career of attacking business regulations as well as the public funding of education.

CLARENCE THOMAS

The right slams affirmative action for making distinctions on the basis of race, even as it has developed its own perverse form of affirmative action, consciously selecting nonwhites to front its agenda. Perhaps the right's—and Bolick's—greatest success in this endeavor is Clarence Thomas. When Bolick went to the EEOC in the mid-1980s, he arrived as a special assistant to Thomas, then the chair of the Commission. Bolick helped Thomas win confirmation to a second term as EEOC chair, despite his record of having cut civil rights enforcement dramatically, of having ended almost all group-based claims of discrimination, and of having lambasted civil rights leaders for their proclivity to "bitch, bitch, bitch, moan and whine."[34] Bolick also helped shepherd Thomas's confirmation as an appellate judge in 1990, and was key to his confirmation to the Supreme Court just over a year later.

Following his standard playbook, Bolick helped put Thomas on the highest bench in the land by emphasizing not Thomas's abilities, but his blackness. Most memorably, when Thomas responded to Anita Hill's credible and detailed accounts of sexual harassment with a strident denunciation portraying himself as a victim of a "high tech lynching," he was trading on race to save his nomination. Race scholar Richard Ford lists Thomas's wail about lynching as a rightwing instance of playing the "race card": "Thomas—a corrosive skeptic of accusations of racism during his tenure at the EEOC—cried racism the moment his nomination was in jeopardy. When the chips were down and the stakes were high, this staunch defender of colorblindness shamelessly played the race card."[35]

But in fact Thomas did not wait until the chips were down to play up race. Rather, his invocation of lynching was only one episode in a larger confirmation strategy that placed race front and center. Bolick orchestrated a racial narrative from the inception, for example stressing Thomas's up-by-his-bootstraps personal story of growing up poor and black in Pin Point, Georgia. Bolick also arranged for a busload of poor and black Thomas supporters from his hometown to travel to DC as if on their own initiative, in order to buttress the authenticity of Thomas's Horatio Alger narrative as well as to give the impression of grassroots black support. "The group was entirely stage-managed and recruited, but able, as Bolick put it, to 'monopolize the media at the time people's impressions were being formed about Thomas.'"[36] Thomas's "blackness" was at the heart of his candidacy. This is not to say he was nominated solely because he was black; no doubt his conservatism and his political connections were essential as well. He would not have gained a seat on the Court, though, had he been white. The hollow protestations by George H.W. Bush that he had nominated the most qualified candidate notwithstanding, Thomas's blackness explains not only his selection to fill the seat vacated by Thurgood Marshall, but the strategy Thomas employed to win confirmation.

Today, the practice of putting forward nonwhite faces has penetrated GOP politics. Herman Cain is one example, for "Cain continued the Republican Party's 'Southern Strategy' by serving as a mouthpiece for mean-spirited denouncements against blacks and the poor."[37] Others abound, and bid likely to increase. When Jim DeMint resigned from the Senate after the 2012 election to lead the Heritage Foundation, South Carolina's Republican governor appointed a black Tea Party conservative, Tim Scott, to fill his seat. Simultaneously, looking forward to 2016, Republicans immediately began elevating to prominence another nonwhite senator, Florida's Marco Rubio, again a staunch conservative who gained office as a darling of the Tea Party. Scott and Rubio illustrate somewhat distinct dynamics in terms of the strategy behind elevating minority mouthpieces. Scott, like other conservative African Americans in the GOP, holds office with virtually no black support. His blackness probably serves less as a way to appeal to African American voters than as a talisman that allows white conservatives to prove—to others and to themselves—that they could not possibly be racist.[38] Rubio's Latino identity likely does double duty, helping both to ward off concerns over racism, and also affirmatively helping the GOP to appeal to Latino voters.[39] Despite these slight differences, Scott and Rubio share a core similarity: both benefit from a rightwing racial politics that has recently learned to push nonwhite faces forward. Criticizing affirmative action, Clarence Thomas once disparaged integration efforts as no more than racial aesthetics, attempts to create pleasing color palettes and nothing more. Ironically, Thomas's own elevation fits that charge, as the right continues to darken its public face without changing its underlying politics.

On the right, colorblindness operates like a weapon, picked up when opportune but set aside when inconvenient. Witness in this respect Bolick's quick aboutface from using race to boost Thomas to condemning race-consciousness to defeat Lani Guinier. Just two years after Bush selected Thomas to sit on the Supreme Court, Clinton nominated Guinier to be the nation's lead civil rights attorney. One of the few African American professors at an elite law school, Guinier had headed the NAACP Legal Defense Fund's voting rights section and had written thoughtfully on democracy and the protection of minorities. But in a *Wall Street Journal* editorial that helped torpedo her nomination, Bolick accused Guinier of promoting "a complex racial spoils system" and described her as "a pro-quota, left-wing extremist."[40] Whereas Guinier did advocate race-consciousness, she opposed any fixed set-asides that resembled actual quotas. Nevertheless the "quota" charge carried heft as a rightwing buzzword long used to mischaracterize race-conscious remedies. Going one better, the *Wall Street Journal* added to the quota falsehood an even more tendentious and ugly term, selecting as a title for Bolick's editorial "Clinton's Quota Queens."[41] Guinier's nomination staggered under the weight of the "quota queen" obloquy, which conjoined an assault on affirmative action with the stereotype of black women as obnoxious and demanding welfare cheats. In Guinier's words, "I became Reagan's welfare queen tooling around the neighborhood in her Cadillac, mocking the hard work of others and the hard labor undertaken to produce this democratic system."[42] When Clinton failed to defend Guinier, and refused to allow her to defend herself, her nomination failed. Bolick was only too happy to prosecute Guinier on the charge of race-consciousness—notwithstanding that he himself relied on race to promote Thomas and advised using non-white plaintiffs to front conservative causes.

Shifting Sympathy

When Bolick wrote in 1990 about using black children as sympathetic plaintiffs, he did so to urge an evolution in conservative strategy. For too long, Bolick argued, insurgent conservative groups had held themselves out as representing aggrieved whites. Instead, he advocated, they could gain ground by pushing to the fore the "black schoolchild" over the "white firefighter who loses a promotion." More than two decades later, it's not clear that Bolick's intuition remains accurate about which of these two figures elicits more public sympathy.

When Obama nominated Judge Sonia Sotomayor for a position on the Supreme Court, she suffered fierce attack from the right. Sotomayor came under greatest fire for having once said that identity matters in how one judges the world. In her words: "I would hope that a wise Latina woman with the richness of her experiences would more often than not reach a better conclusion than a white male who hasn't lived that life."[43] Sotomayor's poor phrasing opened her up to attack, since it implied a qualitative ranking with Latinas making "better" rather than possibly different decisions than whites. Yet Sotomayor intended to espouse no hierarchy, nor did she mean that one's race deterministically shapes one's ideas. Sotomayor was simply arguing that experience and perspective—which are shaped by many things, surely including race, gender, and class—necessarily inform how judges (and everyone else) think about the difficult questions they confront. Because identity matters, this daughter of working-class Puerto Rican parents argued that judges have an obligation to consider their perspective, drawing from it what they can, while always attempting to transcend its limitations. Eliding these nuances, however, conservatives pounced: Sotomayor had said "Latina" and "white," and under their version of colorblindness, that made her remarks tantamount to racism.

Attracting slightly less attention, though more relevant to Bolick's sense of who most elicits public sympathy, conservatives also attacked Sotomayor for ruling against white firefighters in a high profile case. The firemen had alleged that the decision of New Haven, Connecticut, to set aside a poorly designed promotion exam, rather than to promote those who had done well under it, reflected racial discrimination. New Haven responded that the exam, which was only loosely connected to firefighting, produced racially skewed results that would lead to the almost exclusive promotion of whites. This outcome was not only racially divisive in a municipality with a large nonwhite population, New Haven argued, but it would expose the city to a lawsuit for racial discrimination against minority firefighters. Sotomayor agreed with New Haven, only to be overturned when the Supreme Court's five-justice conservative bloc sided with the complainants.[44]

Bringing this fight to Sotomayor's confirmation hearing, conservative senators elicited testimony from the lead plaintiff in the case, white firefighter Frank Ricci. Speaking before banks of microphones and cameras taking his tale to a national audience, Ricci related his narrative as one of vile discrimination and vindicated civil rights: "My colleagues and I have faced numerous discriminatory practices and policies that have been imposed by our department which has sadly and repeatedly succumbed to racial agendas and political pressure. . . . It was only through resort to the courts that our rights have been vindicated and that we gained what we were entitled to but previously were denied because of the color of our skin."[45]

Ricci's rendition of the conflict betrays many of the hallmarks of conservative racial discourse. Pressure to integrate the New Haven fire department emerged as "racial agendas and political pressure." Race itself reduced to "the color of our skin." Missing was any context, especially the long, bitter history of racial exclusion that has kept many fire departments, including New Haven's, disproportionately white. Instead, whites became the real victims of racial discrimination, and liberal government loomed as their greatest enemy.

Yet Ricci's testimony also warns of new lows to come. First, Ricci was not complaining about affirmative action, so long a target of conservative ire. Instead, Ricci sued—and at the Supreme Court won—because he felt that laws preventing racial discrimination had in fact discriminated against him. New Haven argued that civil rights laws required it to consider the racial impact of its promotion practices, and to review those practices carefully. Since the problematic promotion exam only roughly related to the jobs in question, New Haven concluded that it should set aside the results. But the conservative justices disagreed. Instead, they ruled that considering racial impact in order to avoid potential discrimination itself constituted racial discrimination. That bears repeating, though the logic induces vertigo: to consider race, even in order to *avoid* discrimination, is discrimination. The Supreme Court's long battle against affirmative action has almost been won. But the war will not stop. Instead, it seems likely to widen, broadening to an effort to gut laws that address racial discrimination. The Court's 2013 decision striking a crippling blow against the Voting Rights Act further exemplifies this developing campaign.[46]

Beyond legal doctrine, Ricci's well-received Senate testimony also seems to herald an important shift over the last few decades in how the public views whites who claim to be victims of reverse racism. Bolick in 1990 had a sense that whites who challenged racial remedies were viewed with disfavor by many, coming across as disgruntled at best and bigoted at worst. In contrast, plaintiffs like Frank Ricci are now feted as courageous heroes. To be sure, Ricci's narrative is not troubling because he's a bigot. It's disconcerting because, rather than seeing himself as harmed by a test and promotion procedure that ill-served everyone, he cast himself in the role of a racial victim.[47] Rather than give credence to New Haven's professed desire to fashion a fair promotion procedure, Ricci claimed to have been betrayed by a government knuckling under to self-serving pressure from minorities. It's disheartening that this story of white victimization, long part of the narrative of resistance to racial integration, has now attained sufficient cultural credibility to be accepted—and in turn sanctified and broadcast—by the highest court of the land as well as by the US Senate.

Dog whistle politics currently trails innovations in rightwing litigation strategy, only recently fully embracing techniques proposed in the 1990s of pushing nonwhite faces forward. When dog whistling catches up to the newest trend in colorblind litigation, it will find that the next evolution has gone back to putting whites at the forefront of racial complaints. The public seems long past the point of seeing white opponents of integration efforts as disgruntled and maybe even biased, and seems instead inclined to see them as sympathetic figures victimized by liberal racism.

Certainly, the solicitous treatment given to Abigail Fisher fit this pattern; she was the young white woman selected as the lead plaintiff in the 2013 University of Texas affirmative action case. It did not seem to matter that an aggressive conservative money machine backed her, and that she herself lacked the grades and test scores to have gotten into UT Austin, whether or not that institution practiced affirmative action.[48] Instead, her plain face, seemingly bare of makeup, her strawberry blonde bangs, and her heartfelt tale of a dream shattered by unfair racial quotas, seemed to tug at the nation's heartstring. Affirmative action was just wrong, the emotional narrative insisted, if it harms an innocent young person like Fisher. There seemed little appetite for stories showing she was not in fact harmed, and even less for explorations of the many young Americans helped by affirmative action. The nonwhite faces, and the white faces too, of those who have benefitted from integration remedies were never seen. Instead, a rightwing advocacy organization launched Fisher's story as one of racial discrimination against an innocent white, and a conservative majority—on and off the Court—accepted it at face value.

7

Makers and Takers:
The Tea Party
and Romney

Dog whistle politics surged after 2008. We see it in the Tea Party, and in how the Romney campaign conjoined racial demagoguery and robber baron politics, attacking Obama on welfare while favoring tax cuts for the rich, deregulation, and slashed social services.

After the 2008 election, many believed the Southern strategy was over and the power of the GOP broken.[1] In 2010, Republicans surged back. A modest resurgence was predictable; past history shows that a governing party that controls both the presidency and Congress routinely loses seats during mid-term elections. But the Democrats' "shellacking," to use President Obama's description, went well beyond the predicted losses, demonstrating instead a reinvigorated GOP. By all accounts, energy flooded back into conservative politics in the form of the Tea Party, a fast-spinning tornado of grass roots organizations, billionaire funders, and a partisan rightwing media juggernaut, Fox News. The voters who surged to the polls in 2010 to resurrect the moribund Republicans were energized to vote for the Tea Party, not the GOP—though nonetheless everyone they elected turned out to be a Republican. At the height of their revolt, "strong" Tea Party supporters amounted to one out of every five adults.[2] The intensity of support may have moderated, but even after the 2012 election, 23 percent of the public continued to have a "favorable" view of the Tea Party.[3]

■ THE TEA PARTY

What fueled the Tea Party tornado? Commentators have struggled to answer that question, blown off balance by the movement's swirling currents and the random rubbish it picked up. How to explain a backlash made up predominantly of older voters deeply concerned with protecting Medicare, yet fiercely energized to slash government? Maybe the Tea Party partisans were so disorganized and unsure of themselves that conservative operatives easily duped them, argued one critic.[4] What to say of the reappearance of John Birch-style paranoia, and even the rehabilitation of the John Birch Society itself, among voters on average more educated than the electorate as a whole? Maybe this is part of a deeper historical cycle largely independent of current dynamics, insisted another.[5] What accounts for a movement comprised in almost equal parts of social conservatives and libertarians, where the former yearn to stamp religion on every public surface and ache to see the state regulate contraception, abortion, and marriage, while the latter loathe religious infiltration of public life and fiercely oppose state intrusion into private lives? Maybe it's a genuine grass roots uprising of common folks, opined a third.[6] These answers all had two things in common: none was particularly persuasive, and all gave short shrift to the power of race. What happens if we look at the Tea Party through the lens of dog whistle politics?

THE RANT

On February 19, 2009, just weeks after Obama's inauguration, an obscure correspondent for CNBC delivered a blistering rant against a bailout program proposed by the new president to help shore up the faltering economy.[7] Rick Santelli's target wasn't the trillions of dollars in cash infusions and loan guarantees that George W. Bush gifted to the mega-banks—corporate behemoths that, having wrecked the economy, were nevertheless deemed "too big to fail."[8] Rather, he was incensed about Obama's proposal to create a modest fund to help individual homeowners make their mortgage payments and stay in their homes. From the floor of the Chicago Mercantile Exchange, Santelli lashed out, castigating the central government for "promoting bad behavior," and bellyaching that this was an effort "to subsidize the losers' mortgages." Why not instead "buy cars and buy houses in foreclosure and give them to people who might have a chance to actually *prosper* down the road, and reward people that could carry the water, instead of drink the water," he fumed. Santelli's complaint was clear: undeserving, unworthy people got themselves into a mess—and now Obama planned to reward them by taxing average, decent, hardworking Americans. Still shouting, Santelli turned from the camera to the traders on the floor who had been cheering his diatribe: "This is America! How many of you people want to pay for your neighbors' mortgage that has an extra bathroom and can't pay their bills? Raise their hand." As the traders booed, Santelli faced the camera anew, demanding to know, "President Obama, are you listening?" Santelli then capped his tirade by venturing that he might host "a Chicago Tea Party in July. All you capitalists that want to show up to Lake Michigan, I'm going to start organizing."[9]

Set aside that Santelli was calling for a revolt of the "capitalists" against the "losers," hardly a typical start for a populist uprising. Focus instead on the notion of a "Tea Party." The reference, of course, was to the 1773 Boston Tea Party, famously allied in folklore with the slogan "no taxation without representation." The symbolic power here was twofold: First was simply the appeal to the revolutionary era as a sacred moment that in turn sanctified contemporary politics. This tracks a dynamic on the right that the historian Jill Lepore terms "historical fundamentalism": "the belief that a particular and quite narrowly defined past—'the founding'—is ageless and sacred and to be worshipped; that certain historical texts—'the founding documents'—are to be read in the same spirit with which religious fundamentalists read, for instance, the Ten Commandments . . . and that political arguments grounded in appeals to the founding documents, as sacred texts, and to the Founding Fathers, as prophets, are therefore incontrovertible."[10]

The other symbolic strength lay in the slogan "no taxation without representation." When Santelli groped for language to express his opposition to Obama's proposed homeowner bailout, "tea parties" were already standard fare on rightwing menus. During the 1990s, rightwing groups had used the tea party imagery to protest taxes generally. In 2008, the term achieved even greater circulation on the far right, as the quixotic presidential campaign of the libertarian Ron Paul held rallies labeled "Tea Parties."[11] Yet if Santelli used an established term, he clearly struck a newly powerful chord. His rant went viral, and Tea Party rallies occurred across forty cities within the first eight days after Santelli's outburst.

Certainly some of the theme's power came from its opposition to taxes, especially taxes presented as subsidizing "bad behavior." This was the familiar dog whistle complaint that money from hardworking Americans was being siphoned off to reward minority freeloaders. A few months earlier, rightwing provocateur Ann Coulter had tied this theme directly to the foreclosure crisis, penning an article titled "They Gave Your Mortgage to a Less Qualified Minority."[12] The right was building a narrative that blamed poor nonwhites, not powerful banks, for crashing the financial sector, and Santelli was echoing this absurdity.

But the visceral force of the tea party framing also stemmed from the "without representation" element. When Obama won the presidency in 2008, he did so in a commanding fashion, winning the electoral vote 365 to 173 and taking 53 percent of the popular vote. It would seem ludicrous to claim that the new president did not "represent" the country; of course many did not vote for him, but it's axiomatic in a functioning democracy that the person who wins the majority of the vote is elected to represent the entire population. Yet "without representation" resonated powerfully. Not only did Santelli's supporters resent paying taxes to support society's "losers," they seethed that Obama was not *their* president; he did not represent *them*. The fire that put many Tea Partiers into the streets in 2009 and into the voting booths in 2010 was a fury at Obama himself—an opposition so deep it led many to firmly believe that Obama could not legitimately be president at all. An article of faith among Tea Partiers held that Obama was born outside the United States, and so was constitutionally barred from holding the presidency. This canard resisted repeated efforts to debunk it, no doubt because it was rooted less in reason than in the firm faith that this man simply could not lawfully be President of the United States.[13]

What Role for Race?

Why were Tea Partiers so incensed about Obama, so implacably opposed to his presidency? In one of the best studies of the Tea Party to date, Harvard sociologist Theda Skocpol and graduate student Vanessa Williamson closely investigated the movement, and concluded that despite the many contradictory positions of those in the uprising, virtually all were united in their hostility toward Obama. Barack Obama is "virtually the Devil incarnate for Tea Partiers," they reported.[14] But again, why this intense animosity?

Don't answer "racism," the Tea Partiers insist. At rally after rally, Tea Partiers ridiculed the idea that race explained their opposition to Obama. At a demonstration in Chicago, speakers "continually repeated that the Tea Party was not 'about race'—a message that received roars of approval from the nearly 100 percent Caucasian crowd."[15] At a rally in Boston, a black singer in a cowboy hat took the stage, warming up the crowd by shouting "I am not an African American." Strutting back and forth, he yelled "I am Lloyd Marcus, AMERICAAAAAN," drawing the word out to three times its normal length. Marcus then led the raucous crowd in singing what he termed the "National Tea Party Anthem," much of which centered on racial absolution: "When they call you a racist because you disagree," Marcus belted out, "that's just another one of their nasty tricks to silence you and me." Segueing to call and response, Marcus demanded of the crowd, "Are you all racists?" Fervently they screamed back "NO!" Breaking cadence, the black singer reassured them, "I know you're not."[16] The Tea Partiers know to an absolute moral certainty that they're not racists; indeed, they're the racial victims, constantly being falsely accused of racism.

Virtually every commentator who assessed the Tea Party noted the startling racial demographics of the activists—they were almost all white. A 2010 poll found that only 3 percent of Tea Partiers were Hispanic, while a meager 1 percent were black and 1 percent were Asian.[17] And virtually every commentator recorded the ubiquitous prevalence of caustic views on topics closely connected to race, for instance welfare, immigration, and Islam. Most then further noted that the Tea Partiers furiously denied that they were racist. And there, for the most part, the analyses stalled.[18] For instance, Skocpol and Williamson ended a section entitled "Racism in White, Black, and Brown" with an extended account of Mandy Hewes, a white Tea Party activist from Virginia who generously opened her home to foster children from abusive households, including a young black boy who came into their lives at 13, and whom Mandy lovingly referred to as her son. "The stereotype of Tea Party activists as unreconstructed racists—as people who react to politics and policy only through racial oppositions—simply does not jibe with the life story of this very conservative white woman who opens her home to minority teenagers from troubled backgrounds," Skocpol and Williamson concluded.[19]

No doubt they're correct that very few Tea Partiers, so earnest and insistent in denying racism, were what these scholars call "unreconstructed racists"—a term that seems to conjure hooded figures from the past, or violent neo-Nazi skinheads today. Indeed, the story of Mandy Hewes provides an important corrective to some of the liberal invective often used to describe Tea Party supporters. Scathing critics caricatured Tea Partiers as "relatively well off and Middle American (not particularly disadvantaged), very predominantly white, significantly racist, militaristic, narcissistically selfish, vicious in [their] hostility to the poor, deeply undemocratic, profoundly ignorant and deluded, heavily paranoid, [and] wooden-headed."[20] This is obviously overwrought and unfair. On the contrary, the vast majority of Tea Partiers were regular folks. But that does not mean that they entirely escaped racism's scourge. I'm reminded of my travels in South Africa and Namibia where I met kind people who nonetheless held deeply racist views—people I imagine just like Mandy Hewes. To acknowledge the basic decency of the Tea Partiers is a good place to start, not to end, a conversation about racism and dog whistle politics.

Tea Party fury may not have come from old-style, hate-every-black-person racism, but it nevertheless stemmed from the racial hostilities mobilized by dog whistle politics. To be sure, some Tea Partiers would have been out there screaming for the dismantling of social welfare programs no matter what, as part of the fringe opposition to the New Deal that had never fully gone away.[21] But this fringe did not suddenly move to the center of American politics on its own. Rather, dog whistle racism helped bring it back. The vast majority of those identifying with the Tea Party were not dyed-in-the-wool Goldwaterites and last-gasp Birchers. They were Wallace voters and Reagan Democrats. They were persons stampeded by racial anxieties into fearing government and demonizing liberalism.

Consider the core concerns of the Tea Partiers. At root, four hatreds animated the movement:

- Welfare. The stock dog whistle frame of government payouts to the undeserving taken from the taxes of the hardworking suffused Tea Party rallies, with the raucous crowds absolutely certain which side of the equation they represented (Social Security income and Medicare benefits notwithstanding). "You are not ENTITLED To What I have EARNED," proclaimed the signs they waved at rallies.[22]
- Undocumented immigrants. Brown-skinned hordes taking over the country served as a focal point for fears about welfare and crime.[23] Pithily combining the immigrant, welfare, and crime themes into a single vicious slogan, a sign at a Tea Party rally in San Diego proclaimed "Freeloading Illegals are Raping U.S. Taxpayers."[24]
- Arab Muslims. More than as a foreign threat, this hobgoblin represented the enemy within the nation.[25] Invoking the modern know-nothing spirit of the Tea Party, one protester in Manhattan thrust aloft a sign proclaiming "All I Need to Know About Islam I Learned on 9/11."[26]
- Barack Obama. Obama represented for many the perfect storm of the above animosities.[27] Because he embodied so many evils, no slander seemed strong enough, a dynamic that contributed to Tea Partiers frequently comparing Obama to Adolf Hitler, perhaps the closest Western analog to evil incarnate. "Obama = Hitler" read one widely reproduced poster; a more ambitious version of the metaphor claimed "The American Taxpayers are the Jews for Obama's Ovens."[28]

The contradictions others have noted in the Tea Party, so difficult to resolve without reference to race, become intelligible when looked at through the lens of dog whistle politics. Tea Partiers could oppose big government yet insist that Social Security and Medicare were sacrosanct because they continued to see "welfare" as something liberals doled out to lazy nonwhites. They weren't hostile to the New Deal programs on which they relied; on the contrary, like generations before, they supported core New Deal values and many safety net programs. What they resented was the sense that their taxes were being wasted on undeserving minorities. Likewise, John Birch theories could recrudesce because over the past decades these hysterical fears of a dire threat from government gained credibility by being repeatedly tied to stories about the state forcing unwanted integration and being in hock to special interest racial groups. Finally, social conservatives and libertarians could come together because they did so against liberalism as a common enemy: for "traditional" conservatives, the enemy was liberalism and its effort to force tolerance of minorities (and other disfavored groups); for libertarians, the target was liberalism's drive to regulate individual behavior, including by limiting "freedom of association" or the right to racially discriminate. The pervasive concerns about welfare, crime, illegal aliens, Arab Muslims, and a black president strongly suggested that it was racial anxiety that provided the heat roiling the many disparate currents within the Tea Party.

THE POLITICIANS AND BILLIONAIRES BEHIND THE HATE

Even granting the existence of considerable grassroots energy, the Tea Party would not have happened without contributions from opportunistic politicians as well as the moneyed interests that threw their weight behind the rebellion. In 2010, numerous Republican candidates eagerly embraced and promoted the Tea Party brand. Some like Rand Paul, the son of the libertarian Ron Paul, were no doubt quite rightwing—and also steeped in white racial resentments.[29] Others like Scott Brown, the moderate Republican Senate candidate who won Edward Kennedy's seat in Massachusetts, probably married into the Tea Party out of convenience. The advantage was clear: while the GOP was a tainted brand after the Bush years, there was widespread enthusiasm behind the Tea Party. In a 2010 survey of Tea Party partisans, just over half were willing to own the Republican label.[30] Many preferred to call themselves independents. Their actual independence was a fiction, though. If they were "independent," it was because these Tea Partiers were to the *right* of the GOP and resented its supposed capitulation to Washington politics, not because there was a chance they might vote for Democrats. In the voting both, Tea Partiers consistently pulled the lever for Republicans, and on Tea Party coattails the GOP regained the House and came out of 2010 resurrected and emboldened.

Beyond Republican politicians looking for a new label, from the outset rightwing advocacy groups rushed to take advantage of the ire represented in the popular embrace of Rick Santelli's rant. They saw in this outburst a new opportunity to move their agenda further into the mainstream of American politics, cloaking their plutocrat-friendly priorities in the mantle of populist rage. The institutional far right moved quickly to provide financial resources, organizational capacity building, talking points, and speakers to the emerging movement. It's doubtful the Tea Party could have coalesced and exercised much influence without the varied resources provided by moneyed elites—resources that allowed funders not only to shape the ideology of the Tea Party, but also to handpick many of the political candidates Tea Party groups came to endorse. According to a Republican campaign consultant, David and Charles Koch, petro-chemical billionaire backers of rightwing causes, "gave the money that founded [the Tea Party]. It's like they put the seeds in the ground. Then the rainstorm comes, and the frogs come out of the mud—and they're our candidates!"[31] As investigative journalist Jane Mayer concludes, "the anti-government fervor infusing the 2010 elections represents a political triumph for the Kochs. By giving money to 'educate,' fund, and organize Tea Party protesters, they have helped turn their private agenda into a mass movement."[32] Or as David Axelrod, a senior adviser to Obama, acidly remarked, "this is a grassroots citizens' movement brought to you by a bunch of oil billionaires."[33]

Unfair and Hyper-Partisan

The Tea Party also found a crucial ally in rightwing media, from shock radio to the editorial page of the *Wall Street Journal*. Chief among these was Fox News, cheerleading every step of the way. In 2010 Fox carried all ten of the top most-viewed cable news programs in the country, with nearly one quarter of all Americans reporting that they regularly watched Fox News. These one-in-four Americans tended to be older and were almost all white, with less than two percent of Fox viewers identifying as African American.[34] Many of Fox's most outspoken partisans, such as Rush Limbaugh and Sean Hannity, also reached millions more via their radio programs.

Fox News picked up the Tea Party theme within a week of Santelli's mid-February rant, celebrating and exaggerating the rallies that almost immediately followed across the country.[35] During the month of March, Fox News began to *advertise* upcoming Tea Party rallies that would occur on Tax Day, April 15. "Advertise" seems apposite, because Fox was hardly reporting on news; these events had not yet happened. Instead, it seemed to be promoting the upcoming rallies, promising that its celebrities would be broadcasting live from different venues: Glenn Beck from the Alamo in San Antonio; Neil Cavuto in Sacramento, California; Greta Van Susteren in Washington, D.C.; and Sean Hannity from Atlanta, Georgia. Fox pushed the rallies through hundreds of promotional announcements. These ads, purportedly touting the channel's upcoming coverage of the events, served to recruit and fire up participants. Here's a script from one of the spots:

> ANNOUNCER: April fifteenth, all across the country, Americans are making their voices heard. In California, Texas, Georgia, Washington, D.C., citizens are standing up and saying "no" to more taxes and demanding real economic solutions.
>
> April fifteenth: As Tea Parties sweep the nation on Tax Day, we're there with total fair-and-balanced coverage—live. What is the fate of our nation? We report. You decide.[36]

In the delicate formative period when a Tea Party movement would either gel or fade, Fox nursed the incipient revolt: As Skocpol and Williamson concluded, "Fox served as a kind of social movement orchestrator, during what is always a dicey early period for any new protest effort."[37] The result was a Tea Party movement organized, cheered on, celebrated, and amplified by Fox News, and made up overwhelmingly of Fox News viewers.

Fox's role as midwife to the Tea Party reflects the vision of the mastermind behind Fox News, Roger Ailes, and tracing his rise offers additional insight into how Fox connects with conservative dog whistle politics. In 1968, the young Ailes was an executive producer of *The Mike Douglas Show*, and was present when candidate Richard Nixon arrived in the studios for a guest appearance at the beginning of the campaign season. Nixon was nervous about this appearance because during the first-ever televised presidential debate in 1960, between he and the telegenic John F. Kennedy, television had been unkind to Nixon. The hot lights had made him sweat, and the bright glare caused his dark eyes to recede and his jowls to overshadow his face; some thought that first debate ultimately cost Nixon the 1960 election. Now, as he waited for his cue to walk out on stage, he bemoaned the whole enterprise, remarking "it's a shame a man has to use gimmicks like this to get elected." A self-assured Ailes shot back, "television is not a gimmick, and if you think it is, you'll lose again." Within a few days, Nixon's campaign hired him to help get their candidate elected.[38]

Ailes' first innovation was to fabricate town-hall style meetings under tightly controlled environments. The press was excluded from these events, to keep them from reporting on things like the special lighting favoring Nixon, the cameras, the pancake powder, and the warm-up man giving pre-appearance instructions to the audience of Nixon loyalists posing as disinterested citizens—"Now, when Mr. Nixon comes in, I want you to tear the place apart. Sound like ten thousand people. I'm sure, of course, that you'll also want to stand up at that point. So what do you say we try it now? And let me hear it."[39] With the supportive crowd as a backdrop, Nixon would field questions from and banter with a small panel of voters. Those on the panel were not paid actors, but Ailes vetted them carefully, and assembled them with a keen eye toward projecting a demographically sanitized version of America. In his 1969 exposé on the Nixon campaign, *The Selling of the President*, Joe McGinniss described one of these staged events in Philadelphia.[40] He captured Ailes saying that the panel couldn't have more than one African American, and Ailes was also reluctant to include a Jew, explaining that the Nixon campaign wanted "to go easy on the Jews for awhile." Yet Ailes was not just constructing an idealized racial montage. He also wanted to trigger white anxiety directly, and hit upon a casting idea to do so: "A good, mean, Wallaceite cabdriver. Wouldn't that be great? Some guy to sit there and say, 'Awright, Mac, what about these niggers?'"[41] The plan was for Nixon to abhor the statement and then to endorse a "moderate" version of the opinion. Ailes worked a nearby taxi stand till he found his cabby, though in the end his plant disappointed by asking about foreign policy.

Ailes' showmanship helped propel Nixon to victory, and also further deepened the Madison Avenue product-placement feel of modern campaigns. After Nixon's victory, Ailes served as an adviser to the White House and the Republican National Committee, while also beginning his own production company pitched to Republicans seeking election. His next career step, though, was perhaps even more directly influential on the evolution of Fox News.

Lewis Powell's galvanizing memo on conservatism in the United States had warned big business that "national television networks should be monitored."[42] Joseph Coors, the ultra-conservative beer magnate, resolved to go one better; rather than monitor the news, he would fabricate it and thus provide a "corrective" to network news he saw as being slanted toward the left. Coors' production company, Television News Incorporated, initially struggled to find and retain news staff, with many TVN reporters believing that the Coors family wanted a rightwing news network. Indeed Coors did, even going so far as to have Heritage Foundation officials interview potential TVN employees. Two years in, Coors hired Ailes to be the network's news director. According to one

TVN staffer, "the Coors people trust Ailes because of his affiliation with the Republicans, and because he's not a newsman. They don't trust newsmen." TVN was before its time, both in terms of the costs of producing and distributing news, and also in terms of the market for its partisan newscasts. In 1975, the enterprise folded.[43] Nevertheless, an early model for a partisan news organization had been tested, and Ailes was there to lead and to learn.

Two decades later, in 1996 media magnate Rupert Murdoch hired Ailes to run a new start-up, Fox News. At the outset, some effort was made to maintain independence between the reporters and the commentators, who were relentlessly hostile to Bill Clinton's presidency and, later, unrestrained cheerleaders for George W. Bush. By Obama's 2008 election, Fox News was a behemoth, the undisputed champion of cable news. Also by then, the flimsy wall between the news and opinion sections of Fox had crumbled.[44] The whole endeavor became a hyper-partisan enterprise that reflected Ailes' politics. As Rush Limbaugh exulted at a dinner honoring Ailes in 2009: "One man has established a culture for 1,700 people who believe in it, who follow it, who execute it. Roger Ailes cannot do everything. Roger Ailes is not on the air. Roger Ailes does not ever show up on camera, and yet everybody who does is a reflection of him."[45]

Under Ailes' influence, Fox has engaged in incessant race-baiting. Consider the following brief catalog. Fox has trafficked in racially tinged attacks on Obama, including the spurious claim that he was educated in an Islamic madrasa; that he harbors "a deep-seated hatred for white people" and is "a racist"; that his father was "a wife-beating alcoholic who didn't bother to get a divorce before marrying the next woman and having a few more kids"; and the ad nauseam insinuation that Obama is not a US citizen.[46] Fox also repeatedly depicts immigrants as criminals and threats to national security, while hyping fears of a de facto invasion and the possible annexation of the Southwest by Mexico.[47] In addition, Fox actively foments the Arab Muslim caricature, repeatedly linking Islam to terrorism and inflaming passions against Muslim mosques and cultural centers in the United States. Here's Glenn Beck's tirade against a proposed Islamic cultural center in lower Manhattan, for Beck hallowed ground as the general location of the collapsed World Trade Center towers: "If you wanted to unite people, you don't spit in their face. You don't spit in their face. . . . After you've killed 3,000 people, you're going to now build your mosque on there, really?"[48]

Beyond a seemingly intentional policy to agitate the public with racial propaganda, Fox News also demonstrates a strong propensity to propagate falsehoods about liberal policies. Perhaps the most striking example is the claim aired numerous times on Fox that the health care reform passed under Obama would include "death panels," medical tribunals that, according to Glenn Beck, would "tell Grandma and Grandpa . . . how and when to die." This macabre lie captured the imagination of many, with a September 2009 poll showing that 41 percent of respondents were convinced death panels were part of the health reform bill.[49] Research shows that Fox News viewers are systematically misinformed about key public policy issues, leading viewers to develop undue animosity towards liberal governance. After the 2010 elections, those "who watched Fox News almost daily" were much more likely than non-viewers to believe significant falsehoods about the stimulus plan, the state of the economy, the health care law, climate change, and taxes.[50]

Connecting Fox back to the Tea Party movement, Fox helped to foment an activist cadre agitated by racial provocations and misinformed about key facts. Much of the racial hysteria swirling among Tea Party supporters seemed connected to propaganda pumped out by Fox. Likewise, many of the false facts about government programs and policies, and about the president himself, grew out of Fox reporting. The Fox audience and the Tea Party warriors were often the same persons.

* * *

To summarize the discussion of the Tea Party, the movement reflected the confluence of four forces: First, the anger and fear of everyday white folks, a few of them Goldwaterite holdovers or principled libertarians, but most Reagan Democrats—persons whose political conservatism was directly molded by racially infected fears of a liberal government run by a black president. Second, opportunistic Republicans seeking a new label for a damaged brand. Third, rightwing billionaires like the Koch brothers, with their well-funded propaganda machines, who saw in the fear and anger directed at Obama a new opportunity to cast their agenda in populist terms. Finally, Fox News and the rightwing media machine more generally, which promoted the movement and also helped racially agitate and misinform its soldiers. Reviewing all of this, we can now answer a basic question: was the Tea Party driven by conservatism or by race? The answer is emphatically yes. The Tea Party that reenergized the GOP in 2010 and that implacably attacked Obama turned out to be a familiar nemesis of liberalism and the middle class—even if most of its street-level partisans were middle class themselves. Inextricably combining conservatism *and* racism, the Tea Party was almost wholly a creature of rightwing dog whistle politics.

■ VOTE SUPPRESSION

Racial demagoguery and culture-war politics do not exhaust the tactics used by the right to end-run democracy. The same drive is also evident in efforts to suppress the votes of the poor and of nonwhites.

In 2008, Catherine Engelbrecht helped found a Tea Party group, King Street Patriots, and became obsessed with the possibility that fraudulent voting was putting the wrong people in charge. Engelbrecht describes herself as someone who was long apolitical, raising two children, attending church, and running a small business with her husband in Texas. "Then in 2008, I don't know, something clicked," she said, adding, "I saw our country headed in a direction that, for whatever reason—it didn't hit me until 2008—this really threatens the future of our children." Soon after its founding, Engelbrecht's group received funding from Americans for Prosperity, an organization backed by the billionaire Koch brothers. The King Street Patriot's initial focus was the congressional district in Houston represented by Sheila Jackson, an African American Democrat. On Election Day in 2010, dozens of members showed up in the district to challenge voters. Predictably, "the influx of white election observers in black neighborhoods caused friction with voters and poll workers, bringing back memories of a time when racial intimidation at the polls was commonplace in the South."[51] Jackson went on to win in this heavily Democratic district, but not before calling in the Department of Justice to investigate voter intimidation.

By 2012, Engelbrecht's group had evolved into True the Vote, a national organization dedicated to ferreting out "voter fraud."[52] It hardly seemed to matter that there is no evidence illegal voting occurs on anything greater than a freak-of-nature scale. Despite intensive, highly motivated efforts to find voter fraud, the data suggests that voter impersonation happens with roughly the same frequency that persons are struck and killed by lightening.[53] Nevertheless, by the summer and fall of 2012, True the Vote was teaching volunteers how to challenge voters across the country. In one training session in the swing state of Ohio, a senior adviser "unleashed her vitriol" at those protesting the close scrutiny they were giving to black communities, complaining that "when anybody pays a little bit of attention to the fact that there's a high level of fraud coming out of the African-American communities, they say: 'Oh, you're a racist. You don't want black people to vote.'"[54] Yet underlying the panic that crystalized with Obama's election in 2008, there does seem to be a queasy despair that minorities are using the ballot box to steal the country.

True the Vote also agonized over voting fraud—and even legal voting—by welfare recipients. During the fall of 2011, True the Vote hosted conservative columnist Matthew Vadum, author of a blistering essay entitled "Registering The Poor To Vote Is Un-American."[55] Vadum's thesis:

> Registering them to vote is like handing out burglary tools to criminals. It is profoundly antisocial and un-American to empower the nonproductive segments of the population to destroy the country—which is precisely why Barack Obama zealously supports registering welfare recipients to vote. . . . Encouraging those who burden society to participate in elections isn't about helping the poor. It's about helping the poor to help themselves to others' money.[56]

Sounding a similar note, rocker and rightwing activist Ted Nugent published an op-ed in the *Washington Times* immediately after Obama's re-election urging the country to "stop the insanity by suspending the right to vote of any American who is on welfare. Once they get off welfare and are self-sustaining, they get their right to vote restored. No American on welfare should have the right to vote for tax increases on those Americans who are working and paying taxes to support them. That's insane."[57]

True the Vote and Engelbrecht demonstrate that the campaign against voting fraud is intimately connected with dog whistle concerns, yet to focus on True the Vote is to capture only the most recent activist gloss. Practices of vote suppression go much deeper and spread much further. For instance, many states still have on the books laws from the era of convict leasing that strip convicted felons of the right to vote. Far from becoming outdated and ineffective in reducing nonwhite voting power, the modern war on crime dramatically increased the disempowering impact of such laws. A 2008 report from the Brennan Center for Justice warned that because of felon disenfranchisement laws, "three in ten of the next generation of African-American men can expect to lose the right to vote at some point in their lifetime."[58]

In the wake of Obama's 2008 election, the GOP became even more aggressive in seeking to disenfranchise minorities and the poor through various mechanisms, including restrictive voter ID laws. In 2011, 38 states introduced legislation likely to impede voting by these groups. This extraordinary number reflected a concerted effort on the part of some Republican officials—and their billionaire backers—to drive down voting by Democratic constituencies. "One of the most pervasive political movements going on outside Washington today is the disciplined, passionate, determined effort of Republican governors and legislators to keep most of you from voting next time," Bill Clinton admonished in the summer of 2012. Clinton warned, "There has never been in my lifetime, since we got rid of the poll tax and all the Jim Crow burdens on voting, the determined effort to limit the franchise that we see today."[59] Spearheading the effort was the American Legislative Exchange Council (ALEC), with its members introducing copycat legislation in state houses across the nation. Financed partly by the Koch brothers, ALEC was founded by Paul Weyrich, who also co-founded the Heritage Foundation. Weyrich memorably outlined his perspective on voting during the election cycle that first put Reagan into the White House. Speaking at the Southern Baptist Convention in 1980, Weyrich told supporters "I don't want everybody to vote." Making sure no one missed the point, Weyrich continued: "As a matter of fact, our leverage in the elections quite candidly goes up as the voting populace goes down."[60]

Adding to their arsenal, gerrymandering provides another way for conservatives to secure power. In the 2012 election, in only the second such reversal since World War II, the party whose candidates collectively won the popular vote ended up a minority in the House of Representatives. Through gerrymandered districts, the Republicans won control of the House by a 234 to 201 margin, yet the Democrats cumulatively received 1.4 million more votes.[61] The GOP much more than the Democrats has been assiduous in carving out favorable districts, and by this stratagem alone they may continue to control the House and thus obstruct the will of voters for years to come.[62]

In the summer of 2013, the Supreme Court effectively gutted the core enforcement mechanism of the Voting Rights Act, the federal statute that in the runup to the previous election had proved critical in blocking the efforts of Republican-controlled legislatures to disenfranchise minority voters through ID laws and other strategies. Enacted in 1965, the design of the VRA reflected a core insight: racial discrimination constantly evolves. In keeping with this, the Act did not stop with listing proscribed practices, but went on to provide that any changes in voting by jurisdictions with an established history of minority disenfranchisement had to be reviewed before they could take effect. The five-justice conservative majority rendered this provision inoperable by declaring that it treated the covered jurisdictions unfairly—times have changed, the majority lectured, and so, Congress must change the coverage formula.[63] Neither this Congress, nor any we are likely to have anytime soon, is likely to do so, as the conservative justices knew full well. But still, the majority had a point, and it's the point emphasized by the Act itself: times change, and so do techniques for suppressing the votes of minorities. Today, far from being restricted to Southern states, efforts to drive down voting connected to racial conservatism are now a national phenomenon, and these schemes target not just minorities but the poor as well.

What's the relationship between dog whistle politics on the one hand, and vote suppression and gerrymandering on the other? Conservatives use dog whistling to fool a large swath of voters, and deploy the other tactics to reduce the voting power of everyone else. In each case, these strategies reflect a disdain for democracy as an inconvenience to be manipulated or, failing that, directly thwarted.

■ ROMNEY AND RYAN

On the one-year anniversary of Occupy Wall Street's eruption onto the national stage, a year to the day after protesters took over Zuccotti Park in lower Manhattan to theatrically condemn growing income inequality in the United States, a video began to circulate of Republican presidential candidate Mitt Romney addressing wealthy donors at a $50,000-a-plate fundraiser. With timing this impeccable, it was tempting to think it was a spoof, a brilliant piece of performance art. But, no, it was real: here was Romney talking to the mega-rich, most of the video blurred but Romney sharply in focus.

> There are 47 percent of the people who will vote for the president no matter what . . . 47 percent who are with him, who are dependent upon government, who believe that they are victims, who believe the government has a responsibility to care for them, who believe that they are entitled to healthcare, to food, to housing, to you-name-it. That that's an entitlement. And the government should give it to them. And they will vote for this president no matter what.[64]

Romney's incredulous tone made health care, food, and housing sound like luxury goods being pilfered by the lazy. He continued: those people "pay no income tax" and "so our message of low taxes doesn't connect." His bottom line: "my job is not to worry about those people. I'll never convince them they should take personal responsibility and care for their lives."[65]

The 47 percent figure apparently came from a Tax Policy Center report that found that 46.4 percent of households paid no income tax in 2011. Yet over 80 percent of those households paid taxes for Social Security and Medicare, sometimes totaling over 14 percent of their wages, meaning some paid taxes at a higher rate than Romney.[66] This was not a detail Romney cared to admit. Instead, as the *New York Times* editorialist David Brooks observed, "Romney, who criticizes President Obama for dividing the nation, divided the nation into two groups: the makers and the moochers."[67] It is not clear whether Romney believed his own country-club prattle of winners and losers, or simply believed that this is what the millionaires in his audience wanted to hear. Either way, it was a testament to the triumph of dog whistle politics.

How so, if Romney disparaged half the country and never mentioned race? On one level, the answer lies in the language of dependency, entitlement, and lack of responsibility. It's clear from his larger campaign that Romney understood the power of such coded language. He seemed to learn from the primary contest, where Newt Gingrich made hay by lambasting Obama as the food stamp president. Seeking to make welfare a major issue in the race, during the 2012 summer Romney produced several TV ads slamming Obama for allegedly ending the requirement that welfare recipients actively seek employment. "Under Obama's plan, you wouldn't have to work and wouldn't have to train for a job. They just send your welfare check and 'welfare to work' goes back to being plain old welfare," said one ad.[68] This claim was factually false, though the facts hardly seemed to matter because the public was responding, so Romney kept hammering away at welfare for weeks after the charge was debunked.[69] During this crucial season, his campaign poured half their precious advertising dollars into the welfare ads.[70] "We're not going to let our campaign be dictated by fact-checkers," one Romney pollster infamously blustered.[71] It was for this relatively crude racial demagoguery that many commentators criticized Romney. His welfare ads were sharply attacked as dog whistle politics by a range of figures, from established scholars such as Thomas Edsall to media commentators like Chris Matthews and Joan Walsh.[72]

But there is another level of dog whistle politics evident in Romney's campaign, a deeper connection far more consequential to the middle class yet completely unseen by most critics. Romney's true debt to dog whistle politics lay in his ability to garner widespread support while espousing plutocratic priorities. Like a reincarnated Barry Goldwater tilting against the New Deal, Romney cast himself as a champion of the middle class, promising rescue from the economic crisis and a new era of prosperity. But what were his actual proposals? Favoring sweeping pronouncements over revealing detail, Romney reiterated three themes: he would slash taxes (while also balancing the budget); he would prune away government regulation and even excess government itself, liberating the engine of private enterprise; and he would pare government entitlement programs that transferred resources to the least productive elements in society. These were hardly prescriptions likely to help the great bulk of the middle class, especially if understood as families with incomes below six figures. Instead, Romney effectively campaigned on the promise to enact the policy preferences of society's moguls: tax cuts for the rich; deregulation; reduced social spending.

Even more than Romney, his anointed running mate, the young Wisconsin representative Paul Ryan, espoused extreme policies. Consider Ryan's proposed budget plan. A version passed the House of Representatives in the spring of 2012 on a near party-line vote, thus making clear during the campaign season the Republican Party's priorities. Talking of budget deficits in apocalyptic terms, Ryan proposed huge cuts to Medicaid, a program that covers the medical expenses of many disabled and elderly Americans—cuts so deep that potentially 28 million people would have lost medical coverage.[73] He further proposed reducing food stamps for poor families and college aid to students. Perhaps most explosively, he advocated converting Medicare's guarantee of health care for the elderly into a system of vouchers with a fixed value, which would have effectively ended the guarantee of medical care and left many retirees struggling to cover rising costs in their waning years. In all, 62 percent of his budget savings were to come from cuts to aid to the poor—a figure that does not include the savings from restructuring Medicare.[74] "More than any other politician today," Robert Reich wrote in a scorching rebuke, "Paul Ryan exemplifies the social Darwinism at the core of today's Republican Party: Reward the rich, penalize the poor, let everyone else fend for themselves. Dog eat dog."[75]

Pushing beyond reducing social spending, Ryan's budget threatened to suffocate the federal government overall. According to a Congressional Budget Office report, Ryan's budget path anticipated by 2050 the virtual end to all federal government aside from Social Security, a much-reduced health care system, and an engorged defense establishment. "That includes [cutting] everything from veterans' programs to medical and scientific research, highways, education, nearly all programs for low-income families and individuals other than Medicaid, national parks, border patrols, protection of food safety and the water supply, law enforcement, and the like."[76] Ryan and the GOP seized on supposedly dire budget deficits to justify drastically shrinking the federal government "down to the size where it could be drowned in a bathtub," to retrieve Grover Norquist's imagery. To this extent, the budget was a fake, a set of ideological commitments in the form of budget, but completely unworkable as a genuine fiscal blueprint. Few believed that cuts this draconian would be enacted, let alone indefinitely sustained. Nevertheless, Ryan's budget was completely genuine in indicating hostility toward government as a political priority.

The budget also revealed another priority: tax cuts for the very wealthy. Despite all the scare talk of a debt doomsday that necessitated reduced social spending and government's virtual elimination, Ryan's budget included sweeping tax cuts that dwarfed his proposed savings, cuts that threatened to *add* $4.6 trillion to the federal deficit over the next decade.[77] Moreover, these tax rollbacks were to be exclusively geared to the wealthiest Americans. The nonpartisan Tax Policy Center estimated that under Ryan's plan individuals earning more than $1 million a year on average would be able to keep an additional $295,874 annually.[78] Meanwhile, by eliminating deductions especially valuable to the working poor and the middle class, Ryan's plan would have effectively *raised* taxes on the vast majority of citizens.[79]

Ryan's budget might be a laughing matter if he were just another rightwing think tank mercenary, like those at the Heritage Foundation who apparently helped prepare his proposal.[80] (Gushing over Ryan's selection, a research director at the Heritage Foundation swooned that Ryan "is the good think-tanker-as-politician."[81]) Ryan's budget might still be good for a rueful chuckle if he had been selected as a vice-presidential candidate *despite* his priorities. Yet it seems that it was precisely his budget that made Ryan a bold, attractive choice to Romney. With his forthright call to stiff the poor, reward the exceptionally rich, and virtually eliminate much of government, Ryan energized the conservative base that had its doubts about the maybe-moderate Romney—who after all had overseen a push toward universal health insurance as the governor of liberal Massachusetts. In terms of popular support, Ryan was a Tea Party favorite, with his boyish good looks, his limpid blue eyes, and his sincere promises to reduce government and abolish taxes on the rich. More importantly, Ryan also came with the support of rightwing kingmakers and think tanks, groups among whom Ryan but not Romney moved easily.[82] Ryan became the vice-presidential candidate because of, not despite, his severe social vision, his cynicism in invoking the national debt to hurt the poor while vitiating taxes for the wealthy, and his singular ability to propose budget fantasies with a straight face and a firm voice.

In their talk of makers and takers, Romney and Ryan were mouthing the shibboleths of an extreme, even anarchic vision of society. In this vision, the rich are justified in disdaining the poor; in revering themselves as the true producers; in retreating to their gated compounds and neighborhoods to insulate themselves from contact with the unwashed; and in hoarding their immense wealth for themselves and their children, dispossessing the masses. It was a nineteenth century vision nurtured through the twentieth century by a few socially delusional billionaires, convinced, like Romney himself, that "I have inherited nothing. Everything I earned I earned the old fashioned way."[83] It was, in a word, the vision of *Atlas Shrugged*, Ayn Rand's fantasy world in which the great industrial titans retreat to their fortified valley while the world of the moochers comes crashing down around them.[84] "I grew up reading Ayn Rand," Ryan said in a 2005 speech, openly touting a romance with Rand that began predictably in adolescence. "It taught me quite a bit about who I am and what my value systems are, and what my beliefs are," Ryan enthused. He even credited Rand with inspiring his political career: "The reason I got involved in public service, by and large, if I had to credit one thinker, one person, it would be Ayn Rand. And the fight we are in here, make no mistake about it, is a fight of individualism versus collectivism."[85]

Individualism versus collectivism? Loony! Or so the American public thought in the 1950s and 1960s when members of the John Birch Society mouthed these hyperbolic words, back when they were jousting with Eisenhower's expansion of Social Security and Johnson's Great Society programs. Yet half a century later, nearly 60 percent of whites voted for a Republican ticket wedded to this regressive, dated vision. Romney won the votes of three out of every five white voters; won among white men, white women, and white youth; and won a majority of the white vote in every state in the union save four. Only two candidates have done notably better among whites since dog whistling began: Richard Nixon in his 1972 landslide and Ronald Reagan in his 1984 re-election. The power of contemporary dog whistle politics is manifest when Romney and Ryan could campaign as an amalgam of Goldwater and Rand, and by doing so win a supermajority amid white voters. Nothing testifies to dog whistle racism's transformation of American politics over the last half century so much as the recent willingness of three out of five white voters to support tax cuts for the super-rich, reduced social services for everyone, and a dramatic rollback of all government.

Of course dog whistle racism was not the sole factor at work over the last five decades. Major dislocations in the national and global economy played important roles, as did the increasing penetration of money in the political system. In addition, politicians and plutocrats have always used more than just race to stampede voters. Consider the following round up of Ryan's positions: "Though best known as an architect of conservative fiscal policy, Representative Paul D. Ryan has also been an ardent, unwavering foe of abortion rights, has tried to cut off federal money for family planning, has opposed same-sex marriage and has championed the rights of gun owners."[86] Abortion, contraception, same-sex marriage, guns—each of these too has emerged as an indispensable culture war prod used to whip up voter frenzy by politicians indebted to society's magnates and at war with the New Deal.

While it hasn't been dog whistle racism in isolation that transmuted American politics, in the roughly half-century since Goldwater's defeat, it's no accident that hostility toward New Deal liberalism has moved from the fringes to the center especially among whites. Among minorities, 93 percent of blacks, 71 percent of Latinos, and 73 percent of Asians voted against Romney and Ryan. Yet when these politicians talked about makers and takers to broad swaths of the white population, many of them in financial distress and in desperate need of government assistance, they received rousing applause. Dog whistle racism has helped convince many whites, arguably even a majority, that the greatest danger they face comes from a liberal government in hock to minorities, rather than from concentrated wealth and its plutocratic agenda.

The next chapter asks why so many whites fall prey to racial appeals. The one after that asks whether Obama has a good strategy for responding.

8

What's the Matter with White Voters? Commonsense Racism

At base, dog whistle politics exploits race to lure middle-class whites into voting for politicians allied with the rich and powerful. Why do white voters fall for the trick? This chapter explores how race works at the level of those who "hear" dog whistle appeals.

The certainty that Reagan Democrats vote against their own interests runs broadly through liberal complaints about modern politics. Exemplifying this, Thomas Frank persuasively argues that Republicans employ social wedge issues to hoodwink members of the working and middle class. In *What's the Matter with Kansas* (2004), Frank leads an energetic if disheartening romp through the culture-war politics of America's rightward lurch, cataloging the social issues such as abortion, gay rights, school prayer, pornography, guns, and religious fundamentalism that the GOP has married to plutocracy-friendly priorities such as deregulation, privatization, tax cuts for the rich, and slashed social services for everyone else. He's particularly devastating in his insight that the purveyors of cultural conflict depend on a polity continually roiled by social issues, and concomitantly distracted from focusing on the disastrous consequences to their livelihoods that follow from their votes. "The trick never ages; the illusion never wears off. *Vote* to stop abortion; *receive* a rollback in capital gains tax. *Vote* to make our country strong again; *receive* deindustrialization." Frank's trenchant analysis convincingly reveals the various patterns of rightwing demagoguery. And as we now know, race-baiting has been integral to this.

But not according to Frank. On the contrary, he ridicules those who attribute backlash politics in substantial part to race, caricaturing such claims as daft theories about "crypto-racism" or "the protests of 'angry white men.'" This is stale logic, according to Frank. "Ask a liberal pundit what ails the red states," he bemoans, "and he will probably tell you it's all because of racism." This just doesn't hold water, Frank contends. Kansas—and by extension the United States—"cannot easily be dismissed as a nest of bigots. Kansas does not have Trent Lott's disease. It is not Alabama in the sixties." Kansas and country may embrace a lot of crazy, self-defeating antipathies, Frank acknowledges, "but one thing it doesn't do is racism."[1]

Frank is right, but also wrong. He's right that Kansas isn't Alabama in the 1960s. Then again, even Alabama isn't Alabama in the 1960s (exhibit A: arch-segregationist George Wallace repudiated his previous racism on his way to re-election as governor in 1982).[2] Frank is wrong because he fatally misses how quickly and dramatically racism has evolved. In proclaiming that America "doesn't do racism," Frank understands racism as an open endorsement of white supremacy. Hence Frank's reference to Trent Lott. In 2002, the Republican senator from Mississippi gave a speech extolling the 1948 pro-segregation presidential campaign of Strom Thurmond, saying, "We voted for him. We're proud of it. And if the rest of the country had followed our lead, we wouldn't have had all these problems over the years, either."[3] The Lotts of this world—the dwindling number of public leaders foolish enough to publicly avow segregation and white supremacy—are quickly repudiated, including by Republicans. But as we have seen, this is far from the end of racism.

No doubt Frank is correct that for some voters race has nothing to do with their conservative proclivities. Yet it's also overwhelmingly clear that race contributes to broad-based support for regressive policies that wreck the middle class. So how does race convince some white voters to vote against their interests? Or, to paraphrase Frank's evocative title, what's the matter with white voters?

■ WHAT "INTERESTS"?

Before turning to how race might influence voters, let's start with the preliminary question of whether in fact whites necessarily undercut their "interests" when they respond to appeals for racial solidarity. Obviously, if it turned out that some whites had good reasons for voting along racial lines, that alone would go far toward explaining the power of dog whistling. As we shall see, whites *do* have some interests in supporting continued white dominance—but these actual interests are dwarfed by the delusion that racial solidarity will restore a mythical middle-class wonderland.

The allegation that people "vote against their own interests" typically takes the following form: *some voters are led astray by appeals to social concerns and do not recognize their actual economic interests.* This proposition distinguishes between social values on the one hand and pocketbook interests on the other; in doing so, it establishes an implicit hierarchy ranking ostensibly hard-edged economic interests over supposedly mushy social concerns. But frequently social values are deeply held, and also, what's economic and what's social cannot be neatly separated. For instance, explaining why white voters in the North might be open to racial appeals from Republicans, in 1963 political columnists Rowland Evans and Robert Novak offered this analysis: "The white construction worker sees lowering the color bar in his Jim Crow union as a threat to his job. The lower middle class suburbanite, who has invested much of his savings in his home, sees the Negro who wants to live next door to him as a financial threat."[4] Economic and social interests are often intertwined.

Understanding this, we can now ask: what interests might whites have in racial appeals, or more generally, in supporting the continued privileged position of whites? In what follows, I distinguish racial status, class status, and actual economic losses, the better to explain these various elements—but this separation is artificial, as in practice these often overlap.

Racial status. Consider how whites benefit from the social prestige associated with being white. It's easiest to see how this operates by looking to the past, to racial episodes not presently shrouded by racial commonsense. Consider Little Rock, Arkansas, in the fall of 1957, when federal troops arrived to help force school integration. Arkansas Governor Orval Faubus had promised that "blood would run in the streets" before black children would enter Little Rock's Central High School, and when some children first tried, a howling mob of angry whites and the fixed bayonets of the Arkansas National Guard turned them back. Under the protection of federal troops, nine young African American students tried again, finally marching into the main building between phalanxes of soldiers protecting them from the furious crowds.

What aroused the white mob? Yes, many reacted out of hatred, yet beneath that something deeper operated. The crowds massed primarily to protect a social order that draped whites in the velvet robe of unquestionable superiority. Reared in the cradle of white supremacy, integration violated what many whites perceived as the natural order, a hierarchy so thorough it saturated the Southern milieu. In this context, the concept of black equality was truly radical, for it promised to upend the entire social world. Many whites experienced this as an affront—a violation of their obvious superiority, an attack on their exalted status. In turn, this triggered strong emotional responses: anger, rage, fear, and fury surged to the surface. Yet all too often, we construe the emotions as the source of the reaction rather than as an expression of a deeper conflict. Racial bile did not lead many whites to oppose integration. Rather, threats to their supremacy made many whites oppose and indeed hate integration.

Class status. Throughout this book we've talked in terms of a broad economic middle class to describe the breadth of those who suffer from assaults on New Deal liberalism. Here, it's important to note that class divisions nevertheless exist within this range, and within the white middle class these divisions interact powerfully with race. Again, Little Rock helps lay this bare.

When Central High was the only white high school, race obfuscated class lines among whites, as the children of laborers attended school with the children of doctors and lawyers. Their proximity, and their whiteness, suggested less social distance than class divisions otherwise might imply. In the midst of resisting integration, however, Little Rock opted to build a new public high school in the more affluent northwestern part of the city. Opening in the fall of 1957, the new school took the wealthier students who had previously attended Central, just as Central began to integrate. Those left behind felt that "working-class whites became the guinea pigs in the integration experiment at Central."⁵ Little Rock demonstrates in microcosm a larger dynamic: the white working class has largely shouldered the costs of school, neighborhood, and job integration, while white professionals have mainly avoided integration by retreating to private academies, gated suburbs, and protected professional worlds. Their ability to flee integration reflects both the resources available to better-off whites, as well as the greater sway they exercise over government. As a result, well-off whites have experienced integration only on their own terms—in controlled settings, such as elite colleges and universities, and with only token numbers of nonwhites. Beyond these managed interactions with integration, well-off whites remain the most racially isolated group in the United States.

Where race previously obscured class divisions among whites, now it came to exaggerate them. For many whites, the measure of whether they've made it increasingly turns on being able to set the terms with which they associate with minorities. Social critic Rich Benjamin describes one version of this, explaining how for many middle-class whites, by the 1990s everything good in life seemed to depend on having enough money to escape to what Benjamin describes as "Whitopia"—"a constellation of small towns and so-called 'exurbs' that are extremely white . . . communal pods that cannily preserve a white-bread world, a throwback to the imagined past with 'authentic' 1950s values and the nifty suburban amenities available today."[6] In contrast, dystopia came to mean places peopled by nonwhites. To suffer downward class mobility meant having to rub shoulders with nonwhites at every turn—even if one lived in the same house, worked at the same job, and sent one's kids to the same schools that, when all white, had marked middle-class status.

Actual economic losses. Beyond the loss of status, working-class whites also suffered material losses associated with integration. Poorer whites who lacked the financial resources to resist the pressures of integration slowly lost exclusive control of their neighborhoods, schools, and workplaces, their most valuable possessions. They rightly viewed these as sources of their well-being and launching pads for their children: homes that held most of their wealth; neighborhoods that supplied a sense of community; jobs that delivered decent pay and maybe someday had a place for one's child; schools that seemed like escalators to take the next generation higher. This was about more than status. This was about access to union jobs, government mortgages, decent schools, effective public services, and government-funded amenities like nice public parks and swimming pools—all of which had been reserved for whites, often formally and in any event by social sanction.

Having to share these resources with nonwhites was costly—in the same way that having to share a single pie with more people means smaller slices for everyone. This zero-sum result was not inevitable; a political establishment committed to fostering integration could have offset these costs, or even provided resources to grow the pie for the lower- and middle-class, white and nonwhite alike. But the reality was otherwise, and the pattern set in Little Rock continued throughout the country: rather than integration bringing more resources into working-class white communities, it often brought less. Public dollars that had once paid for everything from good schools to swimming pools dwindled once voters came to perceive minorities as the beneficiaries—often as a function of dog whistle politics on the local level.[7] As a result, whites who lacked the financial resources to escape integration often found themselves confronting more claims on the same—and very often fewer—resources.

To be sure, this is a highly artificial way to talk about integration's costs. Whites did not greet the newcomers simply as more folks moving into the neighborhood; rather, race profoundly distorted their reactions in numerous ways. We'll turn to that in a moment. For now, though, the point is that whites had an interest in opposing integration completely apart from racial antipathy: first, integration created more demands on their schools, neighborhoods, and jobs; second, integration often lead to cuts in resources.

Imagined losses. There are some actual interests—racial status, class status, and material losses—that may cause whites to support politicians who signal racial solidarity. But these interests are dwarfed by a racial imagination that often heaps blame on nonwhites for almost every reversal in the fortunes of the white middle class over the last 50 years. Illustrating the power of imagined losses more than of real harms, though lower-class whites have encountered the greatest costs from integration, the defection among whites from the Democratic Party has *not* been led by the working class. Among whites, anti-black hostility seems largely *disconnected* from "direct racial threats to whites' private lives (to their jobs, their neighborhoods, their children's schooling, their families' safety)."[8] Rather, it has been principally those able to racially isolate themselves that have left the Democratic party in the greatest numbers.[9] The retreat of wealthier whites to suburbs did not reduce racial conservatism, it led to its acceleration.[10] Dog whistle politics has convinced a number of whites to vote their fears about minorities, and yet, for those prone to do so most aggressively, their fears have little basis in the reality of their segregated lives.

There's a classic film from 1993 that can help us see the exaggerated scale of the blame many whites put on minorities. In *Falling Down*, Michael Douglas's character, William Foster, descends into a violent racial rampage. The movie grounds Foster in the economic malaise that resulted from the Reagan era, when financial deregulation led to an economic recession that rattled the country for years. In Foster's backstory, he has been fired from his defense industry job, leaving him marooned and unable to find an engineering position in the wounded economy. Foster has spent months mimicking the routine of going to a nonexistent job, seeking to preserve as long as possible his dignity and even his sanity. He eventually loses his grip, though, in encounters with nonwhites that precipitate Foster's mental breakdown. Stumbling through Los Angeles in a short-sleeve button-down shirt complete with pocket protector and pens, nonwhites he can neither avoid nor fathom accost Foster at every turn: the rude Asian grocer, the threatening Latino gangsters. Foster turns increasingly violent—but no old-style racist, for good measure he shoots a white supremacist among others in his bloody rampage. Nevertheless, it's nonwhites, in their aggressive disrespect toward him, who symbolize the destroyers of what he nostalgically mourns: a safe world of polite white people with good jobs, nice homes, and tidy lawns.

Many whites seem to follow Foster in blaming minorities for much of the hardship in their lives. Integration began in earnest in the late 1960s and early 1970s, as one of the longest sustained periods of economic growth in the United States slowed and the dislocating forces of globalization and deindustrialization gathered speed. In these years, whites began to suffer a number of shocks to their livelihood: factory closings, stagnating wages, increasing inflation, and eroding pensions. These economic challenges have only increased over the last 40 years, including during the recession in the late 1980s and, of course, in the Great Recession of 2008. The causes have been complex, including major structural changes and important shifts in government policy—shifts that partly reflect the power of dog whistle politics. Yet the very magnitude and complexity of the forces behind the worsening economic plight of the white middle and working class have impeded straightforward analysis.

In this vacuum, nonwhites—relatively powerless and widely demeaned, though also steadily increasing in numbers—became a convenient scapegoat. Many whites came to attribute job losses, shrinking savings, and declining opportunities to integration specifically and nonwhites generally. Recall how Michigan Democrats who defected to Reagan perceived their woes: "Blacks constitute the explanation for their vulnerability and for almost everything that has gone wrong in their lives; not being black is what constitutes being middle class; not living with blacks is what makes a neighborhood a decent place to live."[11] Or reflect on the plaintive Tea Party wail, "We want our country back." Presumably they mean back from a black president, and a return to a national Whitopia.

This imagined ideal gains the status of paradise not simply from the absence of nonwhites; rather, its halcyon quality stems from the misapprehension that reducing the presence of nonwhites will bring back an America in which hard work and playing by the rules guarantees financial stability and a secure retirement. Many older whites nostalgically pine for the days when a solid work ethic meant a good job, a decent home, a new car every few years, an affordable college education for the kids, and a nice vacation by the lake or seashore every August. Their children may not want to return to a *Leave It to Beaver* world, but still yearn for a society of increasing opportunities for people like themselves, a vision that tends to erase most minorities. These imagined worlds—the one recalled from the past by the older generation and the one wished for by those starting out—are fairytales.

But even so, in their shared celebration of work, stability, and upward mobility, we can recognize the kernel of these dreams: the ache for a world of middle-class prosperity. This desperation for economic security helps bring into sharp relief the dramatic losses that the middle class has suffered over the last five decades. The way forward is through a return to liberal governance. Yet, partly due to the insistent badgering of dog whistle politics, many whites imagine instead that the challenges in their lives stem from the increasing presence of nonwhites, and can best be solved by further reducing the power of activist government.

■ HEARING THE DOG WHISTLE

Imagining that minorities are the root problem in society makes many whites receptive to dog whistle appeals spreading that message. But what does it mean to "hear" a racial dog whistle? Do those who respond clearly perceive a message of racial salvation? Or instead are most whites unaware of the racial solicitations to which they nevertheless respond? I've mentioned before the contention that, for most whites, racial appeals work on the level of commonsense. Let's explore that further.

Seeking to discover precisely how coded racial appeals work, Princeton politics professor Tali Mendelberg closely studied the Willie Horton campaign strategy that helped elect George H.W. Bush in 1988.[12] The Horton episode provided something of a natural experiment for testing whether race-baiting is unconsciously or instead clearly heard because it operated in two phases, one in which race was implicit and the other where it was expressly foregrounded.

In keeping with dog whistle strategy, when the Bush team introduced the Horton story—a convicted murderer released on furlough who assaulted a couple, raping the woman—the campaign left the crucial racial element to be conveyed by images, but took great pains to never say expressly that Horton was black and his victims were white. Likewise, media stories on Horton and the furlough program very rarely referenced race directly. Reporters seemed to be following a colorblind script, refusing to mention what lay plainly in view. The net result was that, up until about two weeks before the election, race provided the emotional punch of the Horton story, but no one talked about Horton and race openly.

That changed on October 21, when civil rights leader and Democratic powerhouse Jesse Jackson charged at a press conference that the whole Horton affair stood at the heart of a larger strategy to stir racial animosities, saying, "There have been a number of rather ugly race-conscious signals sent from that campaign."[13] While Dukakis himself avoided the issue, within a couple of days the presidential nominee's running mate seconded Jackson's charge. Dukakis's campaign manager then went on record with the *New York Times*, stating that "There is no stronger metaphor for racial hatred in our country than the black man raping the white woman," and adding, "if you were going to run a campaign of fear and smear and appeal to racial hatred you could not have picked a better case to use than this one."[14]

Having punched race into the campaign, the Bush camp parried the charges, expressing outrage that anyone would allege such despicable behavior. True to the script, Bush also played the aggrieved victim, proclaiming, "there is not a racist bone in my body."[15] The media largely accepted the denials, treating the allegations as desperate Democratic mudslinging. It would take three years, numerous investigations of the campaign, and the Bush administration's repeated hostility toward civil rights, to convince most reporters that the Horton campaign had indeed amounted to intentional racial demagoguery.[16] Notwithstanding the media's tardy arrival at the truth, though, in the days after Jackson first aired the race-baiting accusation, coverage of Horton changed dramatically. For the final two weeks of the campaign, reporters often directly tied Horton to race. They did not credit the allegations of racial pandering, but they nevertheless reported them. Skeptical or not, the media now openly discussed the racial dimensions of the Horton ads and campaign mailings.

To tease out how racial appeals work, Mendelberg examined support for Bush before and after Jackson brought race to the fore. If voters consciously received and welcomed racial appeals, she expected to see support for Bush remain the same or even increase after October 21. After all, if the message of racial solidarity was clear to voters, nothing would change once the cover of racial neutrality was stripped away; if anything, the message would become even clearer. If this was correct, then dog whistle politicians code their race-baiting to escape public censure, but not to fool their intended audience.

But on the other hand, if coded racial appeals worked at an unconscious level, Mendelberg expected support for Bush to fall off once race became foregrounded. She reasoned that if those who respond to dog whistles "hear" race unconsciously, but consciously embrace the national ethos of racial equality, then the eruption of race into consciousness should reduce support for racial demagoguery. In this event, racial code words hide race even from the intended audience.

Mendelberg found that support for Bush rose precipitously during the early phase of the Horton campaign, and then plummeted sharply once Jackson shoved race to the surface. Concludes Mendelberg, "Keeping the message implicit was important to its ability to achieve the intended result of mobilizing whites' racial fears, stereotypes, and resentments. When the racial nature of the message was explicitly pointed out, it lost much of its racial power."[17] This result strongly suggests that most of those who respond to dog whistles do not consciously hear them as racial appeals. They do not say to themselves, *I'm voting for politician W because he's on my racial team.* Rather, dog whistle appeals remain inaudible to most, instead resonating with their unconscious racial anxieties and eliciting support only so long as they remain hidden. It seems that dog whistle politicians manipulate these background views and emotions, but succeed with most whites only so long as the racial appeals stay below conscious recognition.

To test this in a more controlled environment, Mendelberg carefully crafted a psychological experiment, fabricating brief news segments purporting to cover a fictional gubernatorial candidate named "Hayes." In two nearly identical segments, a faux newscaster discussed Hayes's position on welfare, while a background visual depicted black welfare recipients. In the "implicit" version, the script did not reference race directly; the "explicit" version did reference race, by adding the italicized phrases:

> The candidates are taking very different positions concerning New Jersey's welfare budget. Hayes says that people, *especially African Americans,* take advantage of welfare at the expense of hard-working taxpayers. He claims that welfare has become a way of life for many, *especially for African Americans,* and criticized New Jersey's above-average rates of welfare cheating. He says able-bodied welfare recipients should have to work in return for benefits.

Mendelberg found that whites holding strongly stereotypical views of blacks were very likely to support Hayes, so long as they did not judge the appeal to be racial in nature. In contrast, once they understood Hayes to be invoking race, their support dropped to the level shown by whites who only weakly subscribed to stereotypical views. Mendelberg summarized her findings thus: "A message is at its most powerful when it contains racial content but is not consciously recognized as racial. A message backfires among the very constituency it targets when it contains racial content that triggers the realization that it is in fact a racial appeal."[18]

Mendelberg understandably took hope from this result. It suggests that dog whistle voters are themselves victims of manipulation, rather than covert racists. It intimates that rather than being committed to racial politics, most whites resoundingly reject it when it's brought into the light. And it implies that a remedy for race-baiting lies readily at hand in public denunciations. "Transforming an implicit appeal into an explicit one is among the surest ways to neutralize it," Mendelberg wrote in her concluding chapter. "The counterstrategy of remaining silent on race in the face of an implicit racial appeal is a losing strategy. More effective is the counterstrategy of bringing race to the surface, of showing the racial meaning of the message and thus preventing the opposition from using race in a deniable way."[19]

Mendelberg's work adds powerful ammunition to the argument that liberals sabotage themselves when they acquiesce to the colorblind demand to avoid all race talk. She makes a very strong case that liberals must instead address racial pandering head on. We'll return to this argument in the solutions chapter, sketching how to effectively name and critique dog whistle frames.

Before leaving this discussion, though, we should temper the optimism that simply calling out race-baiting can defeat the phenomenon. In Chapter Six we outlined how conservatives repulse charges of racial pandering with the "playing the race card" kick, and also with accusations that they've been maligned for being Klan members. Liberals publicly denouncing dog whistling will have to overcome these retorts, and in addition will confront another large hurdle: the resistance of many whites to recognizing racial dynamics.

Consider a startling finding that Mendelberg reports but makes little of: when she asked respondents to judge whether the fictitious news reports invoked race, surprisingly few discerned racial appeals. In the "implicit" case, recall, the newscaster reported that the candidate talked of persons who "take advantage of welfare at the expense of hard-working taxpayers," while the background visuals flashed images of black welfare recipients. Among the white respondents who viewed this clip, only one in five perceived it as "a racial appeal."[20] What then of the "explicit" report, which carried the same background visuals and in addition featured the candidate condemning "welfare [as] a way of life for many, especially for African Americans"? Even here, where race virtually slapped respondents in the face, only half categorized this report as embodying a racial appeal; the other half didn't see it as racial at all.[21] Mendelberg reports that whites temper their response to dog whistle pandering once they understand a political appeal as racial. But it may take quite a bit to get most whites to that point.

Here's an illustration from the 2012 Republican primaries. While stumping in Iowa, a videotape caught Rick Santorum saying the following about food stamps: "I don't want to make black people's lives better by giving them somebody else's money. I want to give them the opportunity to go out and earn their money and provide for themselves and their families." Challenged over these remarks, Santorum subsequently denied that he had said "black," instead lamely claiming he had stumbled over another word—as Charles Blow reported, "Now he's saying that he didn't say 'black people' at all but that he 'started to say a word' and then 'sort of mumbled it and changed my thought.'" Blow's response: "Pause as I look askance and hum an incredulous, 'Uh huh.'"[22]

Santorum surely regretted blurting it out, but the tape is clear, and in addition the statement corresponds to standard rightwing thinking; of course he said "black people."[23]

But more interesting is how Santorum's audience reacted, both immediately and as the controversy gained steam. The crowd in the room did not gasp or object; instead, after Santorum gaffed, the all-white audience reacted with applause. It's unlikely they intended to cheer a racist statement. Instead, they probably failed to note the Freudian slip, instead merely hearing what was already in their minds the minute talk turned to food stamps. Eighty-four percent of those receiving food stamps in Iowa are white, and only nine percent are black.[24] But criticizing the government's welfare policies in race-coded terms has become a staple of dog whistle racism, so routine that the occasional use of express racial language can easily pass unnoticed.

What, then, of the reaction to Santorum once the racial element of his remarks became a source of controversy? It seemed there was little or no backlash against Santorum—not for insinuating that black people were the quintessential welfare recipients, and not for subsequently lying about it either. The linkage of blacks and welfare seemed so self-evident, so "true" to Santorum's target audience, that they seemed to see nothing wrong in his blunder, and no fault in his prevaricating to defend himself. Santorum campaigned as the embodiment of conservative rectitude, from his righteous condemnations of homosexuality down to his earnest sweater vests suggesting old-fashioned honesty and probity. Yet the GOP primary voters seemed to see no hypocrisy in his evident mendacity—most likely, we might surmise, because they knew what he meant, and were certain it was not racially unfair or offensive. Many voters may refuse to recognize even express racial appeals as violating anti-racist norms.

There is a final caution. Making it even more unlikely whites will recognize racial manipulation in action, coded race-baiting continuously evolves. Mendelberg reports that though it took three years, the media eventually came to the consensus that the Bush camp had deployed Horton as a racial tactic. Today, "Willie Horton" serves as a generic reference to political race-baiting, a shorthand term for racial demagoguery. No doubt contemporary reporters benefit from this, standing much more ready to condemn dog whistle racism that uses grainy mug shots and trades on narratives of black men raping white women. This marks genuine progress in combating dog whistle racism. Yet if one traces the phenomenon since its inception with Wallace and Goldwater, one sees not the gradual dissipation but the persistent evolution of racial appeals. Post-Horton, racial entreaties morphed into standard politics during the Clinton administration, and warped anew into hysteria concerning brown foreigners, whether illegals or terrorists, during the Bush years. As with the Willie Horton debacle, all too often today's dog whistle comes to be widely condemned as racism only after the damage has already been done.

■ COMMONSENSE RACISM

It seems that race agitates most whites at the unconscious level. But how? We can answer this in terms of commonsense racism, a concept briefly introduced back in Chapter Two. "Commonsense" evokes the overwhelming ordinariness, pervasiveness, and legitimacy of much social knowledge; it expresses the intuitive certainty that many things are just what they are, widely known, widely recognized, and not needing any further explanation.[25] For many in our society, whites and nonwhites too, racial beliefs operate in this fashion. For many, it simply seems "true," an unquestioned matter of commonsense, that blacks prefer welfare to work, that undocumented immigrants breed crime, and that Islam spawns violence. How is this commonsense generated? Four different forces impel us to think in racist terms. I separate them below to make describing them easier, but in practice they are mutually reinforcing and difficult to distinguish.[26]

SOCIAL LEARNING

The first time I turned on *The Wire*, I abruptly clicked it off. An HBO series built around urban devastation and drug crimes in the burnt wreckage of Baltimore, the show struck me as just another voyeuristic portrayal of ghetto dysfunction. It seemed a slicker version of the jangly reality TV ride-alongs that bring into livingrooms all across the country images of police officers interrogating groups of young black men attired in sagging pants and hoodies, or accosting Latinos leaned up against chain-link fences. More than simply overrepresenting nonwhites among the criminal class, such fodder strips the context from the lives of those it portrays. Oblivious to life stories, the camera reduces complex individuals to the sum total of the behavior that lands them in the lights' glare. Their lives' larger trajectory, including the structural forces that opened and shut various avenues leading to that moment, remain obscured by deep shadows. We don't just learn that nonwhites commit crimes. We learn that they are criminals, and little else.

This is where *The Wire* differs. Despite my initial misgivings, over five seasons the show explored the interconnected lives of drug dealers and cops—and longshoremen, journalists, and bureaucrats—illuminating the complicated humanity of those trapped by forces of urban deterioration. The more complete background shifted the perception of those perpetrating "crimes": now this term seemed to include not only the street hoodlums but also those who would never be charged with breaking the law, yet who in the socially destructive dimensions of their actions seemed at least equally culpable of great social and moral wrongs. The long arc and broad field of view helped lead to a better understanding of those who acted reprehensibly and often self-destructively, while also revealing the responsibility borne and often shirked by those with actual political and economic power.

Comparing *The Wire* to standard media fare—meaning not only Hollywood and TV, but also journalism—helps bring into focus the damage done by most media representations of race. Rather than treat nonwhites as complex persons, the media often reduce minorities to walking stereotypes: rapists, gang members, maids, terrorists, and so forth. White characters, though all too often also flat, nevertheless are typically the only ones allowed to blossom into multifaceted personalities, persons who respond to and also change their relations with others and, on occasion, alter their environment. As a result, media consumers learn to see nonwhites only as racial archetypes, while simultaneously being reminded that whites are unique individuals shaped by and in turn capable of shaping the world around them.

Beyond repeating tired stereotypes, by following the political debates of the day, media representations of minorities also greatly amplify dog whistle themes. In one striking example, media depictions of welfare over several decades tended to carry more black faces during presidential election years, and relatively more images of whites during periods of economic recession when the public was more sympathetic to the need for government assistance.[27] In another example, when Ronald Reagan first began to address unauthorized immigration as a national threat, this issue hardly merited attention among journalists. Within a few years, however, news stories proliferated on this topic, and the overwhelming majority of these used brown faces to illustrate the danger.[28] The adage that an image is worth a thousand words applies to the power of the media to "teach" about race. Often, the lessons are deeply imbued with racist stereotypes that buttress dog whistle themes torn from political campaigns.

The media is one component—albeit a very powerful one—of a larger process of social learning. We begin to learn about race as children, yet even as adults we continue to learn about race through a constant bombardment of messages, images, and storylines from myriad sources. In a society like ours, no one can escape a racial education that often occurs by osmosis, gradually filling one's head with racial understandings of the social world.

In turn, social learning has a self-fulfilling character. Consider a striking experiment conducted several decades ago by Jane Elliot, a third-grade teacher in Riceville, Iowa, a town "so homogenous that many of her students had never seen an African American."[29] The day after the assassination of Martin Luther King, Jr., Elliot struggled to illustrate to her students the significance of King's life. She struck upon the idea of teaching them what segregation meant. Elliot divided her students between those with blue and those with brown eyes. Discriminating first against the brown-eyed children, she put felt collars around their necks to further the differentiation. Then she began to favor the blue-eyed children, seating them at the front of the room, and giving them first choice of the toys at recess. The effects were profound. The brown-eyed children "were humiliated; they huddled together on the playground . . . They said almost nothing in class and barely spoke all day. The blue-eyed students, meanwhile, were relaxed, happy, unself-conscious participants in class."[30] The next day, Elliot reversed the positions, elevating the brown-eyed kids and stigmatizing those with blue eyes. The brown-eyed children returned to being eager learners, but their blue-eyed classmates became downcast and withdrawn. These differences carried through to lessons about arithmetic and spelling. The stigmatized children "barely paid attention. They receded to the back of even these small groups. They spoke only if spoken to. They didn't remember instructions. They were slow to respond. They got a lot of answers wrong." In contrast, on the day these students were favored, "these same students responded like the exuberant, cognitively adept children they apparently were."[31]

Just one day as a disfavored child produced these heart-breaking changes. Imagine the toll of a whole childhood spent facing belittling messages. Now consider how children's responses to years of mistreatment would confirm the very stereotyping that produced the harm in the first place. Withdrawn and anxious from mistreatment, these students' poor performances would only harden the destructive suspicion of their inferiority. The insights of the liberal race theorists from the first half of the twentieth century seem relevant again. As Gunnar Myrdal summarized, "All our attempts to reach scientific explanations of why the Negroes are what they are and why they live as they do have regularly led to determinants on the white side of the race line."[32] Social learning both draws on and reinforces racial patterns.

THE ENVIRONMENT

As with social learning, the environment both teaches about race and has a self-fulfilling dynamic. By the environment, I mean our built world, for instance the narrow streets just north of the University of California, Berkeley, where I teach, which wind up through hills overlooking San Francisco Bay. Gorgeous views complement the varied homes in the area, an architecturally interesting mélange of Tudor, Craftsman, and California Mission style, and the people you see walking their dogs, cycling through the neighborhood, and driving by typically exude the confidence common to privilege—and they are almost exclusively white; a nonwhite face may cause a double-take. Looking further north, though, you spy Richmond, home to oil refineries, urban blight, extreme poverty, and lots of nonwhites. Looking south, you discern Oakland, with a downtown enjoying a renaissance, but also with pockets of intense poverty and spikes of violence, some in black neighborhoods, some in Latino barrios. There's also an Oakland Chinatown, constantly rejuvenated with new immigrants.

Combined with the stereotypes acquired through social learning, these environmental differences make the idea of race seem real, powerful, and supremely relevant. The strong correlation between whites and wealth makes each seem an attribute of the other: wealthy people are white; and white people are wealthy, or soon might be. Likewise, the environment conjoins poverty with nonwhiteness. Poor people are brown and black; black and brown people are poor, or curious exceptions. Sometimes the environment also links race to foreignness: Americans are white; browns and yellows are perpetual strangers. More deeply, these different environments seemingly testify to racial character: white folks keep their neighborhoods nice and work hard to earn the good things in life. In contrast, nonwhites trash their homes and streets, refuse to lift themselves out of poverty, and cling to foreign ways.

All of this seems "obvious," but this very quality of being commonsense depends on the environment obscuring underlying racial processes. It's very difficult to discern the racial advantages that favored those whites who reside in the beautiful North Berkeley abodes: the education and jobs they excelled at through hard work but also with help from racially informed presumptions of competence; the government programs and market opportunities open to their parents and grandparents, but closed by racial barriers to many others. Nor can you readily observe the racial mechanics that over decades have trapped nonwhites in parts of Richmond and Oakland, where areas of concentrated poverty severely limit opportunities, and older generations often have little to pass on in terms of net worth because past segregation in housing, jobs, and education truncated their own potential. Beyond that, it's almost impossible to easily perceive how behavioral norms conducive to success are fostered by settings in which success is possible, while behavioral patterns likely to lead to further marginalization are often encouraged in destructive environments without exits. The social world through which we move reflects centuries of racism that extends right up to the present. But this is hard to grasp in its particulars. Instead, we see clearly only the results, and with the underlying causes hidden, we tend to accept the extant world as a testament to the implacable truth of racial stereotypes.[33] The environment itself seems to confirm the power of race to explain group differences, and also group fates.

COGNITIVE ROUTINES

Social learning and the environment constantly bombard us with racial messages. How do we process this information? To handle the millions of bits of data we daily receive, our brains have developed a number of cognitive routines for efficiently sifting and sorting information. Many of these processes contribute to race's power. Here, I briefly mention three aspects of human cognition that seem especially helpful in understanding the power of race in shaping how we engage others. Yet underlying this discussion is the essential caveat discussed when I first introduced the concept of commonsense racism: while these cognitive elements may be hardwired into how humans think, *race* is not natural to our thinking. Our neural networks may process information in ways that facilitate racial beliefs, but the actual content of our thoughts remain a matter of society and environment.[34]

Categorization. Among our standard repertoire of cognitive tricks, perhaps the most important to race is that the human mind leaps at the chance to categorize others into groups, and then discriminates on that basis. We're deeply accustomed to quickly sorting people into categories, and then to judging individuals in our group much more favorably than others. This dynamic of in-group favoritism and out-group mistreatment operates even when the basis for distinguishing between groups is transparently arbitrary, for instance after a group of children count off, one-two, into opposing teams.[35] Making group distinctions is natural to us, though again the actual groupings reflect social arrangements. The propensity for humans to categorize, and to favor their own while disfavoring others, goes some way toward explaining the power of race in social relations.

Automaticity. Almost equally importantly, the tendency to categorize occurs unconsciously and automatically. Once you gain familiarity with racial groups and their relative social positions—unavoidable knowledge when living more than briefly in the United States—racial misjudgments will occur even before you know it. Indeed, because of race's high social salience and its typically easy visual identification, "of all the dimensions on which people categorize each other, race is among the quickest and most automatic."[36] The social science on this is abundantly clear. As we encounter each other in the social world, our minds have already recognized racial distinctions and activated racial stereotypes, no matter how much we might wish it were otherwise.

Loss aversion. A third cognitive dynamic, albeit one not connected closely to groups, also bears mention. We tend to react to losses very differently from how we respond to unrealized gains. If someone takes $5 from you, you're likely to resent it much more than if someone fails to give you $5 they owe you. Rationally, there should be no difference: in either case, you're out five bucks. Perhaps so, but we nevertheless tend to experience losses more intensely. This dynamic seems relevant to understanding the high level of resentment expressed when whites confront demands for integration. Many take the status quo as a neutral starting point. Certainly this reflects racial ideology, which seeks to assure whites that their superior position is warranted rather than illegitimate. But it seems likely to also reflect a cognitive predisposition to greatly resent any effort to take away what we presently hold.[37] This same predisposition also leads us to undervalue potential gains. Thus, even if gains from integration exceed the losses, the losses will be counted much more heavily in how whites experience them.

MOTIVES

Our minds automatically process information gleaned about race from society and the environment, contributing to a commonsense about race. Contrast this with strategic racists: they interact with race consciously and purposefully. This may lead to a sense that there's a division between those who unconsciously engage with race, and those who do so completely mindfully. This division is too stark. Instead, engagements with race occur along a continuum between fully strategic and fully automatic, with everyone somewhere along that spectrum. This means that strategic racists both manipulate and draw on commonsense ideas. And it also means that commonsense racism involves some element of motivation.

We can start with strategic racism, combining cold calculations and also a reliance on existing racial ideas. We've seen this exemplified in politicians from George Wallace to Mitt Romney, brainstorming over how best to stoke racial grievances; and by William Rehnquist and Clint Bolick, working diligently to harness civil rights rhetoric to enhance the plutocrats' power. Notice here, though, that strategic racism is not simply the purview of presidential candidates and political operatives; instead, it has always functioned at every layer of the social stratum. To give an example, consider Justice Frank Murphy's dissent from *Korematsu v. United States*, a World War II case which blessed the internment of roughly 110,000 persons of Japanese descent, the majority of them American citizens. Murphy vigorously objected, emphasizing the combined racial *and* financial motives of those pushing for prison camps:

> Special interest groups were extremely active in applying pressure for mass evacuation. Mr. Austin E. Anson, managing secretary of the Salinas Vegetable Grower—Shipper Association, has frankly admitted that "We're charged with wanting to get rid of the Japs for selfish reasons. We do. It's a question of whether the white man lives on the Pacific Coast or the brown men. They came into this valley to work, and they stayed to take over. . . . They undersell the white man in the markets. . . . They work their women and children while the white farmer has to pay wages for his help. If all the Japs were removed tomorrow, we'd never miss them in two weeks, because the white farmers can take over and produce everything the Jap grows. And we don't want them back when the war ends, either."[38]

Anson laid bare his ulterior motives for favoring the removal of Japanese farmers, but like all strategic racists, he also at least partially subscribed to the racial antipathies he endeavored to exploit.

From here, motives become more attenuated as persons adopt particular ideas depending not on their material interests but on how these notions protect their self-image and, for the privileged, confirm society's basic fairness.[39] For instance, the dominance of colorblindness today surely ties back to motives, not on the fully conscious level, but in many whites being drawn to conceptions of race that affirm their sense of being moral persons neither responsible for nor benefited by racial inequality. Colorblindness offers whites racial expiation: they cannot be racist if they lack malice; nor can they be responsible for inequality, since this reflects differences in group mores. Colorblindness also compliments whites on a superior culture that explains their social position. In addition it empathizes with whites as racism's real victims when government favors minorities through affirmative action or welfare payments. Finally, colorblindness affirms that whites are moral when they oppose measures to promote integration because it's allegedly their principled objection to any use of race that drives them, not bias. Colorblindness has not gained adherents because of its analytic insight (that race is completely disconnected from social practices blinks reality); rather, it thrives because it comforts whites regarding their innocence, reassures them that their privilege is legitimate, commiserates with their victimization, and hides from them their hostility toward racial equality.

Finally, people seem "motivated" to act racially in the even looser sense of seeking to minimize their discomfort in dealing with race.[40] In contrast to the foundational questions of self bound up in world views, this involves managing immediate anxiety in interactions with others. Seeking to avoid strain or embarrassment, we search for strategies that help us avoid or manage unsettling situations. Here again colorblindness often comes in, though now not as a complex set of ideas so much as an interactional strategy. Many whites find it stressful to engage with someone nonwhite, at least partly because they worry they may come across as prejudiced. In such settings, "one approach many Whites adopt is *strategic colorblindness*: avoidance of talking about race—or even acknowledging racial difference—in an effort to avoid the appearance of bias."[41] Especially in cross-racial encounters, many whites opt to act as if they simply don't see race. Not altogether surprisingly, this often backfires, as their evident discomfort and strained self-management causes them to be perceived as more prejudiced.[42] Motivation, in this context, is less akin to deliberately comparing costs and benefits, or even subtly weighing which ideas protect one's ego, and more like managing anxiety or discomfort.

* * *

The thousand-pound gorilla in American politics is that race convinces many whites to vote against their interests. How does it do so?

To start, framing the question as whites voting against their interests glosses the important fact that, when they respond to racial appeals, some whites *are* voting according to their interests. Along the dimensions of racial and class status, as well as in terms of protecting settled advantages in jobs, neighborhoods, and schools, some whites have actual interests in supporting continued white dominance.

But even granting this, there's strong evidence, including from the Willie Horton episode, that most who "hear" the dog whistle do so only unconsciously. We should be clear that commonsense racism does far more than conscious self-interest to drive the receptivity of most whites to dog whistle appeals. Without entirely dismissing actual interests, it's nevertheless clear that racial pandering works primarily because many whites are susceptible to subtle messages that present minorities as the major threat in their lives. Reflect on how the four general dynamics that contribute to commonsense racism— social learning, environmental influence, cognitive routines, and motives— play out for most whites in a political environment defined by dog whistling and colorblindness.

- Whites learn about race through social learning in a white-dominated society, and integral to this education by osmosis is a massive political effort to subliminally convince whites that they are in peril.

- The environment reflects centuries of white privilege, and this too increases race's subterranean power, making race seem powerfully real, and also, making race a ready way to explain the position of one's group and indeed one's own fate.

- As with all of us, the minds of whites conspire against them: they think along racial lines categorically and automatically in ways very difficult to control, and tend to resent as losses any diminution in their status or privilege. Meanwhile, far from learning to counteract their biased judgments, colorblindness constantly tells whites that the way to get beyond race is to not consciously consider race.

- Finally, even if not motivated in a strategic way, whites are trapped by the desire to protect their self-image as well as the seeming legitimacy of their group position, and thus tend to adopt ideas about race and racism that provide absolution—ideas often crafted by dog whistle entrepreneurs to insinuate minority inferiority and to foster a sense of white victimization.

Dog whistle narratives trade on but also shape commonsense ideas of race, all too easily triggering approbation from whites privileged by race but anxious in a changing world. Rightwing race-baiting works because strategic racists are able to appeal to racial commonsense, ultimately manipulating broad segments of the white population into voting in ways that hurt themselves and wreck the middle class.

9

Obama's Post-Racial Strategy

After decades of dog whistle politics, have liberals devised a workable response? Obama's preferred solution is to avoid insofar as possible becoming entangled by race. But in order to avoid race, he apparently calculates he must keep his distance from liberalism too.

B arack Obama entered the White House in 2009 accompanied by widespread optimism among many liberals. Many reacted as if the helicopter that carried George W. Bush aloft, the crowds below cheering his departure, also allowed a long night to lift. The country's situation seemed dire, with the financial market teetering on the brink of collapse, hundreds of thousands of jobs disappearing, home values falling and foreclosures skyrocketing. Meanwhile, the country was locked into interminable wars abroad: fighting with part-time National Guard soldiers on endless rotations; routinely employing unconstitutional and illegal tactics, including interrogation techniques that qualified as torture under international law; and all while shoveling truckloads of money into private multinationals, Vice President Dick Cheney's Halliburton chief among them. As Obama entered 1600 Pennsylvania Avenue, many believed that all this would end and that the skies would lighten, abroad and at home.

■ A LOST OPPORTUNITY

The very depth of the crises facing the country in 2008 created a rare opportunity to jolt American politics back toward liberalism. During periods of relative stability, inertia largely carries established politics forward. New thoughts and sharp critiques can gain little or no traction because most of the polity views the status quo as safe, secure, and predictable; continuity is almost inevitable, whichever party comes to power. But calamity can change things. What once seemed obvious and right, principally because known and familiar, suddenly becomes potentially wrong and dangerous. An opportunity opens to challenge the stories that have undergirded normal politics; to reveal previous assumptions as misguided; and to offer a new interpretation of history that explains the impending hazards and offers a bold way forward.

This is the opportunity that Obama squandered in 2009. The country was reeling, and the standard rightwing bromides about tax cuts for the wealthy, market deregulation, slashed social services, and a muscular foreign policy offered no promise of respite. On the contrary, after eight years of Republican rule, these policies seemed to be the culprits behind the country's shuddering condition. The conservative prescriptions tied closely to dog whistle politics were knocked to their knees by the profound economic and martial crises they had produced. The moment was ripe for Obama to offer the country a new narrative: one that explained the dangers of unfettered wealth and extolled the potential of government to offer a helping hand.

But beginning immediately with his inaugural address, Obama pivoted from a campaign that had preached "change" to a presidency that promised compromise. There was no grand narrative that would explain what had brought America low, and how it would recover. Instead, to foster compromise and prove his bipartisan bona fides, he began to parrot rightwing descriptions of what ailed America. Rather than laying out a vision for activist government, during his first year Obama frequently gave credence to conservative mythmaking.

To take one example, Obama signed onto the Republican mantra that taxes were too high and agreed to extend tax cuts from the Bush administration that overwhelmingly favored the wealthy. Even when directing resources toward the working class, Obama favored tax rebates as a social policy tool, further entrenching the notion that high taxes plague everyone except, of course, for the tax eaters on welfare. In doing so, Obama not only followed the Republican anti-tax frame, but he showed that liberals had learned nothing about the dangers of obscuring government's helping hand. A more liberal Obama could have channeled aid through direct programs, and would have reminded the populace that tax rates were at historic lows, while reiterating, in the words inscribed on the IRS building in Washington, that "taxes are the price we pay for living in a civilized society."[1] But in a long list of areas—financial reform, job creation, housing, consumer protection, Social Security, Medicare, and deficits, to name some of the most important—Obama shied from giving voice to, let alone implementing, liberal solutions to the worst economic crisis since the

Great Depression. This pattern, set during his initial year in office, ultimately continued through his entire first term. Nobel laureate economist and *New York Times* columnist Paul Krugman would eventually gnash his teeth in frustration, demanding that the administration promote strategic government spending and other liberal solutions to "End this Depression Now!"[2] Yet Obama was not about to risk adopting liberal positions.

The standard excuse for Obama's cautious politics is the straightjacket imposed by strident Republican obstructionism. Without a doubt, the right handcuffed Obama after the elections of 2010 put a reinvigorated GOP in control of the House. The GOP's governing philosophy reverted to the cynical tactics perfected during the Clinton years: use extreme intransigence to create gridlock in Washington, the better to encourage frustrated voters to turn out the president.[3] Even by the fall of 2009, less than a full year after his inauguration, the increasing power of the Tea Party narrowed the range of options open to Obama.

Yet it's false to suppose that conservative power constrained Obama from day one. Obama initially had far more leeway to act than is commonly recalled. When he took office in January 2009, the GOP was in complete disarray, its ideas largely discredited, and its leaders (W., Cheney, McCain, Palin) immensely unpopular.[4] Far from being hamstrung by the right, Obama's refusal to offer a liberal counterweight to rightwing mythmaking may have contributed to the conservative resurgence. The vacuum left by Obama's refusal to embrace liberal ideas and policies allowed conservatives to offer once again their standard story about race and betrayal, big government and victimization. With Obama silent or himself voicing lite versions of these refrains, this became the *sole* coherent narrative out there. The right did not initially fetter Obama. Instead, Obama's decision not to offer the country a renewed liberal narrative contributed to conservative counter-mobilization.

Perhaps Obama failed early on to recognize the importance of a grand narrative, mistakenly assuming he could govern in a relatively liberal fashion while he mouthed conservative maxims.[5] It could also be that Obama held back from embracing more liberal solutions because in his actual convictions—rather than simply in his calculated politics—he was at least centrist if not conservative. More than one disappointed supporter reluctantly reached this conclusion.[6] Other constraints certainly operated: the precarious state of the economy and pressure from corporate players "too big to fail"; the momentum of war; the political risks facing a young president. All of these, singly and in combination, would explain a hesitancy to endorse liberalism that extended back to Obama's first day in office.

But there's another explanation for Obama's flight from liberalism we should also consider, one directly tied to race and dog whistle politics. Obama probably understood that, as an African American Democrat, he physically embodied the right's fear-mongering storyline. Where dog whistle politicians had spent half a century describing nightmares of liberal government pandering to undeserving nonwhites, Obama must have realized that he seemed to offer proof that it was all true, and worse. Here was the specter of a *black* president ready to take the whole country's reins. In this context, coming out swinging as a liberal carried a special risk, since rightwing narratives bound liberalism so closely to give-it-all-to-minorities scare stories. Perhaps this helped convince Obama to avoid staking out strong liberal positions, and encouraged his defensive adoption of conservative rhetoric. He may have calculated that, as judged by the majority of whites, he was already doubly damned, as a Democrat and as an African American; to also embrace activist government likely seemed foolhardy. It's impossible to know with certainty how Obama gauged his positions, of course. But let's turn now to Obama's approach to race, for this strengthens the sense that Obama strategically avoids engaging with race and, connected to this, that this same strategizing leads him to reject a liberal mantle.

■ POST-RACIALISM

Obama's election impelled many to claim that the United States had become a post-racial society, in the strong sense of fully transcending race. For many, race was history. Yes, this version of post-racialism acknowledged, bad things had happened in the past, but that was long ago, and by electing a black president the country had forcefully and forever broken with bygone ways. The day after Obama's election, black conservative Shelby Steele pointedly asked, "doesn't a black in the Oval Office put the lie to both black inferiority and white racism? Doesn't it imply a 'post-racial' America?"[7] Responding to this facile version of post-racialism, in early 2010 Obama remarked, "you know, on the heels of [my] victory over a year ago, there were some who suggested that somehow we had entered into a post-racial America, all those problems would be solved." Then he deadpanned, "that didn't work out so well."[8]

Obama has spent a good portion of his life thinking about race. As Obama eloquently relates in *Dreams from My Father*, he grappled with race during his formative years—wrestling with his identity in Hawaii, exploring "black power" in college, and discovering a racial home when serving as a community organizer in Chicago.⁹ A sophisticated thinker on racial issues, he clearly rejects "post-racial" as a claim that the United States is beyond race. Obama knows all too well that racial bigotry still exists, and that race remains powerfully linked to advantage and disadvantage. "To say that we are one people," he later wrote in *The Audacity of Hope*, "is not to suggest that race no longer matters—that the fight for equality has been won, or that the problems that minorities face in this country today are largely self-inflicted."¹⁰ Certainly, the strident reactions to his presidency have only increased Obama's all-too-personal awareness that race's distorting power continues.

THE GATES AFFAIR

If he rejects post-racialism as a claim that society is past race, however, Obama nevertheless adopts an *approach* toward race that can be considered "post-racial." For Obama, publicly pretending that we are beyond race is a strategy. Consider Obama's first direct engagement with race as president, his response to the arrest of prominent African American professor Henry Louis Gates, Jr.¹¹ Gates, an internationally renowned Harvard faculty member, was returning from a trip abroad in mid-July 2009 when he initially had trouble opening his front door. A cautious neighbor called the police to report seemingly suspicious activity. By the time the police arrived, Gates had secured access through the back entry and had managed to work open the front door. Sergeant James Crowley, a white police officer, questioned Gates at his door, receiving not only proof that Gates was in his own home, but an upbraiding for the interrogation. A verbal altercation ensued, with Gates alleging that the officer acted in a demeaning way, and Crowley claiming that the professor displayed "tumultuous" behavior. Whatever the details, Crowley placed Gates under arrest for disorderly conduct, removing him from his home and taking him in handcuffs to the local police station, where he was held for four hours. Five days later, amid swirling national attention, the Cambridge, Massachusetts, police dropped all charges against Gates.

The next day, in a press conference otherwise dedicated to health care reform, Obama fielded a question on Gates's arrest. After noting that he personally knew Gates and considered him a friend, Obama responded,

> Now, I don't know, not having been there and not seeing all the facts, what role race played in that, but I think it's fair to say, number one, any of us would be pretty angry; number two, that the Cambridge police acted stupidly in arresting somebody when there was already proof that they were in their own home; and, number three, what I think we know, separate and

apart from this incident, is that there is a long history in this country of African-Americans and Latinos being stopped by law enforcement disproportionately. And that's just a fact.[12]

The furor around Gates's arrest, slowly subsiding, now reignited, fueled by the president's comments. A political firestorm immediately enveloped Obama, with some charging him with inappropriately taking sides, and even of being "racist."

Before considering Obama's response to this yowling, note the cautious substance of his initial remarks. Obama did not charge Crowley or the Cambridge police with racism. True, Obama castigated the police for acting "stupidly," but he tied that to the decision to arrest a person who had already proven he was in his own home. On the issue of race and criminal justice, Obama carefully cabined his point as "separate and apart from this incident." At most, Obama's decision to talk about Gates's arrest and race in the same breath *implied* a connection—a connection Obama shied away from explicitly naming. When Obama initially waded into the matter, he did so gingerly. Avoiding any direct allegation of bias, he did no more than implicitly tie Gates's experience to the patent unfairness of racial profiling, a practice so indisputably objectionable that President George W. Bush had announced in early 2001, "It is wrong, and we will end it in America."[13]

For all his caution, though, a political conflagration quickly engulfed Obama's comments, and in the face of its heat, he retreated. Two days after his extemporaneous remarks, Obama explained that while he still considered the arrest "an overreaction," he recognized that "Professor Gates probably overreacted as well."[14] Describing his own choice of words as unfortunate, Obama praised the professionalism of Crowley, and proposed that he, Gates, and Crowley meet at the White House over beer. The event, subsequently described as the "beer summit," took place at the end of July—with Joe Biden invited to sit in at the last minute, likely to avoid a photo shoot featuring two powerful black men facing down a white cop. The fest apparently produced little more than a stiff civility: "They came, they met, they drank. They did not apologize," the *New York Times* reported.[15]

The Gates affair provides a window into Obama's post-racialism, revealing a core insight: at root, liberal post-racialism is a response to colorblindness. Obama, like mainstream liberals, recognizes that race remains relevant today. Nevertheless, he fears controversies stirred up by colorblind attacks that tar the first person to directly mention race with the charge of racism. To avoid such imbroglios, he adopts a post-racial strategy of avoiding race insofar as possible, and of quickly denying the salience of race on those few occasions when either race cannot be avoided or he slips and inadvertently ventures into the forbidden zone.

Obama followed this trajectory in the Gates brouhaha. Speaking off the cuff, Obama transgressed the post-racial rule, if ever so slightly, by implicitly connecting the arrest to racial profiling. Chastened by the intense reaction, he immediately backtracked, abandoning any larger engagement with race. Obama did not respond by reiterating that profiling was a "fact," let alone by deepening his analysis regarding the salience of race in the crime control system. Rather, not only did he back away from race almost entirely, Obama created a parallel between the conduct of Gates and Crowley, and ultimately between Crowley and himself. As all three sat down for beer, each seemed equally innocent of anything more than a shared propensity to "overreact." In effect, Obama's post-racialism reacted to colorblind jabs by adopting the latter's insistence that race should not be discussed.

LIBERAL COLORBLINDNESS

Because post-racialism has long been widely embraced by liberals—and never more so than today, encouraged by the president's example—we should parse more closely its relationship to colorblindness. As a defense against allegations that liberals are always talking about race and are the real racists for doing so, post-racialism adopts the basic colorblind injunction to avoid race. But can post-racialism otherwise keep its distance from reactionary colorblindness, which sees whites as victims and refuses to remedy racial inequality? Comparing the responses of post-racialism and colorblindness to baseline questions about the nature of race and racism shows that post-racialism tends to confirm important dog whistle themes. We also arrive at a disheartening similarity when we compare post-racialism and colorblindness on the fundamental question of what should be done to promote racial justice.[16]

Race as a product of historical injustices. Unlike colorblindness, post-racialism does not portray race as blood or culture. Rather, post-racialism acknowledges race as a product of an ugly history that continues to carry heavy contemporary relevance. In the midst of the 2008 presidential campaign, an uproar arose over racial statements made by Obama's pastor, Reverend Jeremiah Wright, throwing the candidate on the ropes.[17] Choosing to respond from Philadelphia, the "City of Brotherly Love," Obama delivered a speech on race widely credited with saving his candidacy. In doing so, Obama drew on a vision of race grounded in history:

Legalized discrimination—where blacks were prevented, often through violence, from owning property, or loans were not granted to African-American business owners, or black homeowners could not access FHA mortgages, or blacks were excluded from unions, or the police force, or fire departments—meant that black families could not amass any meaningful wealth to bequeath to future generations. That history helps explain the wealth and income gap between black and white, and the concentrated pockets of poverty that persists in so many of today's urban and rural communities.[18]

According to this insight, race carries social relevance today because of yesterday's discrimination. Obama recognized that to talk of race is not, as in the colorblind conception, to commit the moral offense of racism. Rather, to acknowledge present racial inequality is to recognize a sorry history and its continuing legacy.

Racism as individual bias. Despite locating race in terms of powerful social forces in the past, post-racial rhetoric refuses to connect these to a broad understanding of contemporary racism. It accepts that current inequalities reflect prior injustices. But it rejects, at least in its public claims, any conception of present racism that indicts broad structural dynamics or prevalent cultural beliefs. Instead, in the post-racial vernacular, "racism" seems to refer only to individual bias. Witness Obama's repudiation of the notion that racism helped explain the Bush administration's listless response to the humanitarian crisis driven ashore by Hurricane Katrina. Obama rejected any role for race in the government's laggardly reaction, saying instead "the incompetence was color-blind."[19] Obama seemed to accept that the gross racial disparities evident in New Orleans' Lower Ninth Ward—concentrated poverty, extreme vulnerability, dilapidated homes, people without the resources to flee—partially stemmed from past racism. Yet, at least in his public statements, he severed this earlier racism from any ongoing dynamics of structural discrimination or ingrained indifference to the suffering of blacks. Obama may privately perceive racism as a powerful social force that extends well beyond the personal biases of a few bad apples. Yet in his public performance of post-racialism, he remains silent about how racism continues to structure the status quo, probably concluding that to do otherwise would provoke too much controversy. The net result is that, as with colorblindness, post-racialism refuses to recognize that racism means more than small-minded prejudice.

Two principal harms flow from the decision to talk about present racism exclusively in terms of individual bigotry. First, beyond lending support to the conservative definition of racism as malice, the public focus on individuals pushes post-racialists toward forgetting widespread contemporary racial dynamics. Because they dare not discuss commonsense and structural racism, let alone contemporary dog whistling, post-racialists inevitably tend to lose sight of these forces. Able to talk outloud only about racism as hate, the strategy of staying silent on other forms of racism affects the substance of what post-racialists think.

Second, because post-racialists refuse to acknowledge broader conceptions of racism, they cannot publicly differentiate the racial positions of whites and nonwhites. When structural, cultural, and political factors drop from discussions of race, it becomes much harder to say in what way the social reality of nonwhites differs from that of whites. As a result, like colorblindness when it talks about racial groups as instead ethnicities, post-racialism tends to depict both whites and minorities as occupying a similar social space, neither group more advantaged than the other by racial practices. More pointedly, both nonwhites and whites alike become equally victimized by race.

The most damaging manifestation of this lies in Obama's tendency to treat reactions to racism as the equivalent of racism itself. This technique surfaced in Philadelphia when Obama equated the outrage expressed by Reverend Wright with the prejudice harbored by his own white grandmother. Obama likened "the bitterness and bias that make up [part of] the black experience in America" with "a woman who loves me as much as she loves anything in this world, but a woman who once confessed her fear of black men who passed by her on the street, and who on more than one occasion has uttered racial or ethnic stereotypes that made me cringe."[20] But what makes these two similar? Nonwhites have been and continue to be maltreated in society. A certain amount of anger and bitterness is well warranted. Indeed, as the Harvard philosopher Tommie Shelby writes, "a lack of anger among persons unfairly treated and burdened by injustice would be disquieting, suggesting that the afflicted had either given up hope or lacked self-respect, that they had succumbed to cynicism or surrendered to injustice, and they had ceased to put up a fight."[21] Of course anger that spills over to undifferentiated hatred, as it sometimes does, should be repudiated. But nonwhite outrage proportionate to injustice and appropriately directed is not "bitterness and bias," as Obama described it—and in all fairness ought not to be linked to cringe-inducing "racial and ethnic stereotypes" by whites.

Legitimating dog whistle themes. By emphasizing individual bias and equating reactions to racism with racism itself, post-racialism not only echoes colorblindness, it tends to legitimate dog whistle themes. In his Philadelphia address, for instance, Obama not only linked black umbrage with white antagonism, he did so when that animosity was specifically expressed as opposition to school busing, welfare, and affirmative action.

After explaining that black resentment must be understood in the context of a legacy of racial injustice, Obama claimed that "a similar anger exists within segments of the white community." To explain, Obama drew upon the ethnic argument rooted in colorblindness, recasting whites in terms of "the immigrant experience":

> Most working- and middle-class white Americans don't feel that they have been particularly privileged by their race. Their experience is the immigrant experience—as far as they're concerned, no one's handed them anything, they've built it from scratch. They've worked hard all their lives, many times only to see their jobs shipped overseas or their pension dumped after a life-time of labor. They are anxious about their futures, and feel their dreams slipping away; in an era of stagnant wages and global competition, oppor-tunity comes to be seen as a zero sum game, in which your dreams come at my expense.

The ethnic analogy allowed Obama to deny the very different group positions occupied by whites and nonwhites. By treating whites as immigrants, Obama invoked the notion of ethnic groups all in mutual competition, none more advantaged or disadvantaged than anyone else. Segregated neighborhoods, schools, and workplaces disappeared in this account, replaced by a "zero sum" fray that placed all racial groups on the same level.

In the context of this competition, Obama continued, whites resented ef-forts to force integration, either through busing or affirmative action, and also bristled at any suggestion that racial prejudice might be operating. "So when they are told to bus their children to a school across town; when they hear that an African American is getting an advantage in landing a good job or a spot in a good college because of an injustice that they themselves never commit-ted; when they're told that their fears about crime in urban neighborhoods are somehow prejudiced, resentment builds over time." This was a startling moment in his talk, because Obama seemed to be saying that whites were justified in fiercely protecting their segregated spaces, and rightfully irate over accusations of racial bigotry.

But Obama paused, and acknowledged that these grudges were in fact fanned by politicians, opening the way for a repudiation of this anger and a con-demnation of dog whistle politics. "These resentments," Obama noted, "have helped shape the political landscape for at least a generation. Anger over welfare and affirmative action helped forge the Reagan Coalition. Politicians routinely exploited fears of crime for their own electoral ends." Obama seemed on the cusp of exposing how racial pandering helps fuel, and even fashion, racial resentments over welfare, affirmative action, and crime.

Yet, turning back, Obama returned to his original course and instead gave these complaints legitimacy. "To wish away the resentments of white Americans, to label them as misguided or even racist, without recognizing they are grounded in legitimate concerns—this too widens the racial divide, and blocks the path to understanding."[22] Obama made clear that white animosity is "grounded in legitimate concerns," thus approving of "the resentments of white Americans." In addition, Obama endorsed again the sense that whites suffer injury when their rancor is labeled "misguided or even racist." Then, in talking about widening the racial divide and blocking the path of understanding, Obama retrieved the parallel to black bitterness over discrimination, suggesting that society must acknowledge the propriety of both black and white indignation in order to move forward. The linkage was spurious: black ire at past and present abuse in no way parallels white fury at the prospect of integration. Nor is an irate sense of victimization among whites an appropriate response to calls for social repair.

More than erroneous, the equivalence of black and white anger was dangerous, especially as it tied back to dog whistle politics. By only briefly noting and then passing over how "anger over welfare and affirmative action helped forge the Reagan Coalition," and how "politicians routinely exploited fears of crime for their own electoral ends," Obama effectively resurrected the backlash conception of modern race-baiting.[23] The backlash narrative portrays racial demagogues as opportunistic politicians who take advantage of, but do not themselves foment, racial grievances. Instead, backlash thinking lays white bitterness at the feet of liberalism. It is liberalism's excessive pursuit of integration that supposedly engenders white resentment. Just so with Obama's tale, which rooted the cause for white wrath in welfare, crime, and efforts to promote integration, as well as in unfair intimations of bias. By legitimating white resentment, Obama bestowed upon it a prominent benediction. Worse, he largely exonerated dog whistle politics while faulting excessive liberal zeal for causing a racial backlash.

Perhaps nothing better illustrates how Obama's post-racialism echoes conservative racial politics than the ecstatic reaction of the *Denver Post* to the Philadelphia speech: "Obama's eloquent address revived, for the Democrats, [Martin Luther] King's dream of a colorblind America. No racial quotas; no Jim Crow laws. Just Americans."[24] The *Post* did not seem to appreciate the differences between colorblindness and post-racialism, instead hearing Obama endorse the former—an endorsement it perceived as so robust that the *Post* thought it heard Obama equate affirmative action and Jim Crow racial oppression.

Racial justice. If post-racial rhetoric parallels colorblind discourse, does post-racialism nevertheless deviate in terms of what government actually does? How do post-racialism and colorblindness compare regarding the steps society should take to repair racial injustice? Colorblindness answers that race-conscious action is tantamount to racism, and that in any event group culture rather than racism explains racial inequality, making any reform effort futile. As a result, colorblindness proclaims that justice demands doing nothing.

Post-racialism may recognize that contemporary racial inequality reflects past discrimination, yet this does not translate into an obligation to remedy persistent harms to nonwhites, for example in education, housing, health care, or over-policing. Rather, post-racialism considers efforts at racial repair politically unwise and even counter-productive. The standard post-racial calculus goes something like this: attempting to address racial injustice (1) leads to a backlash that virtually guarantees crippling opposition to the immediate effort; and (2) saps strength from other liberal goals that might otherwise be achieved and that might incidentally help nonwhites. Ergo, everyone is better off, including minorities, when race-targeted efforts give way to more inclusive policies. This has become post-racialism's core policy tenet: race should not be allowed to become a distraction from non-racial issues ostensibly more amenable to political resolution, and which in any event might do more to ultimately budge racial disparities.

Reflecting this calculus, the post-racial flight from race is often expressed as a preference for "universal," rather than race-targeted, policies. For instance, in his second book—published in 2006 when he had his eyes on higher office— Obama argued that "an emphasis on universal, as opposed to race-specific, programs isn't just good policy; it's good politics." To illustrate why, he recounted a formative experience sitting in the Illinois Senate, listening to a black colleague decry racism, only to have a liberal white colleague lean over and complain, "You know what the problem is with John? Whenever I hear him, he makes me feel more white." Calling his white colleague's comments "instructive," Obama translated them as follows: "Rightly or wrongly, white guilt has largely exhausted itself in America; even the most fair-minded whites, those who would genuinely like to see racial inequality ended and poverty relieved, tend to push back against suggestions of racial victimization—or race-specific claims based on the history of race discrimination in this country."[25]

That Obama framed his colleague's sentiments in the heavily laden language of "white guilt" should give us pause. Often when whites use that rhetoric, they make two moves. First, they deploy "guilt" to suggest a notion of individual culpability, and then deny that they bear any *personal* responsibility for past racism. This move sidesteps the fact that many whites continue to benefit from persistent social inequalities produced by past and present racism; more fundamentally, it also misrepresents the issue, which is not one of personal guilt (anymore than it is of personal bigotry), so much as a shared social obligation to remedy injustice. Then, in the second maneuver, after painting themselves as innocent individuals, whites wielding the language of guilt often portray themselves as victims—subject to emotional blackmail by unscrupulous minorities. Those advocating racial reform are presented instead as racial hucksters, cynically seeking the rewards of manipulating others by appealing to their guilt.[26] Regardless of whether Obama intended to summon the full weight of this perspective, adverting to the exhaustion of "white guilt" made it difficult for him to probe more deeply into the dynamics behind many whites' antipathy toward reform efforts. In any event, this is not an inquiry Obama pursued.

Instead, uncritically accepting that whites have largely lost interest in racial justice, Obama drew from his colleague's comments the conclusion that progressives must desist from the direct pursuit of racial justice. They must retire reform efforts centered on "proposals that solely benefit minorities and dissect Americans into 'us' and 'them.'" Rather, in 2006 Obama proposed pursuing "universal appeals . . . that help all Americans (schools that teach, jobs that pay, health care for everyone who needs it, a government that helps out after a flood) . . . even if such strategies disproportionately help minorities."[27]

As president, Obama repeated his preference for universal rather than race-focused solutions, for instance telling black audiences: "I can't pass laws that say I'm just helping black folks. I'm the president of the United States. What I can do is make sure that I am passing laws that help all people, particularly those who are most vulnerable and most in need. That in turn is going to help lift up the African-American community."[28] Then, practicing what he preached, Obama's first administration largely refused to undertake initiatives especially geared to helping nonwhites. The Department of Justice proved something of an exception, ramping up investigations into racial discrimination and taking an aggressive stance against voter disenfranchisement efforts. Apart from this, though, the White House did very little to directly ameliorate the crises engulfing minority communities, including harms directly triggered by the Great Recession. Shunning such efforts formed an essential component of a larger post-racial strategy of disengaging from race as much as possible. After his Philadelphia speech in 2008 and until his heartfelt remarks on the verdict in the murder of Trayvon Martin in 2013, Obama effectively stopped speaking about race to the general public, by one account talking about race less than any Democratic president since 1961.[29] For Obama, to be post-racial meant to eschew any mention of race, and if this meant largely abandoning efforts to specifically promote racial justice, then so be it.

Advocates of both rightwing colorblindness and liberal post-racialism argue for doing nothing to promote racial justice. I do not mean fully to equate colorblindness and post-racialism, for in their underlying intentions, they differ diametrically: colorblind partisans aim to leave racial inequalities unaddressed; post-racialists hope to ameliorate them through universal approaches. Moreover, the racial sensibilities of many liberals speak movingly to past racial injustices and to the current devastation of nonwhite communities. Discussing blighted neighborhoods in his adopted hometown of Chicago, Obama strongly rejects the explanation offered by "conservative think tanks," the colorblind rhetoric that blames "cultural pathologies—rather than racism or structural inequalities." For Obama, these desperate places tell "the stories of those who didn't make it out of history's confinement, of the neighborhoods within the black community that house the poorest of the poor, serving as repositories for all the scars of slavery and violence of Jim Crow, the internalized rage and the forced ignorance, the shame of men who could not protect their women or support their families, the children who grew up being told they wouldn't amount to anything and had no one there to undo the damage."[30] And yet, however powerful his insight and however heartfelt his empathy, post-racial politics nevertheless carries Obama to a terminus close to that of the colorblind ideology he otherwise rejects. Differences in intentions and sensibility notwithstanding, on the fundamental question of what should be done about racial injustice, colorblindness and post-racialism come to the same disheartening conclusion: do nothing.

The result for communities of color has been severe. Reflecting on Obama's post-racial approach, Columbia professor Fredrick Harris issued this indictment just days before Obama's re-election: "the triumph of 'post-racial' Democratic politics has not been a triumph for African-Americans in the aggregate. It has failed to arrest the growing chasm of income and wealth inequality; to improve prospects for social and economic mobility; to halt the re-segregation of public schools and narrow the black-white achievement gap; and to prevent the Supreme Court from eroding the last vestiges of affirmative action."[31] At the end of Obama's first term, 28 percent of African Americans and 27 percent of Latinos were poor; among black and Latino children, over one-third were growing up in poverty. The comparable figures for whites stood at 10 percent, with 13 percent of white children in poverty. Over the decade ending in 2010, whites experienced a 7 percent drop in household income. The same decade knocked down African Americans with a 17 percent drop in family earnings, while Latinos took an 11 percent hit.[32] Post-racialism is not solely responsible for these outcomes, but in avoiding any direct engagement with race, the post-racial strategy has made addressing the plight of nonwhite communities virtually impossible, ensuring that the especially vulnerable position of minorities will persist long into the future.[33]

■ STEERING CLEAR OF LIBERALISM

Post-racialism justifies walking away from direct responses to racial inequality by promising universal approaches, and in doing so, it not only betrays minorities but dupes the middle class more generally. It's not just that post-racialism abandons race-targeted efforts; the overriding impulse to flee from race also guarantees that post-racial liberals will only timidly fight for their vaunted universal solutions. After decades of dog whistle politics, even race-neutral liberal efforts do not escape racial taint: liberalism itself is widely perceived as race-targeted. Thus post-racialism ultimately encourages abandoning not only direct responses to racial inequality, but liberal endeavors too closely associated with nonwhites—which is to say, liberalism in general. Despite Obama's promise to promote universal programs, in his flight from race Obama has jettisoned liberalism as well. Avoiding race so as not to alienate middle class voters, Obama also has sacrificed the middle class.

To see the interaction of racially marked liberalism, dog whistle politics, and post-racial evasion, consider health care reform. Major players in the medical field, including giant insurance companies and more recently HMOs, have for decades warred against government efforts to provide universal access to health care. Tactics have included the standard appeals to freedom of choice, fear mongering about "socialized medicine," and warnings about government paternalism. During the Clinton administration, the drumbeat against infantilization was especially pronounced, aided by casting the "nanny state" in the form of a domineering woman—Hillary Clinton and her proposals for "Hillarycare." In addition, as a progressive initiative closely associated with liberalism, universal health care has long been tarnished in racial terms. One study from 2007 found that voters who measured high in their levels of racial resentment were 30 percent more likely to oppose government-supported health care reform.[34] It's noteworthy that this study predates Obama's emergence as health care reform's public face, and thus betrays the underlying racialization of liberal programs that has resulted from decades of race-baiting.

Obama's health care proposal, already tainted as a liberal program, then suffered targeted racial attacks, for instance in constant references to "Obamacare." Reform opponents embraced that derisive appellation to brand and tarnish the effort; in trumpeting this phrase, they were blowing a dog whistle. Superficially, the label seemed race-neutral, a gibe mocking Obama personally. Yet just as Hillarycare invoked gender stereotypes, for some Obamacare triggered racial reactions. A few liberal pundits advised repurposing this negative label, altering Obamacare into Obama Cares, thus emphasizing the positive aspects of personal empathy and governmental compassion. But the underlying charge was racial and could not be addressed through notes of liberal concern—on the contrary, the confluence of liberalism and race made the subliminal message behind "Obamacare" especially damaging: *here comes a black man to get government involved raising taxes on you in order to fund even more giveaways to minorities.* Obama Cares was less likely to alter the basic dog whistle message than to accentuate the suspicion that Obama cares—about minority loafers and not white taxpayers. Or, to glimpse dog whistle politics working on a different level, recall that the fracas over Obama's comments on the Gates arrest came in the midst of the health care debate. In the middle of a national debate on the numbers of Americans without adequate health care and what we might do about it, the right began attacking Obama as a racist. This fit squarely within dog whistle politics, supplanting a substantive focus on liberal reforms with baleful racial accusations.

After decades of coded racial appeals, even seemingly race-neutral programs such as health care reform are widely perceived, and quickly attacked, in highly racialized ways. The health care debate made abundantly clear that the universal solutions that Obama promises will move the country forward cannot be promoted without a debilitating brawl over race.

Yet how has Obama responded? Certainly not by objecting to racial demagoguery. In November 2009, a survey showed that half of all Americans recognized that "race was at least a minor reason" behind opposition to medical care reform.[35] This is a remarkably high number for a country not notably perceptive about contemporary dog whistling. On the other hand, the influence of race on the health care debate was deep: from 2007 to 2009, the impact of racial resentment on opposition to health care reform *doubled*.[36] For his part, though, Obama repeatedly denied that race had anything to do with opposition to his proposals. No doubt he knew better, but calculated that he would lose more by challenging race than by leaving racial attacks uncontested. Seemingly following the dictates of post-racialism, Obama decided not to defend health care reform from coded race-baiting.

In addition to an unwillingness to address racial entreaties directly, Obama's post-racial strategy also included an active campaign to keep progressive allies quiet on race. The White House put out a message to liberal organizations and civil rights groups: support the president, stay patient, don't mention racial injustice or respond to racial provocations. The administration saw this as necessary to keep itself from being pulled into any affray, and to protect itself, it was willing to threaten its allies: stay silent, or risk getting frozen out by the White House. Even as the Great Recession was taking an especially terrible toll on nonwhites, and even as dog whistle blasts were rising to an ear-splitting crescendo, the administration commanded progressives to stay away from race. Almost all of the mainstream liberal think tanks and foundations readily acquiesced; many of them had already internalized post-racialism as a strategy, and the president's admonition to stay quiet on race seemed like good logic. Among the civil rights groups, frustration prevailed. Many felt vexed that the president took them for granted, and by refusing to move forward on racial justice, had even betrayed their trust. But a sense of supportive loyalty nevertheless prevailed, and these groups also largely remained silent. The Obama administration repeatedly retreated when confronted by rightwing racial broadsides, but played hardball to ensure quiet on racial issues by progressive organizations. Post-racialism among liberals has become a strategy of silence, and also of silencing.[37]

What Should Obama Do?

A year into Obama's first term, professor and cultural critic Michael Eric Dyson famously quipped that Obama "runs from race like a black man runs from a cop." Dyson instead argued that Obama should run toward it: "I think that we should push the president.... What we have to do is ask Mr. Obama to stand up and use his bully pulpit to help us. He is loath to speak about race."[38]

I disagree. It's a dubious strategy to strong-arm Obama into addressing racial justice issues in order to "help us," as Dyson implored. Likewise, it's doubtful that pressuring Obama to call out racial demagoguery makes good political sense. As a Democratic president and especially as an African American one, Obama cannot address issues of race—of racial injustice, let alone of racism in politics—without coming under withering attack. Dog whistle politics has gelled into a strong commonsense linking Democrats and liberalism with unwarranted solicitude for nonwhites, and also painting those who challenge racism as the true divisive figures in society. This commonsense was shaken by the crises of

2008, and might have shattered had Obama robustly endorsed liberalism in his first months in office and then consistently worked with allies to renew liberal programs that helped the middle class. But he missed this historic opportunity and dog whistle politics came storming back, perhaps stronger than ever. Today, racial suspicion of Obama is intense, even with him ducking race whenever possible. It would almost certainly metastasize were Obama to speak out on white racism. It's simply too much now to ask Obama to overcome those dynamics during his presidency.

Moreover, even if obvious, it bears emphasis: Obama managed to get health care reform passed without repulsing his racial attackers. Though he dropped the single-payer system with the greatest promise, Obama nevertheless laid the groundwork for extending health insurance to perhaps 30 million Americans, the greatest expansion of social legislation since Johnson's Great Society. The point is not that post-racialism forecloses the possibility of liberal reform. Obviously, moderate progress can still be made.[39] Nor is the point to reject post-racialism as a strategy in favor of relentlessly engaging race in every circumstance. Sometimes, avoiding racial explosions provides the wisest course.

Rather, the point is that the "solution" to dog whistle politics offered by post-racialism has real and drastic costs to nonwhites as well as to the middle class in general. To avoid contentious debates about race, post-racialism dictates that we not address racial problems directly. Beyond that, post-racialism cautions against full-throated endorsements of liberal programs, since today these are inevitably associated with race. Finally, it warns against responding directly to race-baiting. Though in the short run post-racialism might be an appropriate strategy for achieving limited liberal gains, in the long term post-racialism offers no solution to dog whistle politics or persistent racial injustices. Instead, in imitating colorblindness and endorsing dog whistle themes, post-racialism perversely ensures that racial demagoguery will remain a major limit on liberalism for years to come, to the continuing injury of the middle class.

Democrats having been fleeing race for decades, when they have not been affirmatively blowing the dog whistle themselves, and during that time rightwing munitions have kept pounding away at government with constant racial insinuations. Throughout, the liberal sages repeatedly offered the same stale post-racial advice: avoid racial divisions and focus on universal solutions. Like Obama, they understood that the right has mobilized broad populist antipathy toward progressive governance through racial politics. But they feared to contest this directly. Instead, they hoped that if they just ignored it—or even imitated it—dog whistle politics would not do too much damage. Mass incarceration and mass deportation, the economic calamity confronting many in the middle class, the return of robber baron-era levels of inequality, and the increasing threats to once sacrosanct welfare programs like Social Security and Medicare—all of these testify to the error of going mute in the face of dog whistle racism. Proactive strategies are needed if dog whistle racism is to be defeated. There are things Obama, and all of us, can do to fight dog whistle politics.

Conclusion

To End Dog Whistle Politics

How can we bring dog whistle politics to an end? One perennial suggestion is to wait it out. This has not worked, and will not work. Instead, here are recommendations for proactive responses addressed to liberal politicians, civil rights organizations, progressive foundations and unions, and concerned individuals.

The summer after he took over the presidency from the slain John F. Kennedy, Lyndon Johnson signed into law the 1964 Civil Rights Act, the most sweeping piece of civil rights legislation passed in the twentieth century. According to his aide, the president knew this was a historic accomplishment with a steep price to be paid: "When he signed the act he was euphoric, but late that very night I found him in a melancholy mood as he lay in bed reading the bulldog edition of the *Washington Post* with headlines celebrating the day. I asked him what was troubling him. 'I think we just delivered the South to the Republican party for a long time to come,' he said."[1] As a Southerner, Johnson expected there would be a significant but temporary backlash. He failed to anticipate that the GOP would purposefully construct a strategy around covert racial appeals that would encompass the whole country and would endure for more than half a century. Johnson himself won that fall, but his 1964 election marked *the last time* a majority of whites voted for a Democratic presidential candidate. Republicans have carried white majorities in every presidential election since, typically by commanding margins. When and how will it end?

■ DEMOGRAPHY WILL NOT SAVE US

The backlash conception popular a couple of decades ago intimated that dog whistle politics would dissipate as the older generation reared under open white supremacy passed from the scene. This didn't happen. Nevertheless, today we're being told much the same thing: take heart, for changing demographics will solve this problem. That's unlikely.

RACE AND THE REPUBLICAN PARTY

Conservatives cannot simply walk away from racial pandering, as they've been too successful in making race integral to modern conservatism. Pause for a moment and consider just how central race has become to the Republican Party. Nine out of ten of its voters are white, as are 98 percent of its elected officials across the country. And to be clear, that 98 percent figure comes from 2008, *before* the racially anxious Tea Party rebellion remade local Republican organizations.[2] More than one of every three residents of the United States today is not white. In that context, the level of homogeneity achieved by Republicans just doesn't happen by accident; it has taken tremendous effort to transmogrify the GOP into the "white man's party."

More fundamentally, the white identity of conservatism lies in a tendency to see the world in terms of race. It's not simply that the vast majority of Republicans have fair features and European ancestry. Rather, it's that many whites affiliate with the GOP because it resonates racially with how they perceive themselves, others, and government. Conservatives cannot and will not pivot on a dime, for dog whistle politics is not just a strategy, it's now a formative element of American conservatism. In the United States, race is now the single most powerful divide between liberal and conservative self-conceptions. According to Edward Carmines and James Stimson, two of the foundational scholars on the political realignment that has transpired over the past decades, "if we ask simply, what do we know if we know someone avows a position on the liberal-conservative continuum? we answer that more than anything else we know that person's views on race."[3] Race provides the filter through which most white conservatives make sense of society and its problems.

Beyond these numbers and the ideology that produced and sustains them, the racial identification of the Republican Party will endure even if, however unlikely, the national GOP genuinely seeks to dump dog whistle racism. The rapid racial changes in the United States make many people nervous. Whites who turned 50 in 2010 were born when the country was 90 percent white, and they may well remember a homogenously white community from their youth. But if they live in California or Texas, or in any number of the nation's largest cities, they're already a racial minority. Many whites may be comfortable with these changes, or even welcome them, but many do not. This is especially true among older whites, who are less likely to personally know or be familiar with nonwhites, and are more likely to see themselves in direct conflict with them.[4] The older population frets over whether the government will have the funds to cover Social Security and Medicare and worries that resources they need are being diverted to provide services for younger folks, more of whom are non-white. Among demographers, this looming conflict is expressed in short hand as "gray versus brown."[5] For decades, the GOP has positioned itself as offering racial succor to those whites—elderly or otherwise—casting about for security. It's unlikely that state-level Republicans will set aside this comparative advantage in appealing to a demographic group that will likely remain anxious for some time, and this in turn will have long-term national ramifications.

Evolving Dog Whistle Themes

Rather than fading from the scene, dog whistling will evolve. Since the days of George Wallace, demagogues have been quick to adapt when crafting new coded racial appeals, while the public has been slow to condemn these entreaties, typically failing to recognize them as racial until long after they've already done their damage. Crime, forced busing, welfare, taxes, affirmative action, immigration, terrorism—what's next? Current trends suggest education and China.

The public schooling of children has long been a focus of dog whistle politics. Public education provides easy race-baiting opportunities and in addition it is also a favorite bugaboo of anti-government conservatives. In terms of race-baiting, where once "forced busing" offered a favorite dog whistle, the fact that public schools now are highly segregated by race and in many areas primarily serve nonwhites has allowed public education to be recast as exemplifying white tax money being wasted on unruly minority youths. Then, in terms of conservative politics, schools constitute both the enemy and an opportunity. They are a natural target as an expensive social-service, but the very funds going to education also represent an attractive opportunity to divert public money to private corporations. Schools are also well suited for the more camouflaged form of rightwing racial politics that seeks to push nonwhite faces at the fore; conservatives can argue that they are attacking public education because they care so deeply about protecting nonwhite kids.

Consider the pitch on education offered by House Majority Leader Eric Cantor, a Tea Party favorite, put forward after the 2012 elections temporarily motivated the GOP to rebrand itself as committed to serving minorities: "I've talked about a man who is a dad here in the inner city of the District of Columbia who, all he wanted was to find a safe place for his kids to learn. . . . I think what we care about, and what he cares about, is his kids."[6] Cantor's proffered solution? Provide direct funding to parents looking to pull their children out of public schools.[7]

This might seem to be an instance of genuine concern for families with children trapped in failing schools, but on a deeper level it harks back to the tactics of Clint Bolick, who in the 1990s proposed using black children as fronts in efforts to defund public schools.[8] In this retooled version of conservatism, the use of young nonwhite faces obfuscates an agenda that remains unchanged: attack liberal government for wasting money on social services like education. Yes, pulling money out and giving it to parents might help some households, although the evidence shows charter schools on average perform more poorly than public schools. More fundamentally, direct subsidies to parents facilitate (white) flight from public schools, cripple funding for public school systems, and redirect state money into private hands.

Beyond helping to obscure this agenda, the use of nonwhite children also masks how dog whistling continues. For many whites, "public school" itself operates as a dog whistle term, connoting a dangerous nonwhite place that consumes vast resources yet fails to educate masses of young delinquents. This connotation traces back to the civil rights era when conservatives framed integration as making schools unsafe for white children, and over the decades—as whites fled, schools resegregated, and student bodies in many districts became almost exclusively nonwhite—this ulterior meaning has only grown more potent. The main problem, according to Cantor, is terrible schools in DC, and abysmal public education more generally. By saying he wants to help nonwhite children, Cantor adds another layer of veneer; how can this be racial pandering, when all he wants to do is help minorities? But beneath the veneer, conservative dog whistling blasts along: government serves minorities, and fails them; liberalism wastes white tax dollars; fear government, trust the market.

Economic competition with China may also soon mature into a major dog whistle theme. During the 2012 presidential debates, China constituted the one peril on which Mitt Romney and Barack Obama could agree, with both candidates taking aggressive swipes at that economic powerhouse. On one level, this reflected genuine conflicts of interest between the United States and China, implicating important domestic policy considerations. On another, though, it risked capitalizing on xenophobia. All too easily, the economic threat from China can morph into a perceived racial one as well. Consider a particularly over-the-top 2012 Super Bowl attack ad by Republican Senate candidate Pete Hoekstra against Senator Debbie Stabenow. The ad ultimately provoked cries of insensitivity and even racism, apparently contributing to Hoekstra's loss. Nevertheless, the commercial highlights the racial possibilities in barbs over trade with China. In the ad, set to Chinese music, an Asian actress wearing a conical wicker hat rides into view in a rice paddy; stopping in front of the camera, she smirks to the audience in broken English, "Thank you, Michigan Senator Debbie Stabenow! Debbie spend so much American money, you borrow more and more, from us. Your economy get very weak, ours get very good. We take your jobs." Staying on script, when he was subsequently criticized for the ad Hoekstra retorted that he was not racist, while his campaign manager kicked back that "democrats talk about race when they can't defend their records."[9]

If the economy continues to stagger and if China continues to rise, we will likely see more and more dog whistling around China, and for similar reasons perhaps around India as well. In turn, along with these coded appeals we should also expect to see increasing hostility toward Chinese and Indian Americans, and—because racial animosities rarely prove especially discerning—likely toward Asian Americans in general. It has certainly happened before. In 1982, at the height of anti-Japanese rancor stoked by politicians warning of Japanese economic competition, Vincent Chin, a Chinese American, was murdered in a hate crime in Detroit. The perpetrators were white employees of a Chrysler plant that had recently laid off workers; the killers allegedly told Chin before bludgeoning him with a baseball bat, "it's because of you little mother fuckers that we're out of work."[10]

RECRUITING NONWHITES

Dog whistle politics will also likely evolve in the direction of recruiting support from some segments among the nonwhite population. Those who anticipate demography rescuing the Democrats, for instance the political scientists Shaun Bowler and Gary Segura in their book *The Future Is Ours*, do so on the assumption that nonwhites will continue to support the Democratic Party at rates similar to those demonstrated in 2012. But even they concede that "if minority voters move even slightly in the direction of distributions that mirror those of whites, Democrats are sunk."[11] In other words, small defections can tilt the balance sufficiently to create new openings for a GOP that repeatedly attracts a supermajority of whites. The election of a young black president may have helped secure nonwhite loyalty and a sense of personal investment in the Democrats, but other trends suggest caution. For instance, there seems to be a long-term pattern of disaffiliation by African Americans from the Democratic Party, which has long taken their "captured" support for granted.[12] Between 1968 and 2004, the numbers of blacks identifying as Democrats fell from roughly 90 percent to 60 percent.[13]

With respect to Latinos and Asians, a distinct pattern emerges. These groups are comprised overwhelmingly of recent immigrants and their children. Beyond the heterogeneity this implies, it also means that significant segments within these populations have yet to be socialized into party affiliation, or even into political participation. Growing up, many white and black Americans develop an affinity for a political party around the dinner table; this happens with far fewer Asians and Latinos born in the United States to immigrant parents. As a result, Latinos and Asians are far less likely than whites or blacks to identify with either party. Recent surveys show that roughly one third of Latinos and Asians identify as Democrats. But half either identify as independents or indicate no preference between the parties.[14] The political scientists who have done the greatest amount of work in this area conclude: "What this means is that the future of the minority vote, and consequently the balance of power in American politics, is still very much up for grabs. If either party wants to attain dominance, it ignores this segment of the American population at its own peril."[15] Recent history demonstrates the portable support among Latinos for the different parties. George W. Bush, who made a point of reaching out to Hispanics, won 35 percent of their vote in 2000, and 45 percent in 2004.[16] Had Romney polled as well among Latinos, rather than raising their ire by calling for "self-deportation," he may well have won the election. Making this point in scathing terms, on election eve Florida GOP operative Ana Navarro bitingly remarked, "Mitt Romney self-deported himself from the White House."[17]

Expanding Who Counts as White

In reaching out to Hispanics and Asians, the GOP may do more than reach out to nonwhite groups; it may contribute to a long-term transition in the very definition of who counts as white. Consider George Wallace's evolution on this issue. A hundred years ago, firm racial lines elevated Anglo-Saxons over the supposedly degenerate races from southern and eastern Europe, lines that only dissolved in the North in the decades after World War II.[18] The South, however, with fewer immigrants and a deeper commitment to an express ideology of white supremacy, clung more tightly to racially derogatory views of "swarthy" European races. One can hear an echo of this in Wallace's inaugural speech from 1963: just before he endorsed segregation now, tomorrow, and forever, he celebrated "this Cradle of the Confederacy, this very Heart of the Great Anglo-Saxon Southland."[19] As Wallace sought to move onto a national stage, though, he met resistance from those who accused him of disparaging eastern and southern Europeans as "lesser breeds." To counteract this challenge, Wallace began touring the North with Alabamans of Polish, Greek, Jewish, and Italian descent in tow. He did so to reassure these groups that they too shared in a collective white identity: "Speaking as racial victim to racial victim, [Wallace] drew them into the collective identity he described, articulating their interests as whites who were being betrayed by the federal government and made vulnerable to blacks, who by definition became their political enemies, just as they were his."[20] A pioneer of dog whistle racism, Wallace reconciled himself to pulling into the white fold those he seemingly regarded as "lesser breeds." Perhaps this too is a lesson other dog whistlers will learn.

How might expansions in who counts as white play out demographically? The census predicts that whites, 65 percent of the population in 2010, will become a minority by 2045. But this assumes that no Latinos will be included in the white population, a striking assumption given that on the same census, 53 percent of those who identified as Hispanic also claimed to be white.[21] When the census bureau reruns its racial projections and includes white Hispanics in the total tally of whites, it predicts that in 2045, far from whites becoming a minority, whites will number nearly 72 percent of the country's people.[22] (To give some context to this number: in 2013, House Republicans represented districts on average 75 percent white.[23]) In 2045 whites may account for 7 percent *more* of the population than they do today, depending on how white Latinos are counted. The current wisdom is that the white population in the United States is shrinking. But this depends on racial categories staying fixed, and more particularly, on Latinos continuing to be excluded from the white category. If, instead, a segment of the Hispanic population identifies and is seen as white, the next few decades may witness a surge in the country's white population.

It's not far fetched to imagine dog whistle appeals swinging a sizable portion of Latinos into the Republican camp. True, many or perhaps most Latinos—especially those with darker skin, less fluency in English, less education, and those who arrived more recently—will continue to form part of a racial underclass.[24] Notwithstanding this, significant numbers of Hispanics already consider themselves white, and this pattern bids likely to continue. Partly, this reflects conceptions of race that Hispanic immigrants bring with them, as Latin

American countries tend to have broader definitions of who counts as white.[25] Partly, this trend reflects the choices that new immigrants and their children make as they acculturate to a society structured around a white/nonwhite divide that accords much greater status to whites.[26] In addition, there is already a history of some Hispanics organizing themselves as middle-class whites. In the 1950s, leading Mexican American civil rights organizations challenged racial discrimination not on the ground that Jim Crow was immoral, but on the ground that Mexican Americans were white.[27] Like other immigrant groups, they placed themselves on the white side of the color line and were willing to denigrate blacks, and even to support racial segregation, if it helped their own claim to belonging. These same civic groups also supported policies to exclude "wetbacks," a racially derogatory term these leaders endorsed. Now as then, some Hispanics resent how the continuing arrival of new immigrants from Latin America heightens the sense that all Latinos are foreigners, and also fear that darker-skinned immigrants threaten their racial status.[28] GOP operatives often predict some success among Hispanics because of a supposed conservative strain in this group. Beyond that, though, racial dynamics among Latinos will also give dog whistlers some reason to hope, and to begin directing even more resources toward recruiting the right kind of Hispanics.

■ WHAT TO DO

Dog whistle politics is not going to evaporate on its own, not even under the sun of demographic change. To defeat race-baiting and to restore a liberal commitment to use government to help the middle class, proactive efforts are needed. How can different social actors, from politicians to average folks, move us forward?

POLITICIANS

Obama is not in a position to take on race directly. Many liberal politicians will have more leeway, especially if they are white and thus not doubly constrained by politics as well as racial identity. Even beyond directly contesting dog whistle politics, though, there are three things Obama, and by extension all liberal politicians, should be doing.

First, Obama must both articulate and govern according to a positive liberal vision. Either one, without the other, is insufficient. A message without action comes across as politics as usual, while there's also a risk to acting without an accompanying story. Too often, liberals craft programs that provide much-needed assistance but hide government's helping hand, facilitating later attacks by conservatives seeking to convince voters that liberal programs do nothing for them. To give renewed energy to liberalism requires crafting a positive message of where we want to go as a society and how we can get there, and then matching that with corresponding action. Obama began this process in his second inaugural address:

> We do not believe that in this country freedom is reserved for the lucky or happiness for the few. We recognize that no matter how responsibly we live our lives, any one of us at any time may face a job loss or a sudden illness or a home swept away in a terrible storm. The commitments we make to each other through Medicare and Medicaid and Social Security, these things do not sap our initiative. They strengthen us. They do not make us a nation of takers. They free us to take the risks that make this country great.

Having started to voice a liberal vision, Obama now must pursue the initiatives that show people that government makes a positive difference in their lives.

Second, Obama and liberal politicians must give a consistent and coherent account of who the real culprits are. Yes, mobilizing people with an uplifting vision is key, but so too is explaining who is holding us down, and even pushing us downward. With so much hardship in their lives, people want to know whom to blame: as two social critics recently put the point, "resentment abhors a vacuum."[29] Dog whistle politicians, conservative think tanks, and rightwing media sources have made assigning blame their principal task. Liberals should not engage in scapegoating, and indeed should take care to clarify that it is not great wealth itself, or corporations writ large, that are the problem. But by the same token, liberals cannot shy from identifying self-interested billionaires and giant corporations that attempt to distort the democratic process to serve their own narrow interests. Teddy Roosevelt, the great capitalist crusader for progressive government, captured this spirit when lambasting "malefactors of great wealth." Wealth was not their sin. Far from it, the patricians—like Roosevelt himself—had a role to play in contributing to society. But vast inequalities corrode social solidarity, and we must warn against the robber barons—individuals as well as corporations—that use their power and influence to promote only their own interests, with no regard for the damage they do to the rest of us.

Here's the third basic task: liberal politicians must encourage their appointees and allies to address race. If Obama has reason not to speak on race directly, others need to take up that task, both inside and outside the administration. Attorney General Eric Holder and Supreme Court Justice Sonia Sotomayor have taken some heat but have used their positions to stave off attacks from the right and to give voice to concerns about racial discrimination. These sorts of appointments should be more aggressively pursued, even at the cost of some political capital. Beyond that, Obama should support—or at the very least stop discouraging—voices outside the administration willing to raise issues of racial injustice and racial demagoguery. Jesse Jackson wasn't popular with whites who had fled the Democratic party or with the Democratic establishment, but once he criticized the racial politics of the Willie Horton ads, those ads lost some of their power, and support for the Republican candidate stopped climbing. Dog whistle politicians will adjust to increased criticism, perhaps by stepping up their charges that liberals shamelessly play the race card. Yet the research is clear that putting race front and center in voters' consciousness, rather than leaving it operating in the background, helps reduce the power of coded racial appeals.[30] Beyond the research, recent history shows that by staying silent, liberals do not evade race-baiting but merely cede the public square to racial demagogues and their coded trumpeting about race and liberal governance. In today's dog whistle political climate, silence on race spells defeat for liberalism and the middle class.

This is not to say that race is the only social division used to target liberalism. The broader history of culture war politics involves interwoven campaigns assailing gender, abortion rights, sexual orientation, same-sex marriage, religion, the environment, global warming, and guns, among other attacks. Defending liberalism will require more than thinking about how race has evolved over the last half-century. In addition, sustained attention must also be given to other targets of demagogic campaigns, and about how best to respond on those fronts as well.

CIVIL RIGHTS ORGANIZATIONS

In the battle against dog whistle politics, civil rights groups should pursue two distinct goals, one centered on promoting liberalism and the other on sparking a new civil rights movement.

In terms of liberalism, civil rights organizations should aim to clear space for its resurgence, and they can best do so by revitalizing the left pole in American politics. Fortuitously, civil rights groups can reinvigorate the left and create maneuvering room for liberalism precisely by pursuing their core mission of combating racial inequality. Imagine three positions regarding racial justice: a left commitment to directly addressing racial inequalities; a rightwing agenda of reversing civil rights and preserving the status quo; and in the middle, universal liberal programs that only indirectly help minorities. By staying silent on race, the left effectively disappeared: no one was arguing for direct responses to racial injustice. Without a true left, what had been the middle (universalism) came to appear as instead the counterweight to the right's insistence that nothing should be done. This made it easier for conservatives to paint universalism as a left-leaning, radical agenda, and this is where we find ourselves today, with even universalism in peril as Democrats fear being identified with "left" programs that would help everyone. In the short term, then, whether the White House gives its blessing or not, civil rights organizations must vociferously raise racial justice issues, shoving the left back away from the middle. Democrats have long seen civil rights activism as jeopardizing their prospects. But in reality, for Democrats to return to liberalism, they need an angry racial left against which to posture.

To be sure, this is a far cry from the Democrats returning to a commitment to racial justice, and providing a foil for liberal posturing should be understood as an emergency strategy. In the longer term, civil rights organizations must push liberals to directly engage with race again. Liberals must recommit to an ideal of activist government unskewed by racial antipathies. This is not to argue for a post-racial or colorblind universalism, though, but instead for what race scholar john powell calls "targeted universalism."[31] Racial groups are situated differently in the United States in their access to housing, education, decent jobs, professional networks, health care, healthy food, and so on. Solutions to these structural inequalities can be universal in their aspirations—decent opportunities along these dimensions for all—but the policies that will make this a reality inevitably must take into account the differing situations and needs of various groups. Correcting gross racial inequalities is necessary to make good on our social obligation to get beyond racism, and also honors the liberal ideal of helping especially the most vulnerable in society. Beyond the idealism, however, *ameliorating racial inequality is a precondition to ending racial politics.* So long as society remains riven by racial divisions, racial demagoguery will remain a threat to the middle class.

Building on this insight, the broad middle class will best be helped if civil rights organizations set their sights on sparking a new racial justice movement. This will require that they rethink their response to contemporary racism. For decades, racial organizations have assumed that to fight racism they must defend the civil rights achievements of the 1960s, and so they have been conducting an extended rearguard action in the courts and in Congress. Suffering defeats and constantly falling back to fight again, these organizations are presently regrouping from drubbings around affirmative action and voting rights. But these repeated pull backs, combined with the drive to salvage what they can by declaring each rout instead a victory, have combined to skew the vision of civil rights leaders. They increasingly see their core strengths in terms of legal expertise and access to the halls of government, and identify their overarching mission principally in terms of defending civil rights remedies that are ever more wounded, weak, and ineffectual. As a result, year by year civil rights groups have lost sight of how their power ultimately depends on an energized constituency mobilized around racial justice issues, and have also lowered their gaze from more ambitious conceptions of racial equality.

To understand the depths of the changes that need to be made, civil rights activists must recognize that our current situation is less like the 1970s than the 1920s—not in the degree of oppression, but rather, in its *invisibility*. In the 1970s, fights over racial injustice occupied center stage, and even in the face of sharp differences among groups about what to do, all sides conceded that racism was a pressing problem. Today, the right insists that racism against nonwhites is over, most whites seem to agree, and post-racialism convinces even many liberal allies that fighting racism is an unwise distraction. This resembles the 1920s, an era when most whites thought the great racial issue confronting the country— slavery—was safely resolved, and the NAACP campaigned to bring the horrors of widespread lynching into public consciousness as a goad to recognizing the depths of continued racial oppression. Present civil rights organizations need to commit themselves to rebuilding a widespread sense that racism continues to blight society. We should no longer see ourselves as fighting to preserve past successes. Instead, we should envision ourselves at the start of a new civil rights movement, one that must begin by convincing the public that racism yet remains a societal scourge.

The core precondition here is to reclaim and reinvigorate the language of "racism." Liberals have been urging flight from this word for decades, warning over and over that it is divisive and counterproductive—and so it is, if the goal is to assuage the anxieties of Wallace voters and Reagan Democrats. But if the goal is rebuilding a liberal coalition, the word "racism" must be used. The term carries so much power because at root it is a moral indictment: to call something racism is to say it is wrong and society must come together to change it. It's this very power that has made "racism" an object of such fierce struggle over the last half century. In the 1960s, society widely understood "racism" to apply to fundamental structural inequalities; today, for most it means malice and nothing more. This reversal reflects a conservative effort to choke the meaning of racism in a decades-long campaign that went largely unopposed by liberals afraid of losing white votes. Yet they largely lost those votes anyway, or regained them principally by abandoning minorities and liberalism too. The meaning of "racism" goes directly to society's obligations regarding racial justice—and also, to how liberalism is attacked. If liberals don't fight to define what this word means, the right will only too gladly define it for the whole society.

As a particular skirmish in this larger battle, reconsider the phrase "dog whistle racism." In Chapter Two, I defended this term as analytically accurate, but deferred the question of whether it was politically advisable. Let's pick up that point now. When in 1963 the GOP wrestled with the idea of becoming the white man's party, this violated the mores of many party leaders, making some sick at heart. They understood clearly the racial import of the party's actions. "I'm very much afraid," said one Republican official, "we're well on the road to becoming the white supremacy party, and there's no turning back."[32] Where is this sentiment now among Republicans? Two chairs of the Republican National Committee have apologized for the party's use of the "Southern strategy." Where's the apology for preserving notions of white superiority? And outside the GOP, how widespread and how deeply felt is the outrage over conservative racial pandering? As one race scholar notes, even the term "Southern strategy" is a "race-denying euphemism used by Republican operatives, mainstream media analysts, and academic researchers" to occlude what is fundamentally a "white racist strategy."[33] Racism has been at the core of Republican politics for decades, but because "racism" has been truncated to mean malice, and few want to be divisive or counterproductive, almost everyone has shied from naming and protesting this obvious fact. The cost, however, is that this rank injustice continues as normal practice year after year. Civil rights activists and liberals must fight to redefine racism to include unconscious racism, structural racism, commonsense racism, strategic racism and—last but very far from least—dog whistle racism.

Perhaps the existing civil rights organizations will take the lead, or perhaps new organizations taking new forms and adopting new tactics will emerge. This incipient anti-racist effort will not have a popular message—how could it, since it must aim to dispel the popular beliefs rooted in colorblindness that racism is largely over and that we are already a racially just society? But this new movement will take heart in the experience of Martin Luther King, Jr., remembering that he was not widely popular among his contemporaries. Especially as he moved from fighting the formal racism of Jim Crow to the more entrenched versions that endure into our times, his message stirred great insecurity and opposition. This will be the experience of any new civil rights movement attempting to disrupt settled patterns. Crafting a message that polls well is exactly what civil rights organizations must *not* do. Rather, they must lead and they must educate.

Most likely, the place to start lies with nonwhite communities, which have also largely acceded to the idea that racism is yesterday's problem. Even those who are victims of structural racism, trapped by large-scale forces beyond their control, tend to blame themselves. The rage that sparked the civil rights movement seems to have turned inward now that people no longer seem able to situate themselves within a broader history. The malice conception of racism contributes to this, making the impact of race almost impossible to identify in daily interactions that may involve few if any whites, let alone any malevolent bigots. Nonwhite communities also provide crucial organizing targets because conservatives seeking to adjust to the new demographic landscape will increasingly seek to recruit certain sectors within them. Under revamped race-baiting, especially Latino and Asian communities are likely to see their more well-off members enticed by appeals for a new allegiance with whites. Responding to current racial patterns and anticipating likely evolutions both counsel for working immediately in minority communities to reinvigorate outrage over "racism."

FOUNDATIONS AND UNIONS

Liberal foundations and unions have their own work to do. Like civil rights groups, they must help create space in the middle by staking out a more aggressive racial justice stance. In addition to helping liberalism in general, this will help these organizations fulfill their own missions. All too many progressive groups have adopted a version of post-racialism, deciding to ignore racism as a major force in deepening the social problems they are otherwise committed to solving, for instance in education, health, environmental degradation, and the welfare of children. Like other liberal institutions, many foundations have been heavily influenced by the Democratic Party's flight from race, following suit and leaving race behind as well. Unions have their own histories, with some taking more progressive stances on racial issues, and others struggling with unfortunate legacies. Most, however, have also retreated from directly engaging with racial justice.

Yet if the issues these groups care about touch at all upon poverty—and almost all do—then they also inevitably intersect with race. Moreover, if these groups seek help from government, then whatever solutions they propose will certainly be contested in racial terms. Race-baiting is the principal language used to oppose most liberal reforms, and progressive organizations cannot successfully lobby for helpful policies—even seemingly universal or race-neutral initiatives—without being challenged by racial narratives of government gone loco. Public unions in particular today find themselves the targets of aggressive attacks. Some of these are couched in economic terms, for instance highlighting the costs to taxpayers of fulfilling pension obligations. But coursing underneath is also a racial refrain that paints many unions, especially public ones, as havens for unproductive minorities. To protect themselves, and also to make progress on the issues they care most deeply about, unions and liberal foundations must recognize how they too have been stymied by dog whistle racism.

Beyond this, perhaps the principal work that these groups must embrace involves a long-term project to restore luster to liberalism itself. More ambitious than clearing space for liberalism in the short run, foundations and unions must begin an enduring campaign to rebuild a liberal consensus regarding how to help the middle class. For two reasons, progressives have largely stopped defending liberalism. First, paralleling their response to the Democratic demand to back off from race, many have acceded to similar pressure from the Clinton and Obama administrations to tone down demands for New Deal-style solutions to economic challenges. As the country has shifted rightward, many foundations and unions have followed suit, in the process abandoning advocacy for precisely the effective liberal solutions most able to restore the middle class.

Second, and curiously given the country's rightward lurch, many seem to hold a complacent sense that liberalism actually needs little defense. An attenuated version of liberalism still operates as a default position among the nation's intelligentsia, not only among unions and foundations, but from policy groups to the liberal media establishment to college campuses across the country. Partly for this reason, progressive groups seem convinced that, in the marketplace of ideas, liberalism will win out on its own strength.

And most likely liberalism would win out, all other things being equal. But as the ascendance of rightwing think tanks and media conglomerates show, in today's political economy bad ideas thrive with sufficient resources behind them, and good ideas wither from neglect. Following Powell's recommendations and the examples set by the likes of Joseph Coors and the Koch brothers, hundreds of millions of dollars have flowed into promoting notions that primarily serve the interests of the very wealthy. Liberals must acknowledge the skewed nature of the marketplace of ideas, and foundations and unions must step up their commitments to supporting advocacy organizations, think tanks, and grassroots groups motivated to re-engage the increasingly one-sided debates and to bolster liberal ideals.

This need to support liberal ideas extends to supporting universities, starting with the liberal arts programs that help foster the values and critical thinking that undergird liberalism's endorsement of mutual obligation, and extending to professional schools like law, business, and medicine that train many of the country's leaders. Conservatives have been especially effective at pouring money into winning the battle of ideas in law schools. Since the New Deal era, these schools have been fairly liberal in their political orientation. Recognizing this, in the early 1980s conservative funders like the Olin Foundation began a concerted effort to change the character of law schools, principally by using the "law and economics" movement. Their approach was surprisingly simple and effective: provide resources for workshops to create a sense of shared enterprise along with prizes and fellowships to signal professional accomplishment; and simultaneously fund faculty positions for law and economics programs at the most elite schools. In turn, because just a handful of schools produce the vast bulk of law professors hired across the country, this helped to shape the entire legal academy.[34]

How did liberal funders respond? So far, they have not, likely reflecting complacency about the supposedly secure status of liberalism in the idea-generating sectors of society. But this confidence is dangerously naïve, for liberalism is quite fragile at present. Liberal ideas are losing ground not because they lack merit, but because they receive thin backing, even as concentrated funding flows toward promoting conservative views. There's a specific, well-funded political project to defeat liberalism among society's thought leaders. A specific, well-funded political project is now necessary to support liberalism in those institutions that directly shape the perspectives and values of tomorrow's elected officials and tomorrow's voters.

THE REST OF US

Finally, what can individuals do to defeat dog whistle racism? The most basic step is to consciously consider race. The research is clear that colorblindness does not help us overcome racism; on the contrary, colorblindness as a strategy (rather than as a goal) forms part of the problem. Attempting to ignore what one has inevitably already noticed only makes it more difficult to recognize and thus control internalized racial stereotypes. Likewise, averting one's eyes to how race might be operating only makes one more susceptible to dog whistle manipulation. The racial subterfuge of coded appeals that has done so much to wreck the middle class is easy to pierce, but only if one consciously mulls over how race might be involved.

Once the basic step of watching out for race is taken, the next is to raise one's voice. Rightwing racial attacks on liberalism depend on cowing into silence those opposed to continuing racial demonization, thus allowing dog whistle calumnies to spread unchallenged. Connected to this, colorblindness also operates as an etiquette that treats talking about race as impolite and even racist. Those who discuss racism are accused of being the real racists—again, as if pulling a fire alarm means one set the fire, or dialing 911 means one committed the crime. Refusing to be silenced, to defeat dog whistle racism and restore government to the side of the middle class will require as many of us as possible to go ahead and sound that alarm.

For persons of color, this is likely to be especially risky. For minorities in largely white spaces (a description that fits virtually all elite settings), beyond colorblind etiquette there's additional pressure to stay silent. Just as James Baldwin in the 1960s found himself constantly forced to soothe whites made uncomfortable when his skin color drew into consciousness their racial position, so too today. For nonwhites, the price of access to elite environments typically takes the form of a Faustian bargain: receive a warm welcome at least partially offered to show that race no longer matters, but only so long as one does or says nothing that might show that race still matters.[35] Breaking this bargain can carry a steep penalty, including ostracism and an end to professional advancement. Yet accepting the deal makes one an accomplice to social practices that deny, and thus protect, the continued power of racism in society. Challenging dog whistle narratives and, longer term, building a renewed racial justice movement requires raising our voices against a silence that legitimizes racism.

Shifting to the political front, opposing dog whistle racism does not simply mean we should try to elect more Democrats. Virtually every academic critic of dog whistle politics focuses on how the GOP uses race to its advantage, in turn measuring the successful rebuttal of dog whistle appeals by whether Democrats nevertheless manage to retain or gain office. This is the wrong metric. It fails to take account of the extent to which Democrats themselves prevail by picking up the whistle. And it fails to recognize that dog whistle politics has been harnessed to a war on liberalism, a war in which Democratic politicians can be found on both sides. The ultimate goal is not to reassemble a winning Democratic majority. Rather, the goal is to restore a political consensus that sees government not as a handmaiden to mooching nonwhites, but as a powerful tool for promoting liberty and opportunity for all.

To that end, we have to be smarter about whom we support. Initially, the goal of restoring liberalism will entail supporting Democrats, because at least relative to current Republican politicians, on average the Democrats are not so hostile to progressive governance, nor so thoroughly indebted to concentrated wealth. Yet a new and durable Democratic majority carries a distinct risk. If a new Democratic coalition including people of color does emerge—and it may have already—this will be heralded as evidence that the country has fully triumphed over racism. This will reduce the sense of urgency regarding, and indeed will likely increase pressure to stay away from, potentially divisive racial issues that might destabilize the new coalition. In addition to leaving unaddressed the enormous challenges confronting nonwhite communities, the net effect of a renewed liberal consensus to ignore race would be to hold at arm's length liberalism itself. Already we see some leading liberals suggesting that Democrats must continue to "moderate[] their economic and social message," the better to avoid rekindling the "widespread popular disgust with the extremes to which liberal Democrats and New Left movements had gone in the late sixties and the seventies."[36] Arguments like these merely reinvigorate the advice Democratic pundits have been offering since the 1970s: flee from race and flee from liberalism and the middle class too.

Politicians respond to pressure, so we must pressure Democrats to return to liberalism. Some pushing should occur within the party's institutional structures, and some at the ballot box in primary fights between more and less liberal candidates. In addition, generating this pressure will require a renewed commitment to street politics. There's evidence of popular energy poised to surge. Obama's 2008 campaign mobilized a broad coalition of folks ready to fight for progressive governance, though many subsequently sunk back toward frustrated passivity when Obama tacked right. Another demonstration of popular ardor can be found in Occupy Wall Street and its many iterations across the country, Occupy demonstrated that tremendous passion exists around issues of economic inequality, and also showed that social media is creating new mobilizing opportunities and tactics. This insurgency deserves applause, as does the voluntarism that often followed, for instance in response to Hurricane Sandy. Yet Occupy also ultimately had little effect on the country, in significant part because it refused to engage in party politics. Just as the Tea Party formed an insurgency both outside and inside the GOP that forced that party to the right, a renewed commitment to liberalism will require an energized social movement on the streets willing to push, but also willing to accept major financial backing and committed to remaking the Democratic Party from both without and within.

In addition to mistakenly eschewing partisan politics, the Occupy movement also erred in supposing it could challenge economic inequality without engaging racism. It was a curious spectacle, for instance, to see so many white youths in Oakland up in arms about economic injustice but resistant to talking about racism, in a city where wealth and poverty correlate so closely with color. Given the correlation, helping poor people requires addressing racism. More fundamentally, because dog whistle politics has spent half a century building support for reactionary policies through hostility toward nonwhites, addressing racism is now a precondition to helping the broad middle class.

Toward the end of his life, Martin Luther King, Jr., proposed a Poor People's March on Washington that arose out of the black civil rights movement but became a multiracial movement for economic justice:

> There are millions of poor people in this country who have very little, or even nothing, to lose. If they can be helped to take action together, they will do so with a freedom and a power that will be a new and unsettling force in our complacent national life. . . . We will move on to Washington, determined to stay there until the legislative and executive branches of the government take serious and adequate action on jobs and incomes. . . . in fact, a new economic deal for the poor.[37]

Since King proposed the Poor People's March, the need for a multiracial economic justice movement has only become more exigent. In the intervening years, dog whistle politicians have repeatedly used racial frames to blame poverty on its victims, nonwhites and more recently poor whites too, and also to justify tearing down the government programs that aimed to provide a route upward.[38] For activists ready to take to the streets to confront the rising oligarchy, a specific concern with racism must be central to their agenda.

What should we be working toward? In his 1944 State of the Union address, Franklin Roosevelt urged a "second Bill of Rights," including "the right to earn enough to provide adequate food and clothing and recreation," "the right of every family to a decent home," "the right to adequate medical care and the opportunity to achieve and enjoy good health," "the right to adequate protection from the economic fears of old age, sickness, accident, and unemployment," and "the right to a good education." These are the rights that Roosevelt saw undergirding a prosperous and secure middle class. These are the goals to which we as a nation should recommit.

It may seem that by holding aloft King's 1968 Poor People's March, or extolling Roosevelt's second Bill of Rights from 1944, the driving political vision here is backward looking, even perhaps a naïve celebration of a romanticized past. It is not. Instead, my principal call is to restore an interrupted future. In the wake of the Great Depression, we came to appreciate the value of mutual responsibility tied to a model in which government corralled concentrated wealth and served everyone. We came to embrace liberalism in the same way that at the country's founding we tightly clasped liberty, and after the Civil War, equality. We seized on these not just as values, but as aspirations to guide us. Yet as with liberty and equality, so too with liberalism: we failed to live up to our ideals. Among the greatest stumbling blocks in each case, and still today, was race. The years between FDR's first election in 1932 and the end of Johnson's presidency in 1968 marked a giant step forward as US society committed to a vision of government dedicated to building the middle class. But this monumental step nevertheless remained fatally shackled to racism. When dog whistle politics pulled that chain tight, we stumbled in our progress and fell backward. It's time to renew our commitment to moving forward, resolved more than ever to making sure racism doesn't continue to bind our greatest aspirations.

* * *

It took me a long, long time to appreciate Derrick Bell's fundamental insight. A literal reading of his claim that racism was permanent distracted me. Of course racism is not permanent in the sense of unchanging; nevertheless, racism endures and evolves. Also, in rejecting Bell's teaching, I was thinking about myself and about the privileges that I enjoyed. Racism certainly didn't seem fixed and oppressive in my fortunate life. Yet beyond recognizing that racism adapts, Bell also possessed a gentle humanity that lead him to measure racism in the lives of the least privileged among us. He could see racism in the lives of the poor and hungry, the incarcerated, the deported, in the lives of those trapped by social forces beyond their control, both white and nonwhite. More than that, Bell insistently connected the fates of the disadvantaged and the privileged, showing how their diminishment threatened to drag us down and, more uncomfortably, how our status helped to justify their misery. Bell believed, ultimately, in mutual responsibility as a command that we look well beyond ourselves to see our connection to suffering. Coming to his scholarship from the front lines of civil rights work in the Jim Crow South, Bell studied, wrote, and taught about race as a way to touch humanity's pain—its infliction, its endurance, its resistance. Only from there did he seek, all the years he taught, to carve a way forward.

Was he dismayed, even embittered, as I thought when I was a student? He had a right to be. By then, conservative appointees to the Supreme Court and the Reagan administration had undone many of the advances Bell fought for as a lawyer and scholar, and there was no nadir in sight. But in the same book that bemoaned in its title the permanence of racism, Bell closed with an epilogue entitled "Beyond Despair." It seems fitting to award Bell the final word here too, as the best possible response to the deep and evolving challenge of dog whistle racism: "Somehow, as the legacy of our spirituals makes clear, our enslaved ancestors managed to retain their humanity as well as their faith that evil and suffering were not the extent of their destiny—or of the destiny of those who would follow them. Indeed we owe our existence to their perseverance, their faith. In these perilous times we must do no less than they did: fashion a philosophy that both matches the unique dangers we face, and enables us to recognize in those dangers opportunities for committed living and humane service."[39]

Appendix

Percentage of whites voting for the Republican, Democratic, and occasional third-party candidate, plus the GOP percentage of the popular vote and whites as a percentage of all voters. Winning candidates indicated in bold.

	GOP winning margin among white voters	GOP candidate	Democratic candidate	Third Party	GOP share of popular vote	White share of all voters
1960	4%	Richard Nixon 52%	**John F. Kennedy** 48%		50%	90%
1964	−29%	Barry Goldwater 36%	**Lyndon Johnson** 65%		38%	89%
1968	16%	**Richard Nixon** 52%	Hubert Humphrey 36%	George Wallace 12%	43%	89%
1972	40%	**Richard Nixon** 70%	George McGovern 30%		61%	87%
1976	4%	Gerald Ford 52%	**Jimmy Carter** 48%		48%	89%
1980	20%	**Ronald Reagan** 56%	Jimmy Carter 36%	John Anderson 8%	51%	88%
1984	32%	**Ronald Reagan** 66%	Walter Mondale 34%		59%	86%
1988	20%	**George H.W. Bush** 60%	Michael Dukakis 40%		53%	85%
1992	2%	George H.W. Bush 41%	**Bill Clinton** 39%	Ross Perot 21%	37%	87%
1996	2%	Bob Dole 46%	**Bill Clinton** 44%	Ross Perot 9%	41%	83%
2000	13%	**George W. Bush** 55%	Al Gore 42%	Ralph Nader 3%	48%	81%
2004	17%	**George W. Bush** 58%	John Kerry 41%		51%	77%
2008	12%	John McCain 55%	**Barack Obama** 43%		46%	74%
2012	20%	Mitt Romney 59%	**Barack Obama** 39%		47%	72%

Figures for 1960 through 1972 come from The American National Election Studies surveys. Figures from 1976 to 2012 come from the Roper Center for Public Opinion Research.

Notes

Preface

1. J. Christian Adams, "Obama's Beloved Law Professor: Derrick Bell," *Breirbart.com*, March 8, 2012.
2. David A. Graham, "Breitbart.com's Massive Barack Obama-Derrick Bell Video Fail," *The Atlantic*, March 8, 2012.
3. Derrick Bell Interview with David Garrow, January 28, 2010, New York, New York.
4. Jodi Kantor, "In Law School, Obama Found Political Voice," *New York Times*, January 28, 2007.
5. Kenneth Mack, "Barack Obama Before He Was a Rising Political Star," 45 *Journal of Blacks in Higher Education* 99, 100 (2004).
6. Derrick Bell, *Faces at the Bottom of the Well: The Permanence of Racism* (1992).
7. *Id.*, 12.
8. *Id.*, chapter nine.

Introduction

1. Elyse Siegel, "Michael Steele: For Decades GOP Pursued 'Southern Strategy' That Alienated Minorities," *The Huffington Post*, June 22, 2010.
2. Mike Allen, "RNC Chief to Say It Was 'Wrong' to Exploit Racial Conflict for Votes," *Washington Post*, July 14, 2005.
3. Tom Scocca, "Eighty-Eight Percent of Romney Voters Were White," *Slate.com*, November 7, 2012.
4. Shaun Bowler & Gary Segura, *The Future is Ours: Minority Politics, Political Behavior, and the Multiracial Era of American Politics* 66 (2012).
5. Michael D. Shear, "Demographic Shift Brings New Worry for Republicans," *New York Times*, November 7, 2012.
6. "President: Full Results," *CNNPolitics*, CNN.com, December 10, 2012.
7. Jon Wiener, "The Bad News About White People: Romney Won the White Vote Almost Everywhere," *The Nation*, November 7, 2012.
8. Matt Taibbi, "The Truth About the Tea Party," *Rolling Stone*, September 28, 2010.
9. Racial restrictions on liberal initiatives are catalogued in Ira Katznelson, *When Affirmative Action Was White: An Untold History of Racial Inequality in Twentieth-Century America* (2005).

10. Bill O'Reilly, "The White Establishment Is Now The Minority," *Fox Nation*, November 7, 2012.

11. Maeve Reston, "Romney attributes loss to 'gifts' Obama gave minorities," *Los Angeles Times*, November 15, 2012.

12. Carmen DeNavas-Walt, Bernadette D. Proctor, and Jessica C. Smith, U.S. Census Bureau, Current Population Reports, P60–243, *Income, Poverty, and Health Insurance Coverage in the United States: 2011*, at 5 (2012).

13. Hedrick Smith, *Who Stole the American Dream*, at xxiii (2012).

14. Elizabeth Warren & Amelia Warren Tyagi, *The Two-Income Trap: Why Middle-Class Parents are Going Broke* (2004).

15. Emmanuel Saez, "Striking it Richer: The Evolution of Top Incomes in the United States," (Updated with 2009 and 2010 estimates), p.1, March 2, 2012.

16. "S&P 500 CEOs Make 354 Times More Than Their Average Workers: AFL-CIO," *Huffingtonpost.com*, April 15, 2013.

17. Julie Creswell, "Hedge Fund Titans' Pay Stretching to 10 Figures," *New York Times*, April 15, 2013.

18. Joseph Stiglitz, "The 1 Percent's Problem," *Vanity Fair*, May 31, 2012.

19. Larry M. Bartels, *Unequal Democracy: The Political Economy of the New Gilded Age* 3 (2008). This difference caused Bartels to wonder why lower-income groups would vote Republican. Bartels speculates that this stems from patterns of economic growth during election years that have favored GOP candidates. *Id.* at 4.

Chapter 1

1. Dan T. Carter, *From George Wallace to Newt Gingrich: Race in the Conservative Counterrevolution, 1963–1994*, at 23 (1996).

2. Dan T. Carter, *The Politics of Rage: George Wallace, the Origins of the New Conservatism, and the Transformation of American Politics* 11 (1995).

3. Carter (1995), 236, citing J.L. Chestnut & Julia Cass, *Black in Selma: The Uncommon Life of J.L. Chestnut, Jr.*, 117 (1990).

4. Carter (1995), 95.

5. *Id.*, 96.

6. *Id.*, 109. "Wallace was a politician first who embraced racism second." Leonard Zeskind, *Blood and Politics: The History of the White Nationalist Movement from the Margins to the Mainstream* 14 (2009).

7. Michael J. Klarman, *From Jim Crow to Civil Rights: The Supreme Court and the Struggle for Racial Equality* (2006).

8. Carter (1995), 149–151.

9. Carter (1996), 6.

10. *Id.*

11. C. Vann Woodward, *The Strange Career of Jim Crow* 8 (3rd rev. ed. 1974). On the use of "states' rights" as a transitional language between explicit and implicit appeals to race, see Tali Mendelberg, *The Race Card: Campaign Strategy, Implicit Messages, and the Norm of Equality* 72–73 (2001). Mendelberg also discusses other Southern

politicians who early on, some earlier than Wallace, recognized the advantages of coded racial appeals. Mendelberg, 75–81.

12. Carter (1996), 4.

13. Quoted in Donald R. Kinder & Lynn M. Sanders, *Divided by Color* 227 (1996).

14. While national party leaders tended to be racial liberals, Republican state leaders were more likely to oppose civil rights and workplace anti-discrimination reforms. Anthony Chen, *The Fifth Freedom: Jobs, Politics, and Civil Rights in the United States, 1941–1972*, at 243 (2009).

15. Thomas Byrne Edsall with Mary D. Edsall, *Chain Reaction: The Impact of Race, Rights, and Taxes on American Politics* 36 (1992).

16. *Id.*

17. Kim Phillips-Fein, *Invisible Hands: The Businessmen's Crusade Against the New Deal* 127–139 (2009).

18. Jack Bass & Walter Devries, *The Transformation of Southern Politics: Social Change and Political Consequences Since 1945*, at 27 (1976).

19. Jacob K. Javits, "To Preserve the Two-Party System," *New York Times*, October 27, 1963.

20. Robert Novak, *The Agony of the GOP, 1964*, at 171 (1965), quoted in Joseph Aistrup, *The Southern Strategy Revisited: Republican Top-Down Advancement in the South* 28–29 (1996). See also Rowland Evans & Robert Novak, "Future 'White Man's' Party," *St. Petersburg Times*, June 25, 1963, at 9-A ("Far from desiring to out-do Democrats as crusaders for racial equality, substantial numbers of party leaders from both North and South see rich political dividends flowing from the negrophobia of many white Americans. These Republicans want to unmistakably establish the party of Lincoln as the white man's party.").

21. Tom Wicker, "Johnson Bids Congress Enact Civil Rights Bill with Speed; Asks End of Hate and Violence," *New York Times*, November 28, 1963.

22. Joseph Lowndes, *From the New Deal to the New Right: Race and the Southern Origins of Modern Conservatism* 71 (2008).

23. Richard Rovere, *The Goldwater Caper* 141–142 (1965), quoted in Earl Black & Merle Black, *The Rise of Southern Republicans* 139–140 (2002).

24. Lowndes, 68.

25. Rick Perlstein, *Before the Storm: Barry Goldwater and the Unmaking of the American Consensus* 430–431 (2009).

26. Sean Wilentz, "Confounding Fathers: The Tea Party's Cold War Roots," *The New Yorker*, October 18, 2010.

27. Carter (1996), 18–19.

28. Carter (1995), 347.

29. Rick Perlstein, *Nixonland: The Rise of a President and the Fracturing of America* 284 (2008).

30. Mary Frances Berry, "Vindicating Martin Luther King, Jr.: The Road to a Color-Blind Society," 81 *Journal of Negro History* 137, 139 (1996).

31. Anders Walker, "Blackboard Jungle: Delinquency, Desegregation, and the Cultural Politics of *Brown*," 110 *Columbia Law Review* 1911, 1952–1953 (2010).

32. Vesla M. Weaver, "Frontlash: Race and the Development of Punitive Crime Policy," 21 *Studies in American Political Development* 230, 248 (2007).

33. Michelle Alexander, *The New Jim Crow: Mass Incarceration in the Age of Colorblindness* 46 (2012).

34. Joe McGinniss, *The Selling of the President* 23 (1969).

35. Alexander, 44.

36. Molly C. Michelmore, *Tax and Spend: The Welfare State, Tax Politics, and the Limits of American Liberalism* 99–106 (2012). On Nixon's initial hesitancy over whether to adopt the Southern strategy, *see* Paul Frymer, *Uneasy Alliances: Race and Party Competition in America* 103 (1999).

37. Richard M. Scammon & Ben J. Wattenberg, *The Real Majority: How the Silent Center of the American Electorate Chooses its President* 184, 180, 285 (1970).

38. Kevin Phillips, *The Emerging Republican Majority* 22, 39–40, 470 (4th ed. 1970). See also James Boyd, "Nixon's Southern Strategy: It's All in the Charts," *New York Times*, May 17, 1970.

39. Lowndes, 133.

40. Richard Rothstein & Mark Santow, "The Cost of Living Apart," *American Prospect*, August 22, 2012.

41. Frederick A. Lazin, *Policy Implementation of Social Welfare in the 1980s*, at 90 (1987).

42. Aistrup, 5.

43. For an example of this misconception, see Adam Nossiter, "For South, a Waning Hold on National Politics," *New York Times*, November 10, 2008.

44. Boyd; Phillips, 465.

45. Phillips, 471–472.

46. Micah Cohen, "Solid South Reversed, but Still Divided by Race," *New York Times*, October 11, 2012.

47. For examples of this tendency, see Thomas F. Schaller, *Whistling Past Dixie: How Democrats Can Win Without the South* (2006); and Chuck Thompson, *Better Off Without 'Em: A Northern Manifesto for Southern Secession* (2012).

48. Thomas Edsall, "The Decline of Black Power in the South," *New York Times*, July 10, 2013.

49. Bruce Schulman, *The Seventies: The Great Shift in American Culture, Society, and Politics* 105–106 (2001).

50. Mendelberg, 71.

51. The question of what convinces voters to shift parties is interesting to political scientists, and on this level, scholars debate the significance of the Southern strategy, often downplaying its importance on the ground that Democrats continued to hold sway in local elections throughout the South for decades after the supposed rise of the strategy. But from the point of view of assessing the intersection of race, politics, and liberalism, the most pressing questions raised by the Southern strategy do not concern the numbers who once registered as Democrats yet now identify as Republicans or independents. Rather, the core questions center on the ideological consequences of race-baiting in politics, as well as its policy implications.

52. Boyd (emphasis added).

53. *Id.*
54. On the connection between racial reaction and religion, see Joseph Crespino, "Civil Rights and the Religious Right," 90 in *Rightward Bound: Making America Conservative in the 1970s* (Bruce Schulman & Julian Zelizer eds. 2008). On religion and white supremacist movements in the United States, see Michael Barkun, *Religion and the Racist Right: The Origins of the Christian Identity Movement* (1997).
55. Thomas Frank, *What's the Matter with Kansas? How Conservatives Won the Heart of America* (2005).
56. Edward G. Carmines & James A. Stimson, *Issue Evolution: Race and the Transformation of American Politics* 133, 185 (1989).
57. Just as some scholars doubt the significance of the Southern strategy by noting the election of Democrats, others dismiss its power by pointing out the class dimensions of the political realignment in the South. See, for instance, Byron Shafer & Richard Johnston, *The End of Southern Exceptionalism: Class, Race, and Partisan Change in the Postwar South* (2006). Ostensibly, the Republican ascendance in the wealthy, segregated suburbs of the "New South" demonstrates that the real issue is class, not race. But this supposes a neat, and ultimately untenable, distinction between race and class. On the intersection of race, class, and modern conservatism in the suburban South, see Kevin M. Kruse, *White Flight: Atlanta and the Making of Modern Conservatism* (2007).
58. Boyd.
59. Carter (1996), 29.
60. Boyd; Phillips, 470.
61. Richard Hofstadter, *Anti-Intellectualism in American Life* 13 (1962).
62. Phillips himself opposed plutocratic politics, and when the Republican Party shifted decisively in this direction, Phillips wrote in opposition. See, for instance, Kevin Phillips, *Wealth and Democracy: A Political History of the American Rich* (2002).
63. Edsall with Edsall, 9.
64. See Anthony Chen, *The Fifth Freedom: Jobs, Politics, and Civil Rights in the United States, 1941–1972* (2009); and Thomas J. Sugrue, *Sweet Land of Liberty: The Forgotten Struggle for Civil Rights in the North* (2008).
65. Edsall with Edsall, 9.
66. Daniel Martinez HoSang, *Racial Propositions: Ballot Initiatives and the Making of Postwar California* 20 (2010).
67. Thomas Sugrue, *Not Even Past: Barack Obama and the Burden of Race* 36–37, 82 (2010).

Chapter 2

1. Mark Peffley & Jon Hurwitz, "Persuasion and Resistance: Race and the Death Penalty in America," 51 *American Journal of Political Science* 996, 999 n.4, 1002, Table 1 (2007). See also Lawrence Bobo & Devon Johnson, "A Taste for Punishment: Black and White Americans' Views on the Death Penalty and the War on Drugs," 1 *Du Bois Review* 151, 160 (2004).

2. Peffley & Hurwitz, 1006.

3. Dorothy Roberts, "Constructing a Criminal Justice System Free of Racial Bias: An Abolitionist Framework," 39 *Columbia Human Rights Law Review* 261, 268 (2007).

4. US Constitution, Amendment XIII, §1.

5. Eric Foner, *Forever Free: The Story of Emancipation and Reconstruction* 202 (2006).

6. Douglas A. Blackmon, *Slavery by Another Name: The Re-Enslavement of Black Americans from the Civil War to World War II* (2008). Much of the following discussion draws on Blackmon's excellent work.

7. Blackmon, 95, 375, 295, 312–313.

8. Stanley Engerman & Robert William Fogel, *Time on the Cross: The Economics of American Slavery* (1974).

9. Matthew Mancini, *One Dies, Get Another: Convict Leasing in the American South, 1866–1928*, at 3 (1996).

10. Foner, 202.

11. Blackmon, 98. See also David M. Oshinsky, *Worse than Slavery: Parchman Farm and the Ordeal of Jim Crow Justice* 44 (1997).

12. Blackmon, 99, 318, 319, 71, 92.

13. Blackmon, 100, 234. *See* William Cohen, "Negro Involuntary Servitude in the South, 1865–1940: A Preliminary Analysis," 42 *Journal of Southern History* 31 (1976).

14. Blackmon, 380. See generally Mary L. Dudziak, *Cold War Civil Rights: Race and the Image of American Democracy* (2002).

15. Blackmon, 375.

16. Leonard Zeskind, *Blood and Politics: The History of the White Nationalist Movement from the Margins to the Mainstream* (2009).

17. Ian Haney López, "Intentional Blindness," 87 *New York University Law Review* 1779 (2012). For a further discussion of the Supreme Court's conception of racism, both as against minorities and as against whites, see Chapter Four.

18. Stokely Carmichael & Charles V. Hamilton, *Black Power: The Politics of Liberation in America* 4 (1967). Structural and institutional racism can be distinguished: where the former can be said to refer to social structures in general, institutional racism can be understood to describe practices and ideas within particular institutions, or even the way in which practices and ideas become institutionalized. For an extended exploration of the latter understanding, see Ian Haney López, "Institutional Racism: Judicial Conduct and a New Theory of Racial Discrimination," 109 *Yale Law Journal* 1717 (2000).

19. Rakesh Kochhar, Richard Fry & Paul Taylor, "Wealth Gaps Rise to Record Highs Between Whites, Blacks and Hispanics," *Pew Research Center*, July 26, 2011.

20. For an extended discussion of structural racism, see Daria Roithmayr, *Reproducing Racism: How Everyday Choices Lock In White Advantage* (2014).

21. https://implicit.harvard.edu/.

22. john powell, *Racing to Justice: Transforming Our Conceptions of Self and Other to Build an Inclusive Society* 235 (2012).

23. Legal scholarship focused on unconscious racism prominently includes Charles Lawrence, "The Id, The Ego, and Equal Protection: Reckoning With Unconscious Racism," 39 *Stanford Law Review* 327 (1987); Linda Hamilton Krieger, "The Content of Our Categories: A Cognitive Bias Approach to Discrimination and Equal Employment Opportunity," 47 *Stanford Law Review* 1161 (1995); and Jerry Kang, "Trojan Horses of Race," 118 *Harvard Law Review* 1489 (2005).

24. See Mahzarin Banaji & Anthony G. Greenwald, *Blindspot: Hidden Biases of Good People* (2013).

25. I develop this argument in Ian Haney López, "Post-Racial Racism: Racial Stratification and Mass Incarceration in the Age of Obama," 98 *California Law Review* 1023 (2010), where I draw on Douglas Massey, *Categorically Unequal: The American Stratification System* (2008).

26. Barbara Fields, "Slavery, Race and Ideology in the United States of America," 181 *New Left Review* 95 (1990).

27. See generally Audrey Smedley, *Race in North America: Origin and Evolution of a Worldview* (1993).

28. Winthrop Jordan, *White Over Black: American Attitudes Toward the Negro, 1550–1812* (1968).

29. Samuel R. Sommers & Michael I. Norton, "Lay Theories About White Racists: What Constitutes Racism (and What Doesn't)," 9 *Group Processes & Intergroup Relations* 117, 119 (2006).

30. Bruce Western, *Punishment and Inequality in America* 13 (2007).

31. The Pew Center on the States, *One in 100: Behind Bars in America 2008*, at 5 (2008).

32. Western, 15.

33. Paul Butler, *Let's Get Free: A Hip-Hop Theory of Justice* 27 (2009).

34. The Pew Center on the States, 6.

35. Western, 26, 27.

36. Nsenga Burton, "More Black Men in Prison Today Than Enslaved in 1850," *TheRoot. com*, March 30, 2011.

37. Western, 41.

38. Katherine Beckett, *Making Crime Pay: Law and Order in Contemporary American Politics* 38–43 (1997); and Vesla M. Weaver, "Frontlash: Race and the Development of Punitive Crime Policy," 21 *Studies in American Political Development* 230, 239–250 (2007).

39. Michelle Alexander, *The New Jim Crow: Mass Incarceration in the Age of Colorblindness* 49, 55 (2012).

40. Western, 15.

41. Alexander, 139–160. See also Devah Pager, *Marked: Race, Crime, and Finding Work in an Era of Mass Incarceration* (2007).

42. Western, 127.

43. Donald Braman, "Race, Poverty and Incarceration," 16(6) *Poverty & Race* 1, 9 (November/December 2007).

44. Dorothy Roberts, "The Social and Moral Cost of Mass Incarceration in African American Communities," 56 *Stanford Law Review* 1271 (2004).

45. Glenn C. Loury, *Race, Incarceration, and American Values* 27 (2008).

Chapter 3

1. "THE CAMPAIGN: Candidate Carter: I Apologize," *Time Magazine*, April 19, 1976.

2. "Jimmy Carter Doing Damage Control for 'Ethnic Purity' Remarks," *NBC Today Show*, April 9, 1976.

3. An audio recording of the interview, plus background material on its provenance, is available at Rick Perlstein, "Exclusive: Lee Atwater's Infamous 1981 Interview on the Southern Strategy," *The Nation.com*, November 13, 2012.

4. Tali Mendelberg, *The Race Card: Campaign Strategy, Implicit Messages, and the Norm of Equality* 143 (2001).

5. Kim Phillips-Fein, *Invisible Hands: The Businessmen's Crusade Against the New Deal* 111–114 (2009).

6. Ronald Reagan, "A Time for Choosing," October 1964.

7. Jill Quadagno, *The Color of Welfare: How Racism Undermined the War on Poverty* 98 (1994).

8. Kyle Longley, *Deconstructing Reagan: Conservative Mythology and America's Fortieth President* 76 (2007). See also Lou Cannon, *President Reagan: The Role of a Lifetime* 520 (1991) (noting that "Reagan never supported the use of federal power to provide blacks with the civil rights systematically denied to them by Southern states," and opposed the Voting Rights Act of 1965 as "humiliating to the South").

9. Paul Krugman, "Republicans and Race," *New York Times*, November 17, 2007.

10. Bob Herbert, "Righting Reagan's Wrongs?" *New York Times*, November 13, 2007.

11. Michael Goldfield, *The Color of Politics: Race and the Mainsprings of American Politics* 314 (1997).

12. Herbert.

13. Martin Gilens, *Why Americans Hate Welfare: Race, Media, and the Politics of Antipoverty Policy* (1999).

14. "'Welfare Queen' Becomes Issue in Reagan Campaign," *New York Times*, February 15, 1976. See also Kaaryn S. Gustafson, *Cheating Welfare: Public Assistance and the Criminalization of Poverty* 34–37 (2011).

15. Dan T. Carter, *From George Wallace to Newt Gingrich: Race in the Conservative Counterrevolution, 1963–1994*, at 64 (1996).

16. Michelle Alexander, *The New Jim Crow: Mass Incarceration in the Age of Colorblindness* 48 (2012).

17. Thomas Byrne Edall with Mary D. Edsall, *Chain Reaction: The Impact of Race, Rights, and Taxes on American Politics* 153 (1992).

18. Barack Obama, "Obama: Reagan saw that 'we are all patriots,'" *USA Today*, January 23, 2011.

19. Frank Rich, "The Tea Party Will Win in the End," *New York Magazine*, October 14, 2012.

20. Benjamin Page & Lawrence Jacobs, *Class War? What Americans Really Think about Economic Inequality* 59, 62, 66, 69, 72 (2009).

21. Felicia Pratto, Jim Sidanius, Lisa Stallworth & Bertram Malle, "Social dominance orientation: A personality variable predicting social and political attitudes," 67 *Journal of Personality and Social Psychology* 741 (1994); Chris Mooney, *The Republican*

Brain: The Science of Why They Deny Science—and Reality (2012); George Lakoff, *Don't Think of an Elephant: Know Your Values and Frame the Debate* (2004); and Jonathan Haidt, *The Righteous Mind: Why Good People Are Divided by Politics and Religion* (2012).

22. Benjamin Epstein & Arnold Forster, *The Radical Right: Report on the John Birch Society and Its Allies* 27 (1966).

23. Sara Diamond, *Roads to Dominion: Right Wing Movements and Political Power in the United States* 53–57 (1995). In the South, fears of "communism" also connected to opposition to racial equality. George Lewis, *The White South and the Red Menace: Segregationists, Anticommunism, and Massive Resistance, 1945–1965* (2004).

24. Robert Welch, *The Truth in Time* (1966).

25. *Id.* Welch also included several take-over methods, not quoted here, particular to the military fiasco in Vietnam.

26. Michael D. Shear & Michael Barbaro, "Romney Calls 47% of Voters Dependent in Leaked Video," *The New York Times*, September 17, 2012.

27. Epstein & Forster, 96.

28. Sean Wilentz, "Confounding Fathers: The Tea Party's Cold War Roots," *The New Yorker*, October 18, 2010.

29. William F. Buckley Jr., "Goldwater, The John Birch Society, and Me," *Commentary Magazine*, March 2008; Carl T. Bogus, *Buckley: William F. Buckley Jr. and the Rise of American Conservatism* 174–190, 196–198 (2011).

30. John Jeffries, *Justice Lewis F. Powell, Jr.*, 140–142 (1994).

31. Lewis F. Powell, Jr., "Confidential Memorandum: Attack of American Free Enterprise System," August 23, 1971.

32. Powell's memorandum did not come to public light until after his confirmation hearing, when its militantly pro-business orientation sparked controversy. Phillips-Fein, 161–162.

33. *Id.*, 165.

34. Russ Bellant, *The Coors Connection: How the Coors Family Philanthropy Undermines Democratic Pluralism* 45, 72 (1991).

35. Diamond, 133. See also Jean Stefancic & Richard Delgado, *No Mercy: How Conservative Think Tanks and Foundations Changed America's Social Agenda* (1996).

36. Adam Nagourney, "Frum Forced Out at Conservative Institute," *New York Times*, March 25, 2010. Contributing to his apostasy, Frum later wrote an incisive critique of the right: David Frum, "When Did the GOP Lose Touch With Reality?" *New York Magazine*, November 20, 2011.

37. Quoted in "The Political Activity of Think Tanks: The Case for Mandatory Contributor Disclosure," 115 *Harvard Law Review* 1502, 1511–1512 (2002).

38. Without waiting for Reagan's election, the corporate forces mobilized by the Powell memo began to exert their influence during the Carter administration. Hedrick Smith, *Who Stole the American Dream?* 14–22 (2012).

39. Charles L. Heatherly, ed., *Mandate for Leadership* (1981).

40. Bellant, 10; Thomas Medvetz, *Think Tanks in America* 6 (2012).

41. "Remarks to the American Enterprise Institute for Public Policy Research," Ronald Reagan Presidential Library Archives, December 7, 1988.

42. Edsall with Edsall, 168.
43. Joseph Stiglitz, *The Price of Inequality: How Today's Divided Society Endangers Our Future* 71 (2012).
44. Smith, 107–108.
45. Although Reagan would subsequently authorize a number of smaller tax increases, overall, the tax cuts pushed through under his administration dwarfed the tax increases.
46. Frederick Harris, *The Price of the Ticket: Barack Obama and the Rise and Decline of Black Politics* 191 (2012).
47. Quadagno, 195.
48. Suzanne Mettler, *The Submerged State: How Invisible Government Policies Undermine American Democracy* (2011).
49. Molly C. Michelmore, *Tax and Spend: The Welfare State, Tax Politics, and the Limits of American Liberalism* 73 (2012).
50. Heatherly, 447–448, 1083–1084.
51. Carter, 56–57.
52. Lee Cokorinos, *The Assault on Diversity: An Organized Challenge to Racial and Gender Justice* 26–27 (2003).
53. Drew Days, "Turning Back the Clock: The Reagan Administration and Civil Rights," 19 *Harvard Civil Rights-Civil Liberties Law Review* 309, 327 (1984).
54. Joseph Aistrup, *The Southern Strategy Revisited: Republican Top-Down Advancement in the South* 45 (1996).
55. Desmond S. King & Rogers M. Smith, *Still a House Divided: Race and Politics in Obama's America* 125 (2011).
56. Goldfield, 336–337.
57. Edsall with Edsall, 182.
58. *Id.*, 184.
59. Congressional Budget Office, "Trends in the Distribution of Household Income Between 1979 and 2007," at 21, October 25, 2011.
60. Binyamin Appelbaum & Robert Gebeloff, "Who Benefits From the Safety Net," *New York Times*, February 13, 2012.
61. *Id.*
62. Binyamin Appelbaum & Robert Gebeloff, "Even Critics of Safety Net Increasingly Depend on It," *New York Times*, February 11, 2012.
63. Carmen DeNavas-Walt, Bernadette D. Proctor, & Jessica C. Smith, U.S. Census Bureau, "Current Population Reports, P60-243, Income, Poverty, and Health Insurance Coverage in the United States: 2011," at 13, U.S. Government Printing Office (2012).

Chapter 4

1. Po Bronson & Ashley Merryman, "Is Your Baby Racist?" *Newsweek Magazine*, September 4, 2009.
2. Evan P. Apfelbaum, Samuel R. Sommers & Michael I. Norton, "Seeing Race and Seeming Racist? Evaluating Strategic Colorblindness in Social Interaction," 95 *Journal of Personality & Social Psychology* 918 (2008). See also Chapter Eight.

3. Bronson & Merryman.

4. Linda Hamilton Krieger, "Civil Rights Perestroika: Intergroup Relations after Affirmative Action," 88 *California Law Review* 1251, 1279 (1998).

5. Bronson & Merryman.

6. This discussion draws on Ian F. Haney López, "A Nation of Minorities: Race, Ethnicity, and Reactionary Colorblindness," 59 *Stanford Law Review* 985 (2007).

7. Plessy v. Ferguson, 163 U.S. 537, 559 (1896) (Harlan, J., dissenting). The metaphor of "colorblindness" should be more properly regarded as having been introduced into our constitutional lexicon by Homer Plessy's attorney, Albion Tourgée. Mark Elliott, *Color-Blind Justice: Albion Tourgée and the Quest for Racial Equality from the Civil War to* Plessy v. Ferguson (2006).

8. Parents Involved in Community Schools v. Seattle School District No. 1, 551 U.S. 701, 772–773 (2007) (Thomas, J., concurring).

9. *Plessy*, 163 U.S. at 559.

10. Pace v. Alabama, 106 U.S. 583 (1883).

11. Cumming v. County Bd. of Education, 175 U.S. 528, 545 (1899). See Earl M. Maltz, "Only Partially Color-Blind: John Marshall Harlan's View of Race and the Constitution," 12 *Georgia State University Law Review* 973, 989 (1996); Gabriel J. Chin, "The *Plessy* Myth: Justice Harlan and the Chinese Cases," 82 *Iowa Law Review* 151 (1996).

12. Mark Tushnet, "The Politics of Equality in Constitutional Law: The Equal Protection Clause, Dr. Du Bois, and Charles Hamilton Houston," 74 *Journal of American History* 884, 886 (1987).

13. Tinsley E. Yarbrough, *Judicial Enigma: The First Justice Harlan* 229 (1995) (quoting Judge Constance Baker Motley's address at a memorial for Thurgood Marshall).

14. Brown v. Board of Education (Brown II), 349 U.S. 294, 301 (1955).

15. Naim v. Naim, 350 U.S. 985 (1956); see Michael J. Klarman, *From Jim Crow to Civil Rights: The Supreme Court and the Struggle for Racial Equality* 321 (2004).

16. Loving v. Virginia, 388 U.S. 1 (1967).

17. See generally Gerald Rosenberg, *Hollow Hope? Can Courts Bring About Social Change?* (1991).

18. Martin Luther King, Jr., *Why We Can't Wait* 134 (1964).

19. Christopher W. Schmidt, "*Brown* and the Colorblind Constitution," 94 *Cornell Law Review* 203, 234 (2008).

20. Briggs v. Elliott, 132 F. Supp. 776, 777 (E.D.S.C. 1955) (per curiam).

21. Randall v. Sumter School District No. 2, 241 F. Supp. 787, 789 (E.D.S.C. 1965) (citation omitted).

22. Rick Perlstein, *Before the Storm: Barry Goldwater and the Unmaking of the American Consensus* 460–461 (2009).

23. William H. Rehnquist, "A Random Thought on the Segregation Cases," reprinted in 117 *Congressional Record* 440, 441 (1971 (1952)).

24. Perlstein, 461–462. See David G. Savage, *Turning Right: The Making of the Rehnquist Supreme Court* 39 (1992).

25. Perlstein, 461.

26. N.C. State Board of Education v. Swann, 402 U.S. 43, 46 (1971).

27. Regents of the University of California v. Bakke, 438 U.S. 265, 401 (1978) (Marshall, J., concurring in part, dissenting in part) (emphasis added).

28. National Advisory Commission on Civil Disorders, *Report of the National Advisory Commission on Civil Disorders* 1, 11–13 (1968).

29. Griggs v. Duke Power, 401 U.S. 424, 432 (1971). Though *Griggs* turned on a statute rather than the Constitution, at the time no sharp distinction existed in how courts understood discrimination in one context versus the other.

30. Massachusetts Personnel Administrators v. Feeney, 442 U.S. 256 (1979). For a discussion of racism as hate, see Chapter 2. The following discussion draws upon Ian Haney López, "Intentional Blindness," 87 *New York University Law Review* 1779 (2012).

31. McCleskey v. Kemp, 481 U.S. 279 (1987).

32. The Court has occasionally found discrimination, but only when the coalition of conservative justices breaks down and one or more switch to vote with the liberals who do not use the malice test to resolve racial discrimination cases.

33. United Jewish Organizations of Williamsburgh, Inc. v. Carey, 430 U.S. 144, 165 (1977).

34. *Bakke*, 438 U.S. at 291.

35. Gunnar Myrdal, *An American Dilemma: The Negro Problem and Modern Democracy* lxxv, 115–116 (20th anniversary ed. 1962); see also 75 ("White prejudice and discrimination keep the Negro low in standards of living, health, education, manners and morals.").

36. George M. Fredrickson, *Racism: A Short History* 5 (2002).

37. Antonin Scalia, "The Disease as Cure," 1979 *Washington University Law Quarterly* 147, 153.

38. Grutter v. Bollinger, 539 U.S. 306, 355 n.3 (2003).

39. Adarand Constructors, Inc. v. Pena, 515 U.S. 200, 241 (1995) (Thomas, J., concurring) (emphases added).

40. Michael Omi & Howard Winant, *Racial Formation in the United States: From the 1960s to the 1990s*, at 14 (1994). See also Matthew Frye Jacobson, *Whiteness of a Different Color: European Immigrants and the Alchemy of Race* (1999).

41. Stephen Steinberg, *The Ethnic Myth: Race, Ethnicity, and Class in America* 47–48 (1981).

42. David R. Roediger, *Working Toward Whiteness: How America's Immigrants Become White* 25 (2005).

43. Mary C. Waters, *Ethnic Options: Choosing Identities in America* (1990).

44. Nathan Glazer & Daniel Patrick Moynihan, *Beyond the Melting Pot: The Negroes, Puerto Ricans, Jews, Italians, and Irish of New York City* (1963).

45. This analysis draws on the thorough critique of Glazer and Moynihan's work offered in Stephen Steinberg, *Turning Back: The Retreat from Racial Justice in American Thought and Policy* (1995).

46. Glazer & Moynihan, at 49–50.

47. *Id.*, 50.

48. US Department of Labor, "The Negro Family: The Case for National Action" (1965), reprinted in *The Moynihan Report and the Politics of Controversy* 41, 43, 51, 61–63, 93 (Lee Rainwater & William L. Yancey eds., 1967). See also James T. Patterson, *Freedom Is Not Enough: The Moynihan Report and America's Struggle over Black Family Life—From LBJ to Obama* (2010).

49. Daniel Patrick Moynihan, "A Family Policy for the Nation," September 18, 1966, reprinted in *The Moynihan Report and the Politics of Controversy* 385, 393.

50. Charles Murray, *Losing Ground: American Social Policy, 1950–1980* (1984); Charles Murray & Richard Hernstein, *The Bell Curve: Intelligence and Class Structure in American Life* (1994); Dinesh D'Souza, *The End of Racism: Principles for a Multiracial Society* (1995); Myron Magnet, *The Dream and the Nightmare: The Sixties' Legacy to the Underclass* (2000).

51. Charles M. Blow, "Newt's War on Poor Children," *New York Times*, December 2, 2011.

52. Dorothy E. Roberts, "The Value of Black Mothers' Work," 26 *Connecticut Law Review* 871, 877 (1994).

53. Kenneth B. Clark, *Dark Ghetto: Dilemmas of Social Power* 67–74 (1965); Edward Franklin Frazier, *The Negro Family in the United States* (1939).

54. Thomas J. Sugrue, *Not Even Past: Barack Obama and the Burden of Race* 88–90 (2010).

55. Martin Luther King, Jr., "Address at Abbott House," Westchester County, New York (October 29, 1965), reprinted in *The Moynihan Report and the Politics of Controversy*, at 407, 408.

56. *Bakke*, 438 U.S. at 295–296.

57. Matthew Frye Jacobson, *Roots Too: White Ethnic Revival in Post-Civil Rights America* (2006).

58. Thomas Sugrue & John Skrentny, "The White Ethnic Strategy," 171, 174, in *Rightward Bound: Making America Conservative in the 1970s* (Bruce Schulman & Julian Zelizer eds. 2008).

59. See Chapter Three.

60. David O. Sears & Donald R. Kinder, "Racial Tensions and Voting in Los Angeles," in *Los Angeles: Viability and Prospects for Urban Leadership* 51 (Werner Z. Hirsch ed., 1971).

61. John B. McConahay, "Modern Racism, Ambivalence, and the Modern Racism Scale," in *Prejudice, Discrimination, and Racism* 91, 94 (John F. Dovidio & Samuel L. Gaertner eds., 1986). See also John B. McConahay & Joseph C. Hough, Jr., "Symbolic Racism," 32 *Journal of Social Issues* 23, 24 (1976).

62. Donald R. Kinder & Lynn M. Sanders, *Divided by Color: Racial Politics and Democratic Ideals* 105–106 (1996).

63. Lawrence Bobo et al., "Laissez-Faire Racism: The Crystallization of a Kinder, Gentler, Antiblack Ideology," in *Racial Attitudes in the 1990s: Continuity and Change* 15 (Stephen A. Tuch & Jack K. Martin eds., 1997). See also James M. Jones, "Racism: A Cultural Analysis of the Problem," 279, 293, in *Prejudice, Discrimination, and Racism* (John F. Dovidio & Samuel L. Gaertner eds. 1986); and Eduardo Bonilla-Silva, *Racism without Racists: Color-Blind Racism and the Persistence of Racial Inequality in the United States* 28 (2003).

64. Josh Pasek, Jon A. Krosnick & Trevor Thompson, "The Impact of Anti-Black Racism on Approval of Barack Obama's Job Performance and on Voting in the 2012 Presidential Election," October 13, 2012.

65. *Id.* These survey questions originated in the early 1970s in an effort to study "symbolic racism," or what became known as "modern racism." See McConahay;

McConahay & Hough; and Donald R. Kinder & David O. Sears, "Prejudice and Politics: Symbolic Racism Versus Racial Threats to the Good Life," 40 *Journal of Personality & Social Psychology* 414 (1981).

66. Edward G. Carmines, Paul M. Sniderman & Beth C.Easter, "On the Meaning, Measurement, and Implications of Racial Resentment," 634 *The Annals of the American Academy of Political and Social Science* 98, 112–113 (2011).

67. Daniel Cox, E.J. Dionne, Jr., William A. Galston & Robert P. Jones, "What it Means to be American: Attitudes in an Increasingly Diverse America Ten Years After 9/11" at 8–9, Brookings Institution, September 6, 2011. See also Michael I. Norton & Samuel R. Sommers, "Whites See Racism as Zero-Sum Game That They Are Now Losing," 6 *Perspectives on Psychological Science* 215 (2011), suggesting that a majority of whites now accept "the notion that Whites have replaced Blacks as the primary victims of racial discrimination."

Chapter 5

1. Tali Mendelberg, *The Race Card: Campaign Strategy, Implicit Messages, and the Norm of Equality* 135–144 (2001).

2. Dan T. Carter, *From George Wallace to Newt Gingrich: Race in the Conservative Counterrevolution, 1963–1994*, at 76 (1996).

3. Sidney Blumenthal, *Pledging Allegiance: The Last Campaign of the Cold War* 264–265 (1990).

4. Jane Mayer, "Attack Dog," *The New Yorker*, February 13, 2012.

5. Carter, 79. Atwater had help from a young media whiz, Roger Ailes, formerly of the Nixon and Reagan campaigns. We will confront Ailes again in assessing how he remade Fox News into a race-baiting megaphone for the right. See Chapter Seven.

6. Mendelberg, 87.

7. *Id.*, 104.

8. Thomas Sugrue, *Not Even Past: Barack Obama and the Burden of Race* 83 (2010).

9. See Chapter One.

10. Marshall Frady, "Death in Arkansas," *The New Yorker*, February 22, 1993.

11. Michael Kramer, "Frying Them Isn't the Answer," *Time*, March 14, 1994.

12. Anthony Lewis, "Abroad at Home; Black and White," *New York Times*, June 18, 1992.

13. Kenneth O'Reilly, *Nixon's Piano: Presidents and Racial Politics from Washington to Clinton* 410 (1995).

14. *Id.*, 415.

15. Michelle Alexander, *The New Jim Crow: Mass Incarceration in the Age of Colorblindness* 56 (2012).

16. Sugrue, 81.

17. Bill Clinton, "How We Ended Welfare, Together," *New York Times*, August 22, 2006.

18. Clinton also pandered to the right by signing the Defense of Marriage Act, which defined marriage under federal law in terms of opposite-sex couples. Belatedly, he

came to regret this decision. Peter Baker, "Now in Defense of Gay Marriage, Bill Clinton," *New York Times*, March 25, 2013.

19. Alex Seitz-Wald, "Did Romney Want to Get Booed?" *Salon.com*, July 12, 2012.

20. Charles Blow, "Romney in the Lions' Den," *New York Times*, July 11, 2012.

21. Seitz-Wald.

22. Michael Eric Dyson, "Obama's Rebuke of Absentee Black Fathers," *Time*, June 19, 2008.

23. Mark Landler, "It's the President's Message, With President Clinton," *New York Times*, August 23, 2012.

24. Kathy Kiely & Jill Lawrence, "Clinton makes case for wide appeal," *USA TODAY*, May 8, 2008; Adia Harvey Wingfield & Joe R. Feagin, *Yes We Can? White Racial Framing and the Obama Presidency* 60 (2nd ed. 2013).

25. Joe Conason, "Was Hillary channeling George Wallace?" *Salon.com*, May 9, 2008.

26. Kiely & Lawrence.

27. Toni Morrison, "Clinton as the First Black President," *The New Yorker*, October 1998.

28. Anne E. Kornblut, "Civil Rights Pioneer Endorses Clinton," *Washington Post*, October 12, 2007.

29. Frank Rich, "Whitewash," *New York Magazine*, May 5, 2013.

30. Paul Frymer, *Uneasy Alliances: Race and Party Competition in America* (2010).

31. Randall Kennedy, *The Persistence of the Color Line: Racial Politics and the Obama Presidency* 34 (2012).

32. O'Reilly, 408–409.

33. "Where Are They Now: The Clinton Impeachment: Vernon Jordan," *Time*, January 9, 2009.

34. Adam Nagourney, "In Tapes, Nixon Rails About Jews and Blacks," *New York Times*, December 10, 2010.

35. Paul Krugman, "Republicans and Race," *New York Times*, November 17, 2007.

36. Or maybe Clinton deserves less credit than that. Joseph Stiglitz attributes much of the economy's growth during the Clinton years to the tech bubble, with "Clinton's policies of financial market deregulation and cuts to capital gains tax rates (increasing the returns to speculating on the tech stocks) add[ing] fuel to the fire." Joseph Stiglitz, *The Price of Inequality: How Today's Divided Society Endangers Our Future* 87 (2012).

37. Kim Phillips-Fein, *Invisible Hands: The Businessmen's Crusade Against the New Deal* 265 (2009).

38. *Id.*

39. Jordan Fabian, "Obama: More Moderate Republican Than Socialist," *ABC News/ Univision*, December 14, 2012. *See also* Ezra Klein, "Obama revealed: A moderate Republican," *Washington Post*, April 25, 2011.

40. Karl Rove, *Courage and Consequence: My Life as a Conservative in the Fight* 128 (2010).

41. Bush v. Gore, 531 U.S. 98 (2000); David Margolick, Evgenia Peretz & Michael Shnayerson, "The Path To Florida," *Vanity Fair*, October 2004.

42. Eric Lichtblau, "Bush Issues Racial Profiling Ban But Exempts Security Inquiries," *New York Times*, June 18, 2003.

43. Tina Dupuy, "The Man Behind Paul Ryan's Budget Plan Got the Tax Cuts Wrong Too" *The Atlantic*, April 15, 2011.

44. Brian M. Riedl, "Ten Myths About the Bush Tax Cuts," Heritage Foundation, January 29, 2007.

45. Matt A. Barreto, Fernando Guerra, Mara Marks, Stephen A. Nuño & Nathan D. Woods, "Controversies in Exit Polling: Implementing a Racially Stratified Homogenous Precinct Approach," 39 *PS: Political Science & Politics* 477, 477 (2006). While widely accepted, these figures may considerably overstate the percentage of Hispanics who voted for Bush, for reasons Barreto et al. explain.

46. Sugrue, 129.

47. Wingfield & Feagin, 228.

48. Leti Volpp, "The Citizen and the Terrorist," 49 *UCLA Law Review* 1575, 1578–1580 (2002); Moustafa Bayoumi, "Racing Religion," 6 *CR: The New Centennial Review* 267, 288 (2006). See also Muneer Ahmad, "Homeland Insecurities: Racial Violence the Day after September 11," 72 *Social Text* 101 (2002).

49. Adam Liptak, "Justices Turn Back Ex-Detainee's Suit," *New York Times*, May 18, 2009.

50. Ashcroft v. Iqbal, 556 U.S. 662, 668 (2009).

51. *Id.*, 682.

52. See Yaser Ali, "Shariah and Citizenship—How Islamophobia is Creating a Second-Class Citizenry in America," 100 *California Law Review* 1027 (2012); Neil Gotanda, "The Racialization of Islam in American Law," 637 *The Annals of the American Academy of Political and Social Science* 184 (2011).

53. "Transcript, President Bush's Address to the Nation," September 11, 2006, *New York Times*.

54. Deepa Kumar, "Framing Islam: The Resurgence of Orientalism During the Bush II Era," 34 *Journal of Communication Enquiry* 254, 260 (2010).

55. Douglas S. Massey, "The Past and Future of Mexico-U.S. Migration," 251, 256–257, in *Beyond la Frontera: The History of Mexico-U.S. Migration* (Mark Overmyer-Velazquez ed. 2011).

56. Douglas S. Massey, "Racial Formation in Theory and Practice: The Case of Mexicans in the United States," 1 *Race and Social Problems* 12, 19 (2009).

57. Jeff Chu, "10 Questions for Pat Buchanan," *Time*, August 20, 2006.

58. Samuel P. Huntington, "The Hispanic Challenge," 141 *Foreign Policy* 31, 32 (2004). Huntington helps connect the way in which "Arab Muslims" and Latin American immigrants have been constructed as racial threats through the supposedly non-racial language of culture. Huntington early on applied the "clash of civilizations" language ultimately used by Bush regarding the Middle East. Samuel Huntington, *The Clash of Civilization and the Remaking of the World Order* (1996). In 2004, in a new book entitled *Who Are We? The Challenges to America's Native Identity*, Huntington updated this "clash of civilizations" thesis to apply it across the United States-Mexican border.

59. Frank Luntz, "Respect for the Law and Economic Fairness: Illegal Immigration Prevention," *The Principles and Language of Immigration Reform* 16 (Luntz, Maslansky

Strategic Research 2005). For a historical perspective on the construction of the "illegal alien" threat, see Mae Ngai, *Impossible Subjects: Illegal Aliens and the Making of Modern America* (2005).

60. Arizona v. United States, 132 S. Ct. 2492, 2522 (2012).

61. *Arizona*, 132 S.Ct. at 2504. For deeper critiques of the dehumanizing aspect of references to "illegals," see Gabriel Thompson, "How the Right Made Racism Sound Fair—and Changed Immigration Politics," *Colorlines*, September 13, 2011; Lawrence Downes, "What Part of 'Illegal' Don't You Understand?" *New York Times*, October 28, 2007; Charles Garcia, "Why 'illegal immigrant' is a slur," *CNN*, July 6, 2012; and Mónica Novoa, "Open letter from Drop the I-Word to *The New York Times*," October 1, 2012 (Drop the I-Word is a grassroots effort to pressure media organizations and others to cease using this derogatory term).

62. Mary C. Waters & Tomas Jimenez, "Assessing Immigrant Assimilation: New Empirical and Theoretical Challenges," 31 *Annual Review of Sociology* 105, 111 (2005).

63. M. Kathleen Dingeman & Rubén G. Rumbaut, "The Immigration-Crime Nexus," 31 *University of La Verne Law Review* 363 (2010).

64. Leo R. Chavez, *The Latino Threat: Constructing Immigrants, Citizens, and the Nation* (2008); Otto Santa Ana, *Brown Tide Rising: Metaphors of Latinos in Contemporary American Public Discourse* (2002). The Heritage Foundation was publicly embarrassed when it became known that Jason Richwine, one author of its 2013 report questioning immigration reform, opposed immigration because "the average I.Q. of immigrants in the United States is substantially lower than that of the white native population." Richwine elaborated precisely which immigrants he had in mind: "No one knows whether Hispanics will ever reach I.Q. parity with whites, but the prediction that new Hispanic immigrants will have low-I.Q. children and grandchildren is difficult to argue against. From the perspective of Americans alive today, the low average I.Q. of Hispanics is effectively permanent." Ashley Parker & Kitty Bennett, "Critic of Immigration Proposal Cited Lower I.Q. of Immigrants in Dissertation," *New York Times*, May 8, 2013.

65. Thompson.

66. Peter Slevin, "Deportation of Illegal Immigrants Increases Under Obama Administration," *Washington Post*, July 26, 2010.

67. Julia Preston, "Latinos Support Obama, Despite Deportation Policies," *New York Times*, December 28, 2011.

68. Suzy Khimm, "Obama is deporting immigrants faster than Bush. Republicans don't think that's enough," *Washington Post*, August 27, 2012.

69. Thompson.

Chapter 6

1. The following discussion draws on Michelle DeArmond, "Inland GOP Mailing Depicts Obama's Face on Food Stamp," *The Press-Enterprise*, October 16, 2008; Michelle DeArmond, "Fallout Far, Wide over Illustration," *The Press-Enterprise*, October 16, 2008; and Michelle DeArmond, "Obama Bucks Creator Revealed: MN Democrat Tim Kastelein," *The Press-Enterprise*, October 23, 2008.

2. Jayson K. Jones & Ana C. Rosado, "McCain Campaign Says Obama Is Playing the 'Race Card,'" *New York Times*, July 31, 2008.

3. Gladwin Hill, "'WETBACK' INFLUX NEAR THE RECORD; October Figure Second Highest in History—Crime Follows the Illegal Immigrants," *New York Times*, November 22, 1953.

4. Charles Blow, "The G.O.P.'s Diversity Deserts," *New York Times*, March 29, 2013.

5. DeArmond, "Fallout Far, Wide."

6. Debbie Elliott, "'Food Stamp President': Race Code, Or Just Politics?" *NPR* January 17, 2012.

7. "Gingrich Slams Juan Williams in Racial Exchange," *Newsmax.com*, January 17, 2012.

8. Walter Mosley, "'Food Stamp President': Gingrich's Poetry of Hate," *CNN*, January 26, 2012.

9. Elspeth Reeve, "No, You're the Racist, or Blogging About Obama Phones," *The Atlantic Wire*, September 28, 2012.

10. *Id.*

11. *Id.*

12. Juliet Lapidos, "'Obama Phone,'" *New York Times*, October 15, 2012.

13. William Douglas, "Tea Party Protesters Call Georgia's John Lewis 'Nigger,'" *McClatchy Newspapers*, March 20, 2010.

14. Jim Hoft, "Media Lying About Racist Attacks on Black Reps By Tea Party Protesters . . . Video Proof," *Breitbart.com*, March 21, 2010.

15. "Politics of Attack," *New York Times*, October 7, 2008.

16. Natalie Gewargis, "McCain Camp: Obama 'Playing the Race Card from the Bottom of the Deck,'" *ABC News*, July 31, 2008.

17. "Campaigns Trade Barbs, but Who Started It? Surrogates Charge Opponents of Injecting Race into Dialogue," *MSNBC*, August 1, 2008.

18. *Id.*

19. Thomas Byrne Edsall & Mary D. Edsall, *Chain Reaction: The Impact of Race, Rights, and Taxes on American Politics* 78 (1992).

20. "Campaigns Trade Barbs."

21. "I Guess I'm a Racist," https://www.youtube.com/watch?v=i_AGDih9dBQ.

22. James Baldwin, "White Man's Guilt," *Ebony* (1965), reprinted in James Baldwin, *The Price of the Ticket: Collected Nonfiction, 1948–1985*, at 409 (1985).

23. Lee Cokorinos, *The Assault on Diversity: An Organized Challenge to Racial and Gender Justice* 111–112 (2003); "Alan Keyes Doubts Obama's Citizenship," *Courthouse News Service*, November 17, 2008; Carol J. Williams, "9th Circuit Panel Rejects Suit Filed by 'Birthers' against Obama," *Los Angeles Times*, December 23, 2011.

24. Charles M. Blow, "A Mighty Pale Tea Party," *New York Times*, April 17, 2010.

25. Cokorinos, 73–77.

26. See Clint Bolick, *Unfinished Business: A Civil Rights Strategy for America's Third Century* 16, 26–27, 54, 76 (1990).

27. Richard Hofstadter, *Social Darwinism in American Thought* (rev. ed. 1955).

28. Bolick, 54.

29. *Id.*, 136.

30. Adam Liptak, "Corporations Find a Friend in the Supreme Court," *New York Times*, May 4, 2013.

31. Bolick, 141.
32. Regarding traditional civil rights, including laws banning racial discrimination, Bolick favored their repeal because such laws limited "freedom of association," the same principle once used by Barry Goldwater to defend marketplace segregation. Clint Bolick, *The Affirmative Action Fraud: Can We Restore the American Civil Rights Vision?* 19, 41 (1996).
33. Stephen M. Teles, *The Rise of the Conservative Legal Movement* 245 (2008).
34. Cokorinos, 74; Maureen Dowd, "The Thomas Nomination; In an Ugly Atmosphere, the Accusations Fly," *New York Times*, October 12, 1991.
35. Richard Thompson Ford, *The Race Card: How Bluffing About Bias Makes Race Relations Worse* 15 (2008). Herman Cain similarly was also quick to allege racism when his candidacy first began to founder under multiple complaints of sexual harassment. Kimberle Crenshaw & Catharine MacKinnon, "Why Herman Cain Is Unfit to Lead," *New York Times*, November 14, 2011.
36. Cokorinos, 76.
37. Fredrick Harris, *The Price of the Ticket: Barack Obama and Rise and Decline of Black Politics* 181 (2012).
38. Adolph Reed, "The Puzzle of Black Republicans," *New York Times*, December 18, 2012.
39. The spotlight often shown on Bobby Jindal and Nikki Haley may function similarly, to at once highlight the anti-racist credentials of the GOP and to appeal for support among a growing South Asian population.
40. Clint Bolick, "Clinton's Quota Queens," *Wall Street Journal*, April 30, 1993.
41. Michael Isikoff, "Power Behind the Thrown Nominee: Activist with Score to Settle," *Washington Post*, June 6, 1993.
42. Lani Guinier, *Lift Every Voice: Turning a Civil Rights Setback into a New Vision* 37 (2003).
43. Ian Haney López, "Sotomayor's Remark Does Not Make Her a Racist," *San Francisco Chronicle*, June 2, 2009.
44. Ricci v. DeStefano, 557 U.S. 557 (2009).
45. Cheryl I. Harris & Kimberly West-Faulcon, "Reading *Ricci*: Whitening Discrimination, Racing Test Fairness," 58 *UCLA Law Review* 73, 74–75 (2010).
46. Shelby County v. Holder, 570 U.S. __ (2013).
47. As the dissent detailed at great length, New Haven gave an exam that placed undue emphasis on written tests while giving too little weight to skills and leadership—the sort of exam that fire companies throughout the country had long rejected. *Ricci*, 557 U.S. at 633–636.
48. Nikole Hannah-Jones, "A Colorblind Constitution: What Abigail Fisher's Affirmative Action Case Is Really About," *ProPublica*, March 18, 2013.

Chapter 7

1. Adam Nossiter, "For South, a Waning Hold on National Politics," *New York Times*, November 10, 2008.
2. Theda Skocpol & Vanessa Williamson, *The Tea Party and the Remaking of Republican Conservatism* 22 (2012).

3. Mark Murray, "NBC/WSJ poll: Public lowers expectations heading into Obama's 2nd term," *NBCNEWS.com*, January 17, 2013.

4. Matt Taibbi, "The Truth About the Tea Party," *Rolling Stone*, September 28, 2010.

5. Sean Wilentz, "Confounding Fathers: The Tea Party's Cold War roots," *The New Yorker*, October 18, 2010.

6. Ben McGrath, "The Movement: The rise of Tea Party activism," *The New Yorker*, February 1, 2010.

7. Phil Rosenthal, "Rant raises profile of CNBC on-air personality Rick Santelli," *Chicago Tribune*, February 23, 2009.

8. Nomi Prins, *It Takes a Pillage: Behind the Bailouts, Bonuses, and Backroom Deals from Washington to Wall Street* (2009).

9. Tom Blumer, "Rant for the Ages: CNBC's Rick Santelli Goes Off; Studio Hosts Invoke 'Mob Rule' to Downplay," *NewsBusters*, February 19, 2009.

10. Jill Lepore, *The Whites of their Eyes: The Tea Party's Revolution and the Battle over American History* 16 (2010).

11. Paul Street & Anthony DiMaggio, *Crashing the Tea Party: Mass Media and the Campaign to Remake American Politics* 34–35 (2011).

12. Ann Coulter, "They Gave Your Mortgage to a Less Qualified Minority," *Human Events*, September 24, 2008.

13. As late as 2011, one quarter of Americans did not believe that Obama was born in the United States; even three years into the Obama presidency, this number stood at 45 percent of those who affiliated with the Tea Party. Stephanie Condon, "Poll: One in four Americans think Obama was not born in U.S.," *CBS News*, April 21, 2011. For an interpretation of the Tea Party that emphasizes a negative reaction to what Obama symbolizes as a *black* president, see Christopher Parker & Matt Barreto, *Change They Can't Believe In: The Tea Party and Reactionary Politics in America* (2013).

14. Skocpol & Williamson, 28.

15. Street & DiMaggio, 81.

16. http://www.universalhub.com/node/32479. *See also* Lepore, 136.

17. New York Times/CBS, "Poll: National Survey of Tea Party Supporters," *New York Times*, April 5–12, 2010, p. 41; "Polling the Tea Party," *New York Times*, April 14, 2010.

18. For an exception, *see* Street & DiMaggio, 81–83, exploring what they term "the Tea Party's color-blind racism."

19. Skocpol & Williamson, 70.

20. Street & DiMaggio, 9.

21. Skocpol & Williamson, 81–82. Of course, as we've seen, the Goldwater campaign also combined a large dose of racial pandering with its conservative assaults on the New Deal state. See Chapter One.

22. Skocpol & Williamson, 56, 66.

23. *Id.*, 57, 71.

24. "10 Most Offensive Tea Party Signs And Extensive Photo Coverage From Tax Day Protests," *Huffington Post*, December 28, 2009.

25. Street & DiMaggio, 94.

26. Matthew Rothschild, "Rampant Xenophobia," *The Progressive*, November 2010.

27. Skocpol & Williamson, 79.
28. "10 Most Offensive Tea Party Signs."
29. Alana Goodman, "Rebel Yell," *Washington Free Beacon*, July 9, 2013.
30. "Polling the Tea Party."
31. Jane Mayer, "Covert Operations: The Billionaire Brothers Who are Waging a War Against Obama," *The New Yorker*, August 30, 2010.
32. *Id.*
33. *Id.*
34. Skocpol & Williamson, 125.
35. David Brock & Ari Rabin-Havt, *The Fox Effect: How Roger Ailes Turned a Network into a Propaganda Machine* 107 (2012).
36. *Id.*, 111.
37. Skocpol & Williamson, 132.
38. Joe McGinniss, *The Selling of the President: 1968*, at 63–64 (1969).
39. *Id.*, 105.
40. *Id.*, 97–111.
41. *Id.*, 101.
42. See Chapter Three.
43. Brock & Rabin-Havt, 28–31.
44. *Id.*, 84–85.
45. *Id.*, 38.
46. *Id.*, 65, 68, 143.
47. Solange Uwimana, "Report: In Immigration Coverage, Fox Shuns Pro-Immigrant Voices," *MediaMatters.org*, October 27, 2011; Solange Uwimana, "Study: On Fox News, Immigrants Are Synonymous with Criminality," *MediaMatters.org*, October 27, 2011. See also "A Report on the Media and the Immigration Debate: Democracy in the Age of New Media," Brookings Institution, September 25, 2008; "Hannity falsely claims NCLR 'has called for Mexico to annex southwestern states,'" *MediaMatters.org*, February 26, 2009.
48. Jocelyn Fong & Solange Uwimana, "Fox News: Where you can bash Islam with impunity," *MediaMatters.org*, October 21, 2010.
49. Brock & Rabin-Havt, 122.
50. "Voters Say Election Full of Misleading and False Information," *WorldPublicOpinion.org*, December 9, 2010.
51. Stephanie Saul, "Looking, Very Closely, for Voter Fraud: Conservative Groups Focus on Registration in Swing States," *New York Times*, September 16, 2012.
52. Suevon Lee, "A Reading Guide to True the Vote, the Controversial Voter Fraud Watchdog," *ProPublica*, September 27, 2012.
53. Brennan Center for Justice, "Policy Brief on the Truth About 'Voter Fraud,'" September 12, 2006.
54. Saul.
55. Ryan J. Reilly, "Anti-Voter Fraud Tea Party Group Hosts Author Who Thinks Poor Shouldn't Vote," *TPMMuckraker*, November 14, 2011.
56. Matthew Vadum, "Registering the Poor to Vote is Un-American," *American Thinker*, September 1, 2011.

57. Ted Nugent, "U.S. sailed off the 'fiscal cliff' long ago: We created Fedzilla; now it's time to kill it," *Washington Times*, December 3, 2012.

58. Erika Wood, "Restoring the Right to Vote," 7, Brennan Center for Justice (2008). See generally Jeff Manza & Christopher Uggen, *Locked Out: Felon Disenfranchisement and American Democracy* (2006).

59. Ari Berman, "The GOP War on Voting," *Rolling Stone*, August 30, 2011.

60. *Id.*

61. Sam Wang, "The Great Gerrymander of 2012," *New York Times*, February 2, 2013.

62. Thomas Edsall, "The Decline of Black Power in the South," *New York Times*, July 10, 2013.

63. Shelby County v. Holder, 270 U.S. __ (2013).

64. David Corn, "SECRET VIDEO: Romney Tells Millionaire Donors What He REALLY Thinks of Obama Voters," *Mother Jones*, September 17, 2012.

65. Michael D. Shear & Michael Barbaro, "In Video Clip, Romney Calls 47% of Voters 'Dependent' and Feeling Entitled," *New York Times*, September 17, 2012.

66. David Leonhardt, "Yes, 47% of Households Owe No Taxes. Look Closer," *New York Times*, April 13, 2010.

67. David Brooks, "Thurston Howell Romney," *New York Times*, September 17, 2012.

68. Ron Fournier, "Why (and How) Romney is Playing the Race Card," *TheAtlantic.com*, August 29, 2012. On the role of the Heritage Foundation in spurring this line of attack, see Andy Kroll, "Behind Romney's Welfare Attacks, America's Top Poverty Denier," *Mother Jones*, September 13, 2012.

69. "Mitt Romney says Barack Obama's plan for welfare reform: 'They just send you your check,'" *Politifact.com*, August 7, 2012; Ezra Klein, "Race and the 2012 election," *Washington Post*, August 27, 2012.

70. Jonathan Alter, "Romney Campaign Mutes the Racial Dog Whistles for Tampa," *Bloomberg.com*, August 31, 2012.

71. Robert Reich, "Mitt Romney vs. fact-checkers: the welfare law dispute," *Christian Science Monitor*, August 29, 2012.

72. Thomas B. Edsall, "Making the Election About Race," *New York Times*, August 27, 2012; Dylan Byers, "Matthews defends 'dog whistle' accusations," *Politico.com*, September 22, 2012; Joan Walsh, *What's the Matter with White People?: Why We Long for a Golden Age That Never Was* (2012). For a summary of Romney's crude race-baiting during the 2012 election, see Leland Ware, "Mitt Romney's 47 Percent: Race, Class and Ethnicity in the 2012 Election," (forthcoming).

73. Robert Reich, "The Ryan Choice," *Huffington Post*, August 12, 2012.

74. Kelsey Merrick & Jim Horney, "Chairman Ryan Gets 62 Percent of His Huge Budget Cuts from Programs for Lower-Income Americans," *Center on Budget and Policy Priorities*, March 23, 2012.

75. Reich, "The Ryan Choice."

76. Robert Greenstein, "CBO Shows Ryan Budget Would Set Nation on Path to End Most of Government Other Than Social Security, Healthcare, and Defense by 2050," *Center on Budget and Policy Priorities*, March 20, 2012.

77. Howard Gleckman, "Paul Ryan's Budget Plan: More Big Tax Cuts for the Rich," *Forbes.com*, March 23, 2012.

78. Reich, "The Ryan Choice."
79. Paul Krugman, "The Flimflam Man," *New York Times*, August 5, 2010.
80. Skocpol & Williamson, 174.
81. Annie Lowrey, "Conservative Elite in Capital Pay Heed to Ryan as Thinker," *New York Times*, August 17, 2012.
82. Nicholas Confessore, "Ryan Has Kept Close Ties to Wealthy Donors on the Right," *New York Times*, August 13, 2012.
83. Corn.
84. On the right's embrace of Rand, see Jennifer Burns, *Goddess of the Market: Ayn Rand and the American Right* (2009).
85. Jane Mayer, "Ayn Rand Joins the Ticket," *The New Yorker*, August 11, 2012; Leon Wieseltier, "His Grief, and Ours," *The New Republic*, August 24, 2012.
86. Robert Pear, "As Ryan Looks to Focus on Economy, Spotlight Shines on His Other Views," *New York Times*, August 12, 2012.

Chapter 8

1. Thomas Frank, *What's the Matter with Kansas? How Conservatives Won the Heart of America* 7–8, 179 (2005). In his most recent book, Frank continues the theme, for instance reducing contemporary racial hysteria around Obama to "individual prejudice and a handful of name-calling incidents." Thomas Frank, *Pity the Billionaire: The Hard-Times Swindle and the Unlikely Comeback of the Right* 8 (2012).
2. That said, more recently Alabama seems intent on proving that progress on race is ephemeral. Under the control of its first Republican-led legislature since Reconstruction, it has passed numerous racially retrograde laws. See, for example, Kim Chandler, "New lawsuit challenges 'scarlet letter' provision of Alabama immigration law," *AL.com*, February 7, 2013.
3. Thomas B. Edsall & Brian Faler, "Lott Remarks on Thurmond Echoed 1980 Words," *Washington Post*, December 11, 2002.
4. Rowland Evans & Robert Novak, "Future 'White Man's' Party," *St. Petersburg Times*, June 25, 1963, at 9-A.
5. Lani Guinier, "From Racial Liberalism to Racial Literacy: *Brown v. Board of Education* and the Interest-Divergence Dilemma," 91 *Journal of American History* 92, 104 (June 2004). See also Michael Goldfield, *The Color of Politics: Race and the Mainsprings of American Politics* 306 (1997).
6. Rich Benjamin, *Searching for Whitopia: An Improbable Journey to the Heart of White America* 1 (2009).
7. On the racial politics that led many communities to close rather than integrate community pools, see Jeff Wiltse, *Contested Waters: A Social History of Swimming Pools in America* (2007).
8. Donald R. Kinder & David O. Sears, "Prejudice and Politics: Symbolic Racism Versus Racial Threats to the Good Life," 40 *Journal of Personality & Social Psychology* 414 (1981). See also *Racialized Politics: The Debate About Racism in America* 23 (David O. Sears, Jim Sidanius & Lawrence Bobo eds. 2000).

9. Larry M. Bartels, *Unequal Democracy: The Political Economy of the New Gilded Age* 74 (2008).

10. Kevin M. Kruse, *White Flight: Atlanta and the Making of Modern Conservatism* (2007).

11. Thomas Byrne Edsall with Mary D. Edsall, *Chain Reaction: The Impact of Race, Rights, and Taxes on American Politics* 182 (1992); see also Chapter Three.

12. Tali Mendelberg, *The Race Card: Campaign Strategy, Implicit Messages, and the Norm of Equality* (2001).

13. Andrew Rosenthal, "Foes Accuse Bush Campaign of Inflaming Racial Tension," *New York Times*, October 24, 1988.

14. *Id.*

15. Mendelberg, 138.

16. *Id.*, 156.

17. *Id.*, 176–178.

18. *Id.*, 229, 236.

19. *Id.*, 269.

20. *Id.*, 215 n.3

21. *Id.*, 227. Mendelberg argues that Jackson's forcing of race to the surface sufficed to suppress the Horton campaign's effectiveness, even if the media (or by extension voters) did not credit his allegations. *Id.*, 186. This observation lies in some tension with her study, which shows that respondents must *accept* that an appeal is racial before it loses power. Mendelberg also cautions that exposing coded racial appeals often elicits accusations of racism against the critics, and acknowledges uncertainty as to how this might impact the way whites respond to racial appeals. *Id.*, 274.

22. Charles M. Blow, "The G.O.P.'s 'Black People' Platform," *New York Times*, January 6, 2012.

23. The video can be viewed here: http://colorlines.com/archives/2012/01/santorum_says_hes_not_interested_in_helping_blacks_because_they_rely_too_much_on_welfare.html.

24. Ezra Klein, "Gingrich Says Obama is the 'Food Stamp President.' Is He?" *Washington Post*, January 18, 2012.

25. I develop the notion of commonsense racism in Ian Haney López, *Racism on Trial: The Chicano Fight for Justice* (2003), especially in chapter five.

26. I'm grateful to my colleague Vicky Plaut for helpful conservations regarding how material, cultural, and psychological forces combine to give force to racial beliefs. See generally Victoria C. Plaut, "Diversity Science: Why and How Difference Makes a Difference," 21 *Psychological Inquiry* 77 (2010); and John Duckitt, "Psychology and Prejudice: A Historical Analysis and Integrative Framework," 47 *American Psychologist* 1182 (1992).

27. Martin Gilens, *Why Americans Hate Welfare: Race, Media, and the Politics of Anti-poverty Policy* 114, 117, 122 (1999).

28. Otto Santa Ana, *Brown Tide Rising: Metaphors of Latinos in Contemporary American Public Discourse* (2002).

29. Claude M. Steele, *Whistling Vivaldi: How Stereotypes Affect Us and What We Can Do* 26–28 (2011). Frontline would air a documentary on Elliot's experiment, entitled "A Class Divided."

30. Steele, 27.
31. *Id.*, 28.
32. Gunnar Myrdal, *An American Dilemma: The Negro Problem and Modern Democracy* lxxv; see also Chapter Four.
33. Lawrence Bobo & Michael Massagli, "Stereotyping and Urban Inequality," 89, 92, in *Urban Inequality: Evidence from Four Cities* (Alice O'Connor, Charles Tilly & Lawrence Bobo eds. 2001).
34. See Chapter Two.
35. Henry Tajfel & John Turner, "An Integrative Theory of Intergroup Conflict," in *The Social Psychology of Intergroup Relations* 34 (William G. Austin & Stephen Worchel eds. 1979), quoted in Duckitt, 1188.
36. Evan P. Apfelbaum, Samuel R. Sommers & Michael I. Norton, "Seeing Race and Seeming Racist? Evaluating Strategic Colorblindness in Social Interaction," 95 *Journal of Personality & Social Psychology* 919 (2008).
37. Richard Eibach & Thomas Keegan, "Free at Last? Social Dominance, Loss Aversion, and White and Black Americans' Differing Assessments of Racial Progress," 90 *Journal of Personality & Social Psychology* 453, 454 (2006).
38. Korematsu v. United States, 323 U.S. 214, 239 n.12 (1944) (Murphy, J., dissenting). For classic scholarship on working-class strategic racism, see Alexander Saxton, *The Indispensable Enemy: Labor and the Anti-Chinese Movement in California* (1975); and David R. Roediger, *The Wages of Whiteness: Race and the Making of the American Working Class* (rev. ed. 1999).
39. John Jost & David Hamilton, "Stereotypes in Our Culture," in *On the Nature of Prejudice: Fifty Years after Allport* 208, 215–216 (John Dovidio, Peter Glick & Laurie Rudman eds. 2005).
40. The most familiar exploration of this dynamic proceeds under the label "aversive racism." See Samuel L. Gaertner & John F. Dovidio, "The Aversive Form of Racism," in *Prejudice, Discrimination, and Racism* 61 (John F. Dovidio & Samuel L. Gaertner eds. 1986).
41. Apfelbaum, Sommers & Norton, 918. See also Janet Ward Schofield, "The Colorblind Perspective in School: Causes and Consequences," in *Multicultural Education: Issues and Perspectives* 247 (James L. Banks & Cherry A. McGee Banks eds., 2001); and Eric D. Knowles, Brian S. Lowery, Caitlin M. Hogan & Rosalind M. Chow, "On the Malleability of Ideology: Motivated Construals of Color Blindness," 96 *Journal of Personality & Social Psychology* 857 (2009).
42. Apfelbaum, Sommers & Norton, 929.

Chapter 9

1. Jill Lepore, "Tax Time: Why We Pay," *The New Yorker*, November 26, 2012.
2. Paul Krugman, *End this Depression Now!* (2012).
3. Thomas Mann & Norman Ornstein, *It's Even Worse Than It Looks: How the American Constitutional System Collided with the New Politics of Extremism* 31 (2012).
4. Among the many articles from 2008 and early 2009 announcing the demise of conservatism, see George Packer, "The Fall of Conservatism: Have the Republicans

Run Out of Ideas?" *The New Yorker*, May 26, 2008; and Sam Tanenhaus, "Conservatism is Dead: An Intellectual Autopsy of the Movement," *The New Republic*, February 18, 2009.

5. Drew Westen, "What Happened to Obama?" *New York Times*, August 6, 2011; and Matt Bai, "Still Waiting for the Narrator in Chief," *New York Times*, October 30, 2012.

6. Larissa MacFarquhar, "The Conciliator: Where is Barack Obama Coming From?" *The New Yorker*, May 7, 2007.

7. Shelby Steele, "Obama's post-racial promise," *Los Angeles Times*, November 5, 2008.

8. Barack Obama, "Remarks by the President in Remembrance of Dr. Martin Luther King, Jr.," Office of the Press Secretary, January 17, 2010.

9. Barack Obama, *Dreams from My Father: A Story of Race and Inheritance* (2004).

10. Barack Obama, *The Audacity of Hope: Thoughts on Reclaiming the American Dream* 232 (2006).

11. Peter Baker & Helene Cooper, "President Tries to Defuse Debate over Gates Arrest," *New York Times*, July 25, 2009.

12. Katharine Q. Seelye, "Obama Wades into a Volatile Racial Issue," *New York Times*, July 23, 2009.

13. "Racial Profiling," *PBS News Hour*, March 13, 2001.

14. Baker & Cooper.

15. Helene Cooper & Abby Goodnough, "Over Beers, No Apologies, but Plans to Have Lunch," *New York Times*, July 30, 2009.

16. See Chapter Four. Accentuating the connection, Thomas Sugrue describes what I term post-racialism as "strategic colorblindness." Thomas Sugrue, *Not Even Past: Barack Obama and the Burden of Race* 116 (2010). Paul Butler explores the connection between post-racialism and colorblindness, offering an insightful comparison of Obama and Clarence Thomas. Paul Butler, "The President and the Justice: Two Ways of Looking at a Postblack Man," 64, in *The New Black: What Has Changed—and What Has Not—With Race in America* (Kenneth Mack & Guy-Uriel Charles eds. 2013).

17. For background on Reverend Wright, as well as the controversy, see Adia Harvey Wingfield & Joe R. Feagin, *Yes We Can? White Racial Framing and the Obama Presidency* (2nd ed. 2013), chapter five.

18. Barack Obama, "Remarks at the Constitution Center, Philadelphia: A More Perfect Union," March 18, 2008.

19. Janny Scott, "A Biracial Candidate Walks His Own Fine Line," *New York Times*, December 29, 2007.

20. Obama, "Remarks at the Constitution Center."

21. Tommie Shelby, "Justice & Reconciliation: Two Visions," 140 *Daedalus* 95, 103 (Winter 2011).

22. Obama, "Remarks at the Constitution Center."

23. See Chapter One.

24. Sugrue, 53.

25. Obama, *Audacity*, 247.

26. For an extended indulgence of this logic, see Tom Wolfe, *Radical Chic & Mau-Mauing the Flak Catchers* (1970).

27. Obama, *Audacity*, 248.
28. Sheryl Gay Stolberg, "For Obama, Nuance on Race Invites Questions," *New York Times*, February 8, 2010.
29. Ezra Klein, "Race and the 2012 election," *Washington Post*, August 27, 2012, citing a study by Daniel Gillion.
30. Obama, *Audacity*, 252, 253.
31. Fredrick Harris, "The Price of a Black President," *New York Times*, October 27, 2012.
32. Carmen DeNavas-Walt, Bernadette D. Proctor, and Jessica C. Smith, U.S. Census Bureau, Current Population Reports, P60–243, *Income, Poverty, and Health Insurance Coverage in the United States: 2011*, at 8, 14–15, 58–60 (2012).
33. For a moral critique of Obama's emphasis on "universal" solutions, see Shelby.
34. Michael Tesler, "The Spillover of Racialization into Healthcare: How President Obama Polarized Public Opinion by Racial Attitudes and Race," 56 *American Journal of Political Science* 690, 696 (2012).
35. *Id.*, 690.
36. *Id.*, 696.
37. Fredrick Harris, "Still waiting for our first black president," *Washington Post*, June 1, 2012.
38. Casey Gane-McCalla, "Dyson Says Obama 'Runs From Race Like A Black Man Runs From A Cop,'" *Newsone.com*, January 12, 2010. See also Bob Egelko, "Will Obama discuss race in his 2nd term?" *San Francisco Chronicle*, January 6, 2013.
39. For a paean to Obama's liberal triumphs, see Michael Grunwald, *The New New Deal: The Hidden Story of Change in the Obama Era* (2012).

Conclusion

1. Bill Moyers, *Moyers on America: A Journalist and His Times* 167 (2004). There is also the apocryphal story that, upon signing the bill, Johnson turned to an aide and lamented, "we have lost the South for a generation." Clay Risen, "How the South was won," *Boston Globe*, March 5, 2006.
2. Shaun Bowler & Gary Segura, *The Future is Ours: Minority Politics, Political Behavior, and the Multiracial Era of American Politics* 66 (2012).
3. Edward G. Carmines & James A. Stimson, *Issue Evolution: Race and the Transformation of American Politics* 133 (1989).
4. National Hispanic Media Coalition, "The Impact of Media Stereotypes on Opinions and Attitudes Towards Latinos" September 8, 2012.
5. Ronald Brownstein, "The Gray and the Brown: Generational Mismatch," *National Journal*, July 24, 2010. For a discussion of hostility toward youth among Tea Partiers, see Theda Skocpol & Vanessa Williamson, *The Tea Party and the Remaking of Republican Conservatism* 67, 75, 117, 162 (2012).
6. "Transcripts on Meet The Press: February 10: Eric Cantor, Dick Durbin, Kasim Reed, Michael Gerson, Katty Kay, Mike Murphy, Michael Isikoff," *NBCNews.com*, February 10, 2013. See also Frank Rich, "Lipstick on an Elephant," *New York Magazine*, March 4, 2013.

7. Cantor lauded the D.C. Opportunity Scholarship Program, a federally funded voucher system. On the rise of vouchers across the country, see Fernanda Santo & Motoko Rich, "With Vouchers, States Shift Aid for Schools to Families," *New York Times*, March 27, 2013.

8. See Chapter Six.

9. Kathy Barks Hoffman, "Pete Hoekstra Ad Brings Charges of Racial Insensitivity," *Huffington Post*, February 5, 2012.

10. Sheila A. Bedi, "The Constructed Identities of Asian and African Americans: A Story of Two Races and the American Justice System," 19 *Harvard Blackletter Law Journal* 181, 195 (2003).

11. Bowler & Segura, 4. See also John Judis & Ruy Teixeira, *The Emerging Democratic Majority* 11 (2002).

12. On the "capture" of black votes, see Paul Frymer, *Uneasy Alliances: Race and Party Competition in America* (1999).

13. Zoltan Hajnal & Taeku Lee, *Why Americans Don't Join the Party: Race, Immigration, and the Failure (of Political Parties) to Engage the Electorate* 109 (2011). On the political values that animate black voters, see Michael Dawson, *Behind the Mule: Race and Class in African-American Politics* (1995).

14. Hajnal & Lee, 159.

15. Zoltan Hajnal & Taeku Lee, "The Untold Future of American Politics," *New York Times*, June 4, 2012.

16. Matt A. Barreto, Fernando Guerra, Mara Marks, Stephen A. Nuño, & Nathan D. Woods, "Controversies in Exit Polling: Implementing a Racially Stratified Homogenous Precinct Approach," 39 *PS: Political Science & Politics* 477, 477 (2006). The authors also note reasons to suspect that these numbers may be overstated.

17. "Analysis: Romney Done in by GOP's Latino Problem," *ABC/Univision*, November 7, 2012.

18. Mathew Frye Jacobsen, *Whiteness of a Different Color: European Immigrants and the Alchemy of Race* (1998).

19. Dan T. Carter, *The Politics of Rage: George Wallace, the Origins of the New Conservatism, and the Transformation of American Politics* 11 (1995).

20. Joseph Lowndes, *From the New Deal to the New Right: Race and the Southern Origins of Modern Conservatism* 86 (2008).

21. Karen R. Humes, Nicholas A. Jones, & Roberto R. Ramirez, "Overview of Race and Hispanic Origin: 2010," at 6, US Bureau of the Census, March 2011. See generally Ian Haney López, "Race on the 2010 Census: Hispanics and the Shrinking White Majority," 134 *Daedalus* 42 (2005); Clara E. Rodriguez, *Changing Race: Latinos, the Census and the History of Ethnicity* (2000).

22. U.S. Census Bureau, Population Division, "Table 6. Percent Distribution of the Projected Population by Race and Hispanic Origin for the United States: 2015 to 2060," (NP2012-T6), December 2012.

23. Alex Isenstadt, "GOP could pay price for gerrymandering," *Politico.com*, July 1, 2013.

24. Douglas Massey, "Racial Formation in Theory and Practice: The Case of Mexicans in the United States," 1 *Race and Social Problems* 12 (2009).

25. Tanya K. Hernandez, *Racial Subordination in Latin America: The Role of the State, Customary Law and the New Civil Rights Response* (2012).

26. James Baldwin, "On Being 'White' . . . And Other Lies," in *Black on White: Black Writers on What It Means to Be White* 177, 178 (David R. Roediger ed., 1998). For classic histories of this dynamic, see David Roediger, *The Wages of Whiteness: Race and the Making of the American Working Class* (1999); and Noel Ignatiev, *How the Irish Became White* (1996).

27. Neil Foley, "Becoming Hispanic: Mexican Americans and the Faustian Pact with Whiteness," *Reflexiones 1997*, at 57 (Neil Foley ed., 1998); Ian Haney López, "Race, Ethnicity, Erasure: The Salience of Race to LatCrit Theory," 85 *California Law Review* 1143 (1997).

28. For a discussion of how racial categories may evolve over the next couple of decades, see the chapter entitled "Colorblind White Dominance," in Ian Haney López, *White by Law: The Legal Construction of Race* (revised ed., 2006).

29. Paul Street & Anthony DiMaggio, *Crashing the Tea Party: Mass Media and the Campaign to Remake American Politics* 45 (2011).

30. See Chapter Eight.

31. john a. powell, "Post-Racialism or Targeted Universalism?" 86 *Denver University Law Review* 785 (2009); john a. powell, *Racing to Justice: Transforming Our Conceptions of Self and Other to Build an Inclusive Society* (2012).

32. Rowland Evans & Robert Novak, "Future 'White Man's' Party," *St. Petersburg Times*, June 25, 1963, at 9-A.

33. Adia Harvey Wingfield & Joe R. Feagin, *Yes We Can? White Racial Framing and the Obama Presidency* 227 (2nd ed. 2013).

34. Stephen Teles, *The Rise of the Conservative Legal Movement* 181–207 (2008).

35. Devon Carbado & Mitu Gulati, *Acting White?: Rethinking Race in Post-Racial America* (2013).

36. Judis & Teixeira, 3.

37. Martin Luther King, Jr., *A Testament of Hope: The Essential Writings of Martin Luther King, Jr.*, 651 (James M. Washington ed., 1986).

38. For a recent bestseller using the victim-blaming perfected against minorities to similarly indict the white poor, see Charles Murray, *Coming Apart: The State of White America, 1960–2010* (2012).

39. Derrick Bell, *Faces at the Bottom of the Well: The Permanence of Racism* 195 (1993).

Index

Acknowledgments

I've wrestled for many years with the ideas developed here, yet only recently was I drawn to write a book on the subject. Attempt a tome tracing the interconnections since the civil rights era between rising economic inequality, coded assaults on liberalism, and evolutions in racism? Let someone else sift shifting sands. But in the last few years many encouraged me to write this book—and now that the book is done, I can set aside my earlier pangs of resentment and offer my sincerest gratitude to those who pushed me to get this book down on paper. Derrick Bell, of course, got this whole thing started with the invitation to deliver a lecture on race and society. After hearing the lecture, Diane Wachtell convinced me to attempt a book by assuring that I could sketch these arguments in roughly 70 pages. Obviously, that didn't happen. Keeping up the momentum, Janet Dewart Bell along with Art and Anita Johnson then invited me to inaugurate a Derrick Bell Lecture at the University of Oregon. Heather McGhee too helped lull me into a false confidence regarding the project's feasibility. Heather also put me in touch with Andrew Stuart, who would become my agent; Andrew in turn promptly sold the book proposal and thereby locked me into actually sitting down to write. Oxford University Press committed wholeheartedly to the project, so there I must thank the president, Niko Pfund (the editor of my first book many years ago), the acquiring editor, David McBride, and his assistant, Sarah Rosenthal, all of whom blithely assumed everything would turn out well. I'm deeply, deeply grateful to all of them for their good advice and abiding confidence.

Among my colleagues at Berkeley Law, the sheer number who had the fortitude to persevere through early drafts testifies to the wonderful community I have there. These stalwarts include Taeku Lee, Joy Milligan, Vicky Plaut, john powell, Russell Robinson, Bertrall Ross, and Karen Tani, as well as a couple of de facto Berkeley Law friends, Álvaro Oliveira and Richard Rothstein. Other Berkeley colleagues who provided incisive comments and encouragement include Ty Alper, Michelle Anderson, Maria Echaveste, Laurel Fletcher, Melissa Murray, David Oppenheimer, Jeff Selbin, Jonathan Simon, and Fred Smith. Further afield, David Garrow and Ken Mack pitched in by fielding queries about Barack Obama's law school days. Berkeley also employs my terrific faculty assistant, Drew Kloss, who helped in myriad ways large and small. Because it must, Berkeley gave me access to fabulous students, many of whom found themselves trapped into reading draft chapters. In particular, I appreciate the good humor of the students in my spring 2012 Race and American Law course as well as in the seminar I co-taught that semester with Vicky Plaut, Colorblindness: Psychology and Law. Finally, thanks go to Berkeley Law's dean, Chris Edley, who showed remarkable forbearance in supporting a project purporting to describe some of what he saw from the front lines.

More than to any other small group, I'm incredibly indebted to "Team Dog Whistle," the loyal cadre of research assistants on this project: Colin Allred, Sean Darling-Hammond, Liz Jiménez, Rebecca Lee, and Asad Rahim. They read countless drafts, wrote innumerable memos, edited and re-edited tirelessly, and repeatedly pushed me to address tough questions. Liz also put me in touch with a smart and generous interlocutor, Bernard Moore. As part of this elite team, I would also like to induct Jamie Crook. A former student and now a crack civil rights lawyer with Relman, Dane & Colfax in Washington, DC, she prevailed upon the civic good will of her firm for time to bring to bear on this book her fierce editorial skills. Colin, Sean, Liz, Rebecca, Asad, and Jamie deserve more thanks than I can possibly express. They believed fervently in getting these arguments right and in getting them out broadly, and it's their labor more than anyone else's that made these pages accessible. There remain, of course, missteps in the book, for which I alone am responsible (especially since Team Dog Whistle and others probably tried to warn me).

I move in a circle of terrific friends and family members who've all engaged with this project, at least one (Uncle Mike, you know whom I'm talking about) while being restrained by US marshals. Leah Segawa attended the original Bell Lecture, and then inflicted the YouTube video on her friends. Despite an extremely low tolerance for verbosity, Al Lepp closely read the manuscript and provided concrete and helpful advice, larded with strenuous pleas for greater authorial handholding. Rey Rodríguez gleefully amplified Al's exhortations, and also offered his own impassioned insights. A former professor, Mark Leff, slogged through a distressingly rough draft; having seen my college freshman work, he had low expectations that I nevertheless disappointed. Ticien Sassoubre, straddling the real and academic worlds, invaluably encouraged me to ignore the more arcane suggestions made by some readers (no names). Bob

Miller provided irreverent advice and timely examples of new dog whistle eruptions. Tensia was always ready to welcome me home with chilaquiles. My father, Terry, read the book proposal and was thrilled to encounter what he recognized as English; his hope that I might someday find my way back from academic scholarship and again write intelligibly was rekindled. My older brother, Garth, no doubt still incredulous that I'm a professor, from a distance kept urging more vacation time. Chelsea and Lennea, my stepdaughter and granddaughter, assisted with their patience and understanding, as I missed a lot of moments when I should have been with them. On the other hand, Lennea and I did manage to get in a few great surf sessions, sometimes in company with the Woody clan. Speaking of the Woodies, they helped through some very difficult times—and were repaid with water balloons. Truce. Most of all, my love and gratitude to Debbie, my wife, who helped with the ideas, created space for me to write, buoyed me emotionally, read the final draft under severe time pressure and intrepidly offered suggestions for major rewrites, and almost always pretended to believe me when I promised never to work this hard again.

One final acknowledgment: although this project did not yet exist when the Fletcher Foundation awarded me a fellowship in the spring of 2011, the support they provided and, more, the spirit of the award helped guide this book. The Alphonse Fletcher, Sr. Fellowship goes to "scholars, writers, and artists whose work contributes to improving race relations in American society and furthers the broad social goals of the U.S. Supreme Court's *Brown v. Board of Education* decision of 1954." I've tried to do that in this book, repeatedly returning to the theme that integration offers an essential way forward for all of us of every race.